"Baker handles dialogue ⟨...⟩ rply observed slacker-speak to the distinct ⟨...⟩ r' or 'cool.' But it's the elongated silences, pregnant and empty, that carry the story and distinguish the script of *The Aliens*. Where the play most delights is in its nuanced depictions of the relationships between the three men. Neither of these post-Beckett moderns is going anywhere (they haven't even a Godot to wait for), though some pretty monumental events transpire beneath the static surface. Both KJ and Jasper are damaged goods, which tends to make the many small ways in which they take care of each other all the more moving. In the underlying kindness of these stunted lives, Baker gives us rays of hope amid bleak prospects . . . A miniature portrait of America today."

—Robert Hurwitt, *San Francisco Chronicle*

"Baker has as natural an ear for how people really talk—and shut up—as any American playwright of recent years . . . She is the aural equivalent of a good photo-realist painter, someone who makes us see the quotidian in such heightened detail that it looks almost shockingly new . . . She conveys exactly how people speak, and her plays are shaped by an understanding that all conversation is a compromise."

—Ben Brantley, *New York Times*

"*Body Awareness* is marvelously deft and humane . . . Baker has a sharp ear for the deeply painful—and funny—longings squirming under her characters' dialogue."

—David Cote, *TimeOut New York*

"*Circle Mirror Transformation* is absorbing, unblinking and sharply funny."

—Anita Gates, *New York Times*

"Without a doubt, Baker is a highly original talent and a major playwright. Even two days after seeing *The Aliens* I remain teary not only because of the emotional impact of this wonderful play, but from the sense of thrill and privilege at seeing the early work of a writer who may well be a genius. The exploration of character here is painstakingly slow and gentle and utterly persuasive. Baker takes the extraordinary risk of writing intensive silences into the play—some lasting two or three minutes. The effect is amazing. We seem to be experiencing KJ and Jasper's relationship in real time, not theatrical time at all. As each tiny revelation of character and insight is given, we are allowed ample time to reflect upon it as though we had actually heard it from a personal friend. These characters are so real, so authentic, so true-to-life that I felt as though the playwright had been eavesdropping on my most private conversations with my nearest intimates. A masterpiece."

—Charles Kruger, *Bay Area Theatre Examiner*

The

Vermont Plays

———

The

Vermont Plays

Annie Baker

THEATRE COMMUNICATIONS GROUP
NEW YORK
2012

The Vermont Plays is published by Theatre Communications Group, Inc., 520 8th Avenue, 24th Floor, New York, NY 10018-4156

The publication of *The Vermont Plays* by Annie Baker through TCG's Book Program is made possible in part by the New York State Council on the Arts with the support of Governor Andrew Cuomo and the New York State Legislature.

TCG books are exclusively distributed to the book trade by Consortium Book Sales and Distribution.

Library of Congress Cataloging-in-Publication Data
Baker, Annie, 1981–
The Vermont plays / Annie Baker.
p. cm.
ISBN 978-1-55936-389-1 (pbk.)
I. Title.
PS3602.A5842V47   2012
812'.6—dc23   2012006266

Book design and composition by Lisa Govan
Cover design by Mark Melnick

First Edition, May 2012
Fourth Printing, November 2016

Contents

The Aliens

———

*With original music and lyrics by Michael Chernus,
Patch Darragh and Erin Gann*

Production History

The Aliens was developed, in part, with assistance from the Orchard Project, a program of The Exchange (www.exchangenyc.org). *The Aliens* received its world premiere by Rattlestick Playwrights Theater in New York City (David Van Asselt, Artistic Director) on April 22, 2010. The production was directed by Sam Gold with original music and lyrics by Michael Chernus, Patch Darragh and Erin Gann. The set design was by Andrew Lieberman, the costume design was by Bobby Frederick Tilley II, the lighting design was by Tyler Micoleau, the sound design was by Bart Fasbender, the prop design was by Eugenia Furneaux-Arends and the production stage manager was Nicole Bouclier. It was performed by:

JASPER	Erin Gann
KJ	Michael Chernus
EVAN	Dane DeHaan

Characters

JASPER, thirty-one
KJ, thirty
EVAN, seventeen

About the Pauses and the Silences

At least a third—if not half—of this play is silence. Pauses should be at least three seconds long. Silences should last from five to ten seconds. Long pauses and long silences should, of course, be even longer.

An intermission is necessary for about ten different reasons. Each act should run around fifty to fifty-five minutes.

Two More Things

"Andrea" is pronounced "Ahn-DREY-a."

A slash (/) indicates where the next speech begins.

Act One

Scene One

The desolate back patio of a coffee shop in Vermont. A recycling bin. A trash bin. A PLEASE USE THE FRONT ENTRANCE sign.
Jasper and KJ are sitting in the sun at a lone picnic table, their feet up on plastic chairs. KJ has a beard and long hair pulled into a messy bun. Jasper has shorter hair and simmers with quiet rage. He wears sweatpants and sandals.
Jasper is smoking. KJ is drinking a to-go cup of tea.
A long silence.
Eventually KJ starts singing to himself.

                                KJ
I WON'T
WASTE AWAY
WONDERING WHY
I WON'T GO DOWN LIKE THAT
IF I DIE
TIME MACHINES WERE MADE FOR ME
I BELIEVE
IMPOSSIBILITIES

ARE WHAT YOU PERCEIVE
TRIPLE DIMENSIONAL SUPERSTAR
TRIPLE DIMENSIONAL SUPERSTAR
TRIPLE DIMENSIONAL SUPERSTAR

Jasper smokes. A pause.

KJ
I'M A MARTIAN MASTERPIECE
FROM ANOTHER DIMENSION
TIME AND SPACE WEREN'T MEANT FOR ME.
NO I'M NOT DOWN WITH THAT.
TRIPLE DIMENSIONAL SUPERSTAR
TRIPLE DIMENSIONAL SUPERSTAR
TRIPLE DIMENSIONAL SUPERSTAR

Jasper smokes. A long silence. KJ drinks his tea. Then:

KJ
Remember Orion?

Jasper nods.

KJ
He started a wind farm.
Near Marshfield.

Jasper exhales.

JASPER
What does that mean he started a wind farm?

KJ
He started a wind farm. He lives on a wind farm.

JASPER
Wind farm like the big / white—

KJ
The big white spinny things.
(pause)
With like the—on top of a mountain or something.

JASPER
Aren't those owned by the government?

KJ
I don't know. He lives on one.

JASPER
Yeah, but it's not . . . it's just like a bunch of wheels by the side
of the road.

KJ
Yeah.

Pause.

JASPER
So how does he live on one?

KJ
He just does.

JASPER
Who told you that?

KJ
. . . Eli.

Jasper sighs and stubs out his cigarette. KJ watches him, worried.
Another long silence.

KJ
Hey. Uh. Do you wanna talk about it? Or would you rather just,
uh . . .

KJ trails off.

JASPER

Andrea?

KJ nods.

JASPER

Not really.

KJ nods again. A pause.

JASPER

She's crazy, man.

KJ nods again. A pause.

JASPER

It's sad. I mean, it's really fucking sad.

A pause.

JASPER

There's actually something wrong with her.

KJ

Like—

JASPER

Like borderline paranoia or something. Some kind of psychological issue.

KJ nods.

JASPER

So it's actually kind of a relief. It feels like a relief.

KJ

Cool.

JASPER

And ah . . . I don't know. She played games, you know? She was into that shit. She was into Power. And like . . . part of me found it attractive but it was also really / uh—

KJ

That's not good, man.

JASPER

And uh . . . you know, her thing was like . . . that she didn't have a personality anymore? That she'd like "lost her personality." In the shadow of my . . .
But the hilarious thing is that she was the one who like fucking glued herself to my hip. I didn't need that, man. Necessarily. But she made us that. While like still attempting to fuck with my head the whole time and make feel like shit.

A pause. KJ nods again, at a loss. Jasper lights another cigarette.

KJ

I'm sorry.

JASPER

Don't say you're sorry. It's a good thing.
 (*pause*)
I don't need to talk about it.
 (*pause*)
I actually feel bad for her.

KJ watches Jasper, who smokes and refuses to look at KJ. After a while KJ starts squinting up at the sun and opening his mouth a little.

JASPER

What're you doing?

KJ

 (*still squinting*)
. . . Trying to sneeze.

JASPER

What is that / supposed to—

KJ

It helps you sneeze.
Looking at the sun helps you sneeze.

Jasper watches KJ try to sneeze for a while. KJ is unsuccessful.
Eventually he goes back to sipping his tea.
A long silence.
Jasper suddenly kicks a chair over. It makes a terrible noise.

KJ

Whoa.

Five seconds later, the back door to the coffee shop opens. Evan peeks
his head out the door, sees them, then steps outside, in his white
apron. Evan is seventeen and in a constant state of humiliation.

EVAN

Hey.
Um . . .

Jasper and KJ regard him coldly.

EVAN

Hey.
We're not allowed to, uh . . .
    (pause)
Did you guys just kick that chair over?

Jasper and KJ do not respond. Evan waits, in agony, then:

EVAN

Um. So. We're not allowed to . . . people aren't actually supposed
to sit out here.
It's uh, it's like a staff area. You're supposed to sit at the tables
out front.

JASPER

Who are you?

EVAN

Um. I'm Evan.

JASPER

You new here?

EVAN

Uh . . . yeah.

KJ

We know Rahna.

EVAN

. . . Okay . . .

Pause.

KJ

Rahna lets us sit out here.

EVAN

Um. Okay. Uh.
Because I was told that we should not, um . . . that under no /
condition—

JASPER

What's your last name?

EVAN

Shelmerdine.

KJ

*Shel*merdine?

JASPER

. . . Cause you look like this girl I know. You look like you could
be her younger brother.

Evan doesn't know what to say.

JASPER

Emily.

EVAN

Okay. Cool. Yeah, I don't have a sister named Emily.

JASPER

Her last name is Spencer.

Pause.

EVAN

Um . . . would it be okay with you guys to move out front? Cause
it's my second day working here, and I really don't want to get in,
um, trouble.

They both look at him and do not move. Evan stands there for a
while. Like ten seconds. Everyone is very still.
Finally Evan turns around and walks back inside. After a while:

KJ

Does it feel hot to you?
Like especially hot?

Jasper doesn't respond.

KJ

Is it supposed to be this hot in June?

JASPER

It's July.

KJ

Oh yeah?

JASPER

July 2nd.

Pause.

KJ

He was like *twelve*. That kid.

Pause.

KJ

July 2nd. That makes sense.
Cause the other night I heard like . . . preparations or whatever.
People were like setting off fireworks in their backyard.
(pause)
Have you noticed that? That everybody always starts practicing like the week before the Fourth of July? Why do they need to practice?
(pause)
Don't they just *light* it?

Jasper doesn't answer. He touches the pack of cigarettes in his pocket. He drums his fingers on the table.
After a while, he gets up, rights the chair he kicked over, and sits back down.
KJ basks in the sun.
Blackout.

Scene Two

The next day. KJ is sitting by himself at the table. He has another to-go cup of tea. He removes his tea bag from his cup, opens it, pours out a little bit of the tea onto the plastic table, removes a tiny packet from his pocket, and refills the tea bag with the contents of the tiny

13

packet. *Somewhere during this careful operation, Evan comes out the back door in his apron, beleaguered, dragging a huge garbage bag behind him.*

He sees KJ, tries to figure out whether or not to say anything, then lifts up the lid of the garbage bin and dumps the garbage bag in.

KJ turns around, sees him, waves cheerfully, and then goes back to his teabag surgery.

Evan, for lack of a better response, waves back. Then he wipes his hands on his apron and watches KJ. After a while:

EVAN
Don't you mind the smell back here?

KJ
(not looking up)
Can't smell a thing, my brother.

Pause.

EVAN
. . . So Rahna doesn't actually work here anymore.

No response. KJ twists the new tea bag together and puts it back in his cup. Then he takes a small wooden stirrer out of his pocket and starts stirring.
Evan looks at the mess on the table.

EVAN
What are you doing?

KJ
Concocting.

KJ blows on the tea, then tastes it. He smiles.

KJ
Taste it.

*Evan looks dubious, then walks forward, takes the cup, and takes a
tiny sip. He nods and hands it back. A pause.*

KJ

You go to SHS?

EVAN

Yes. I mean. I have one more year left.

KJ

Is Mr. Amato still around?

EVAN
(nervously glancing back toward the door)
Yeah. Um. I had him for World Civ this past year. He's cool.

KJ

I *hate* that guy.

Evan doesn't know how to respond.

KJ

He's still there?!

Evan nods.

KJ

Oh fuck. Someone needs to fucking *kill* that guy.
That guy ruined my life.
Shit. Just thinking about him makes me wanna like strangle a
fucking animal.
Oh man!
That guy is such a *bitch*!

*KJ sips his tea and tries to calm down. Evan hovers for a moment,
not sure what to do, and then goes back inside. The door shuts
behind him.*
KJ sits by himself for a while. He drinks his tea.
Then KJ takes out his cell phone and dials.

KJ

(after a pause)
Where are you.
(pause)
Ah yes.
(pause)
You are on fire, my friend.

He listens while we hear Jasper's voice, quiet at first, get louder and louder as he approaches the patio from a distance and then arrives, scaling any fences/shrubs in his way.

JASPER
. . . and then I realized that he goes to California. And he drives up the coast. And he's got like five bucks to his name but back then that was like fifty bucks. And he drives, right, he drives up the coast and he sees the ocean for the first time in his life. And then he drives to Big Sur. Which is where . . . that's where Henry Miller lived.

Jasper has now reached KJ. They see each other and snap their cell phones shut.

JASPER
So Miller's gonna be a character.

KJ
No shit.

JASPER
Very minor. But he makes an appearance.

Jasper hauls off his backpack and sits down. He looks at the mess on the table.

JASPER
Shroom tea?

                        KJ

Myfriendmyfriend.

Jasper sits down and takes out his cigarettes. He lights one. He seems wound up.
They sit there.
Eventually KJ starts singing.

                        KJ

TWO FIXED POINTS IS A CONSTANT
TWO FOCAL POINTS ARE THE SAME POINT
ECCENTRICITY IS IDENTICAL
THE X-AXIS IS PERPENDICULAR
THE GRAPH DRAWN
IS LATERAL
THE EQUATION
IS LITERAL
WRITE THE EQUATION IN INTERCEPT FORM
RATIO IS SYMMETRY
IS CONSTANT
IS SYMMETRY
THE TURNING POINT IS ALSO
THE AXIS
OF SYMMETRY
EQUIDISTANT FROM THE FOCUS
AN ELLIPSE
IS THE LOCUS
THE ECCENTRICITY OF THE ELLIPSE
IS BLOSSOMED LOTUS

Jasper smokes agitatedly and stares off into the distance. After a while KJ gets out of his chair, lies down on the ground on his back, and elevates his legs on a plastic chair.

                        KJ

. . . Back problems.

                        JASPER

Oh yeah?

                                        KJ
I slept on it weird.

A long pause. Jasper smokes. Suddenly:

                                      JASPER
Did you know that Andrea started dating that guy? You did, didn't
you? You don't have to hide it from me or anything. I'm actually
happy about it.

Pause.

                                        KJ
Wait, what?!

                                      JASPER
She's dating that guy. Sprocket.
She's dating a guy named Sprocket.

                                        KJ
I had no idea.

                                      JASPER
It's cool if you did, man.

                                        KJ
I had No Fucking Idea. I swear to god.

Pause.

                                        KJ
Who's Sprocket?!

                                      JASPER
The tall guy? With the hair? At Noah's party?

Pause.

                                      JASPER
He makes his own pants?

KJ

Oh god.

JASPER

He takes like that fucking Chinese kimono cloth and sews his own pants or something and everybody makes a big fucking deal about it?

KJ

Oh man.

Pause.

KJ

Sprocket.

Jasper stubs out his cigarette.

JASPER

His real name is probably like *Barnaby* or something.

KJ

Ha.
Yes.

JASPER

So you didn't know.

KJ

. . . I did not know.

JASPER

She called me to tell me. Last night.
"In case I saw them together."
  (*short pause*)
I'm telling you, it ended up being one of the best nights of my life. I was just doing nothing, fucking staring out the window, and

then I get this phone call, and she has this like haughty tone, and she's like telling me that . . .
Hold on.

Jasper suddenly leans forward, rests his elbow on his knees, and bows his head. KJ, who is still lying on his back, lifts his head up a little and peers over.

KJ

Are you okay?

JASPER

Yeah. I just had to, like, breathe.

KJ

Whoa.

JASPER

I feel fantastic, though.

KJ, his head still raised, continues to peer over at Jasper, but after a little while his neck gets tired and he puts his head back down. Jasper takes a deep breath and collects himself.

JASPER

Wow. That was like a crazy head rush slash heart attack.
Okay.
So she calls me and delivers The Big News or whatever in the most condescending freakish manner possible, and I call her a cunt, which, if you recall, was like the big no-no word in our relationship, and she says "you promised never to call me that again" and I say ARE YOU ACTUALLY LISTENING TO YOUR-SELF and I hang up.
And then for like five minutes I'm like . . .
Worst five minutes of my life.
Actually. No. Not the worst five minutes of my life.
Bad, though.

KJ

What were the worst five minutes of your life?

JASPER

(ignoring him)
BUT THEN.
I remember something Your. Fucking. Mother. Told me. Over dinner.

KJ

Sandy Jano?!

JASPER

I remember something Sandy Jano told me. She said it like three years ago. When I crashed on your couch.

KJ

Oh yeah.

JASPER

I was like talking to her about how I was always like getting kicked out of places and like sleeping on floors or whatever and she was like: this, uh, this in-between state, this being unstable or whatever, if you accept / it—

KJ

Oh man. Was she talking about her Gender stuff?

JASPER

No. No. She was like: the state of just having lost something is like the most enlightened state in the world.

KJ is silent.

JASPER

And I thought of that last night, and all of a sudden I felt like incredible. I was simultaneously like being stabbed in the heart over and over again with this like devil knife but I also felt *euphoric*. And then I sat down and I wrote like twenty pages.

KJ

In one night?

> JASPER

And they were like . . . the book just . . . it just switched in a totally different direction. He leaves Iowa City! The whole thing was supposed to take place in Iowa City and he leaves! He's goin' to California!

Pause.

> KJ

Awesome.

KJ lifts his legs off the chair and tries to bring his knees down to his chest with some difficulty.
Jasper, trying to hide his disappointment at KJ's lack of a response, takes out another cigarette and lights it.
Evan comes out the back door with a final bag of trash, no apron on, crippled under the weight of a huge L.L.Bean backpack.

> JASPER

Shelmerdine!

Evan nods, trying to look dignified, and throws the bag into the dumpster.

> JASPER

How are you today, Shelmerdine?

> EVAN

Um. I'm good.
Takin' off.

> JASPER

You done already?

> EVAN

Um. Yeah. Eight to three.

> JASPER

. . . You smoke?

EVAN

Um.
Occasionally.
I don't know.

JASPER

Want one?

EVAN
(after glancing behind him at the door)
Uh . . . sure.

Jasper offers him a cigarette. Evan takes it and holds it between two slightly trembling fingers. Jasper holds out a lighter. After a half second of confusion, Evan remembers what to do, leans forward, inhales, lights it, and then steps back.
He smokes passably, taking tiny hits, still wearing his backpack.
Jasper smokes.
KJ is still lying on his back.
After a while:

KJ

Will someone please pass the psilocybin tea?

Jasper ignores him.

KJ

Will someone please pass the psilocybin tea?

Jasper takes KJ's cup of tea and carefully pours it out onto the ground.

EVAN

What's psilocybum?

JASPER

He's obsessed with incorporating shrooms into every food group.

KJ

Shroom karaoke.

KJ laughs. No one else does.

EVAN

Wait. That tea has mushrooms in it? Psychedelic mushrooms?

Jasper nods.

EVAN

He gave me some. He made me drink some!

JASPER

How much?

EVAN

Like a whole sip.

JASPER

You're fine.

EVAN

Shit!

JASPER

You're fine.

EVAN

Do I seem weird?

JASPER

Do you feel weird?

A pause while Evan tries to gauge if he feels weird.

EVAN

No. I don't know.

JASPER

You're fine.

Pause.

EVAN

My friend grew up in Medfield? Massachusetts? And he said there was this guy at his school who like ate a bunch of shrooms and then tied his own hands to a radiator.

(*pause*)

And then they melted off.

KJ

(*still on his back*)

Urban myth.

Evan throws his cigarette on the ground and stubs it out with his sneaker, with some difficulty.

EVAN

Uh. I should probably head home.

(*pause*)

Um. What are your names? If you don't mind me asking.

JASPER

I'm Jasper.

They both look over at KJ. His eyes are closed.

JASPER

And that's KJ.

EVAN

Cool.

Um.

Cool. Yeah.

Um. If you guys like . . . if like my manager like comes in later and sees you guys and gets mad, don't tell him I saw you. I mean, I didn't know about it.

JASPER

All right.

EVAN

Cool.

JASPER

You just working here at The Green Sheep all summer, Shelmerdine?

EVAN

Uh. Yeah. Pretty much. I'm gone next week. But then I'm back.

JASPER

Where you goin'?

EVAN

Uh . . .
I'm a . . . I'm working as a CIT?

JASPER

A what?

EVAN

Counselor-in-training? It's just like a week-long-thing.

JASPER

At a camp?

EVAN

Uh . . . yeah.

JASPER

What kind of camp?

This is the question Evan has been dreading.

EVAN

Uh . . . it's a, uh . . .
It's a Jewish music camp?
Um—

JASPER

Jewish *music* camp?

> EVAN

. . . Yeah.

Um.

I like teach little kids how to play piano and guitar and stuff.

> JASPER

Little Jewish kids.

> EVAN

. . . Yeah. Um. My mom is Jewish.

Jasper thinks about this, then nods.

> EVAN

I went there when I was a little kid.

> KJ

You play guitar?

> EVAN

No. Not . . . kinda. Not that well. Um. More piano.

> KJ

Jasper plays guitar.

Jasper rolls his eyes.

> EVAN

Oh yeah?

> JASPER

I taught myself from, like, a book once.

> KJ

We had a band!

> JASPER

KJ thinks we had a band.

I'm actually a novelist now. I'm writing a novel.

EVAN

Oh. Cool.

KJ

We had a band!

EVAN

What was the name of the band?

JASPER

Oh fuck. Don't get him started.

KJ finally sits up.

KJ

We had many names. Many phases. Many incarnations.

JASPER

We could never agree on a name. We had like fifty different band names.

KJ

The New Humans!

JASPER

Yeah. He really pushed for that one.

KJ

Hieronymous Blast.

JASPER

Oh god.

KJ

Pillowface.
Frog Men.
Electric Hookah.
The Limp Handshakes.
Joseph Yoseph.

JASPER

Cause his great-grandfather was named Josef and mine was named Joseph.

KJ

The JK/KJ Experience.

JASPER

Because he's Kevin Jano and I'm Jasper Kopatch.

KJ

The JK/KJ *Experiment*.

Jasper shakes his head.

KJ

Killer Jamball and the Jolly Kangaroo!
Dharma Machine!
Nefarious Hookah!

JASPER

I wanted us to be called The Aliens.

KJ

No. Boring.

JASPER

After the Bukowski poem. You like Bukowski?

EVAN

Um . . . I don't know him. I don't know his stuff.

JASPER

You ever write poetry?

EVAN

Um. No. I don't know. Not really. In my journal? Sometimes?
No.

JASPER

You gotta read Bukowski.

                              EVAN
Okay.

                              JASPER
He cuts away all the bullshit.

                              EVAN
Cool.

Evan nods, and keeps nodding.

                              EVAN
. . . Bukowski.

                              JASPER
What are you doin' tomorrow night, Shelmerdine?

                              EVAN
Ah—

                              JASPER
You goin' to the fireworks?

                              EVAN
Uh. I don't know. Maybe. I might just stay home.
   (a short pause)
Sometimes the Fourth, like, depresses me.

                              JASPER
Oh yeah?

                              EVAN
Yeah. You know. I don't know. It's like all these families spread
out on the football field? With the glowsticks? And they have that
crappy local marching band. I don't know. It's like anticlimactic
I guess? Like afterwards everyone seems a little disappointed. And
I don't know: it's like, kind of random. Like we explode stuff in the
sky and we look at it in like a group?
   (pause)
And like, I kind of hate America. So I don't feel this like urgent
need to celebrate it or anything.

A pause. Jasper nods thoughtfully.

> EVAN

Not that there's like . . . not like it's a bad thing . . . or like . . .

Evan trails off.

> JASPER

KJ and I are thinking of having a small shindig tomorrow night.

> KJ

A hootenanny.

> JASPER

We might read shit out loud. Sing a few songs.
Although drumming circles are strictly forbidden.

> KJ

Drumming of any kind.

> EVAN

Oh. Cool.

> JASPER

You could join us.

A pause.

> EVAN

Um . . .
Yeah! Okay. Thanks.
Yeah.
Awesome.

> JASPER

We'll see you then. Nine o'clock-ish.

> EVAN

Um . . . where? Sorry. Where is the party?

> JASPER

Here.

                                    EVAN

Oh. Um.
We're really not supposed to . . .
You can't have a party back here.

Jasper stares at him.

                                    EVAN

It's like a loitering thing.

                                    JASPER

I thought you guys were closed tomorrow.

                                    EVAN

Yeah. We are. But it's. We're not supposed to. Be here. Loiter here.

                                    JASPER

Fine.
Don't come.
It's not a big deal.

A pause while Evan stands there, at a loss. KJ lies back down.

                                    JASPER

No need to fret, little man.

                                    EVAN

I just don't know if I can do it.

                                    JASPER

It's cool.

                                    EVAN

Yeah. Um . . .

Jasper has gone cold. Evan sighs, re-shoulders his backpack and starts to walk away.

                                    KJ

    (*sincerely*)
Have fun at band camp!

> EVAN

Uh.

. . . Thanks.

Evan hesitates again, then exits. Silence for a while. KJ is still lying on his back. He starts humming. Finally:

> JASPER

KJ.

> KJ

Yes.

Pause.

> JASPER

Are you freaking out?

> KJ

What?!

No!

> JASPER

You have to tell me if you start feeling weird again, man.

> KJ

No way.

A pause.

> KJ

You know what Sandy Jano would say you're doing?

> JASPER

What?

> KJ

Projecting, man. You're projecting.

Jasper nods bleakly and stares off into the distance. After a while he reaches for his cigarettes. Blackout.

Scene Three

The next evening. The Fourth of July. Twilight.
The sky turns dark as the scene progresses. There is a guitar case
lying inconspicuously in the corner. Jasper is perched on top of the
recycling bin, reading aloud from a wrinkled sheaf of paper. KJ is
sitting in one of the plastic chairs, wearing sunglasses, listening. He
is rapt. Jasper is in the middle of a sentence.

JASPER

—and her bedroom smelled faintly of stale piss and those porcelain bowls of dried rose petals his mother used to put on the back of the toilet, before she died on his fifteenth birthday.

Candace walked over to the window, took a long white plastic rod between her fingers, and twisted it. Sunlight flooded the dusty little room.

"What?" she said, grinning at him. "I got nothing to be ashamed of." He noticed for the first time that her front tooth was chipped, just a little. The right one. Something about that tooth stirred him, made his gut ache.

She had the reddest hair he'd ever seen. It was a dangerous red. It told you to stop and it told you to go at the same time.

She turned around and faced him while he squinted in the sunlight. She stared at him for a while, her eyes moving up and down his face. Then she slowly started rolling her T-shirt up. Her stomach was round and soft, so pale it was almost translucent, with a cluster of tiny hairs below the bellybutton. He surprised himself in that moment by wishing for Allison, for her skinny, childish body, her watery brown eyes, and the way she would sleep with her head pressed so hard against his chest that he'd wake up with bruises in the morning.

But here was Candace, right in front of him, ample and ready, with her flaming torch hair and her ironic smile. She pulled the T-shirt up all the way over her head and revealed two large, pendulous white breasts. Her nipples were big and pink and undefined, like they'd been painted on with watercolors.

"Do you like me?" she asked. "Do you like the way I look?"

"I do," he said, "I do," and he moved towards her / and—

KJ

Holy shit, man. Your novel is turning me on.

Jasper puts down the paper and sighs.

KJ

I mean, it's amazing. It's great literature. It's just giving me a tiny
bit of a boner.
Please. Continue.

Jasper gives him a stern look, then goes back to the piece of paper.

JASPER

"I do," he said, "I do," and he moved towards her and grasped her
hair with his hand, pulling her head back so her mouth opened a
little. She let / out a—

KJ

Oh wait. One thing.
Sorry.
Can I say one thing?

JASPER

Yes.

KJ

The thing about the fifteenth birthday?
I feel like . . . I feel like maybe it's like too much of a coincidence?
That his mom died on his fifteenth birthday. It feels like . . . I'm
supposed to be like: whoa: or something.

JASPER

My mom died on my fifteenth birthday.

Pause.

KJ

She did?

JASPER

Yes. You knew that.

                                    KJ

Whoa. No.
I knew that you were . . . I knew that you were fifteen, man.
I didn't know it was on your birthday.

                              JASPER

It was on my birthday.

                                    KJ

Jesus.
Oh man. That's horrible.
Wow.
Never mind.

A weird pause.

                                    KJ

I'm sorry I didn't know you back then.

                              JASPER

You should be thankful you didn't know me back then.

                                    KJ

    (*shaking his head*)
Jesus. On your birthday.

                              JASPER

I would've kicked your ass.

KJ looks slightly wounded. He takes off his sunglasses and puts them in his lap.

                              JASPER

Okay. I'm gonna skip ahead.

                                    KJ

No!

                              JASPER

Yes.

Jasper flips through the pages.

JASPER

This next part is what I wrote the other night.
After Andrea called.
(a short pause)
By the way, she's left me like five messages since then and I haven't returned any of them.
(another short pause)
Okay.

Jasper starts reading again.

JASPER

He was seeing America for the first time. In a way he'd been thinking about this drive since he was a kid, this drive across America. What did Arizona look like? he used to wonder. Utah? Wyoming? Oklahoma? Illinois? He had imagined, somehow, that each state had a different set of plants and animals, a slightly different color blue in the sky.

But as he drove, as his little Hudson Hornet cranked and moaned across the long flat highways, and he flashed by farm after farm, cornfield after cornfield, desolate truck stop after desolate truck stop with the red flashing lights and the tooth-less man behind the counter and the occasional lonely woman with crinkled eyes desperately trying to catch his attention, as he crossed state line after state line, he realized that most of America looked like . . . most of America.

At this point Evan quietly and nervously enters, over the fence or through the shrubs, wearing his backpack. Jasper doesn't pause or seem to notice him. Evan stands near the edge of the patio, listening.

JASPER

It was beautiful, sure, it moved him, but it repeated itself. You could find the same thing there that you could find here.

And so as he approached California, his dream of California started to fade. He thought of what Miller had told him about the jutting cliffs in Big Sur, the mystical fog, the amethyst waves. But what if it was a lie? Or worse, some kind of delusion? What if Miller was actually living in a cornfield, sleeping on a billboard, writing underneath the glow of another drive-in movie theater?

He not only started to doubt America, but he started to doubt himself. He started doubting the gift that Allison claimed he was born with.

She had first whispered that word a year and half ago, that strange, sacred word, she had whispered it into his ear one morning, and it had sent thrill and terror down his spine.

Genius.

She had breathed the word out, like a sigh, tickling his hair.

And immediately he knew she was right, he'd known it since he was a boy, that word had lived in him before he even knew how to say it or spell it, but after Allison had confronted him with it, made it live in the air, he started to feel a constant, pressing weight on his shoulders and his back.

The loneliness of it.

The loneliness of it could kill him.

He wasn't sure if he believed in a God, but if there was one, He was waiting up there in the sky impatiently, He was putting his finger on his watch and raising his eyebrows and saying:

When's the new painting gonna be finished, son?

When you gonna stop fucking around?

Jasper puts the sheaf of papers down. Everyone is very still.

JASPER

Anyway.

I don't want to like bore you guys or anything.

Hello, Shelmerdine.

KJ leaps to his feet with an uncharacteristic amount of energy.

KJ

WHAT THE FUCK?!

Jasper tries not to beam.

KJ

Whatthefuckwhatthefuckwhatthefuck. Oh my god.

KJ does a little prayer jog around the recycling bin.

KJ

Ohmygodohmygodohmygodohmygod.
Ohmygodohmygodohmygodohmygod.

EVAN

. . . That was really cool.

JASPER

Aw, come on, Shelmerdine.

EVAN

That was really really cool.

Pause.

EVAN

What's, um, what's the main character's name?

JASPER

He doesn't have one.

EVAN

Oh. Cool.

Pause.

EVAN

And uh . . . what's the title?

JASPER

Little Tigers Everywhere.

EVAN

Little Tigers Everywhere. Cool.

JASPER

It's from a Bukowski poem. It's the one that starts out "Sam the whorehouse man / has squeaky shoes"?

Pause.

EVAN

Yeah. I don't know, um. I don't know. I mean, I'm gonna get him out from the library.

Pause. Evan hauls his backpack off and puts it down on the ground. It is somehow an important gesture. Maybe because it is the first time he is asserting himself as here.

KJ

Yes!
Welcome to the Fourth of July!

JASPER

Lookit that. Shelmerdine showed up.
    (to KJ)
Are you surprised?

KJ

Fuck no. Fuck no.

EVAN

Is anyone else coming?

KJ and Jasper suddenly look self-conscious.

JASPER

Uh . . . no.
Eli is being an asshole tonight and going out with—no.

KJ

What's Noah doing?

JASPER

. . . Being an asshole.

Pause.

                              EVAN

Um. I brought some stuff.

Evan kneels down and unzips his backpack.

                              EVAN

Uh.

He removes some Tupperware.

                              EVAN

Brownies. Um. My mom made like three batches of brownies
yesterday for some reason.
Uh.
. . . And this was the only thing I could steal. We don't really have
a, um, liquor cabinet. Um.

He takes a bottle out of his backpack.

                              EVAN

Peppermint Schnapps?

                              KJ

Ooh. *Peppermint.*

Jasper snatches the bottle out of Evan's hand.

                              JASPER

I'll take that.

Jasper shoves the bottle into his pocket.

                              KJ

Aw come on. Are you serious?

                              JASPER

Yes.

KJ

It's the Fourth of fucking July! I can drink Peppermint Schnapps!

JASPER

No you can't.

Evan has no idea what's going on.

EVAN

Um. Sorry. I thought that you guys were gonna . . . I thought you guys were gonna drink.

KJ

(to Jasper)
Are you kidding?

Jasper doesn't respond.

KJ

JESUS.
I'm . . . this is unbelievable.
You're treating me like a child.

Jasper does not budge. KJ walks over to the recycling bin and kicks it.

KJ

FUCK!
(a short pause)
This is so fucking pointless. I could just march over to the liquor store and buy whatever the fuck I want.
I'm thirty fucking years old!

JASPER

Do it.
I'll just go home.

KJ

You wouldn't fucking *know*!

> JASPER

Oh yes I would, my friend. Yes I would.

A pause.

> JASPER

Last time KJ started drinking he went off his meds and starting doing *this* to random people on the street.

He walks over to Evan.

> KJ

Don't do it, you asshole.

Jasper makes a little beak with his fingers and zaps Evan with it on his arm. Evan is startled.

> JASPER

Zhoop. Zhoop. Zhoop. Zhoop.

> KJ

. . . Fuck you.

Jasper takes out his cigarettes and lights one.

> JASPER

What else you got, Shelmerdine?

> EVAN

Um.

Evan reaches into his backpack.

> EVAN

This is kind of dumb. But I thought I'd just . . . I brought sparklers?

Evan takes out a box of sparklers.

EVAN

I mean, they're old. They're from like two years ago.

JASPER

SHPAHKLAHS!

Evan isn't sure how to respond to this.

JASPER

I'm sorry. That sounded like I was imitating a Jewish person or something.
"SHPAHKLAHS!"
. . . I have no problems with Jews, though.

EVAN

Um. Okay.

JASPER

KJ might be like one-eighth Jewish or something, right, KJ?

KJ, standing near the recycling bin, shakes his head sullenly.

JASPER

Or was that just a Sandy Jano theory.
Mm.
   (to Evan)
Sandy Jano is KJ's fantastic mother, with whom he still lives. She's a little, ah, how shall we say it, New-Agey? She's into the New Age? And she like became obsessed with tracing their ancestry back and proving they were Jewish or something.
It didn't really work, though, did it KJ?

No response.

JASPER

They're like Lutherans.

Pause.

JASPER

I'm one-sixteenth Cherokee.

EVAN

No way.

JASPER

. . . And KJ here has dreams that he's black.

Evan isn't sure whether he's supposed to find this funny or not. He looks at KJ, whose face is inscrutable.

JASPER

Tell him.

KJ doesn't respond.

JASPER

Tell him about the dream.

KJ continues to give no response.

JASPER

Like two months ago KJ had this dream that he was like . . . that he was black. He comes to me and he tells me this. And I was like: wait. How'd you know in the dream that you were black? Did you like look in a mirror or something? And he was like: no. I was just hanging out with a bunch of black people and we were like all having a really good time together and laughing and I felt really, um, accepted—

KJ, despite himself, cracks a smile.

JASPER

—and they all really liked me and then I realized that *I* was black. That I was one of them.

KJ

And I was really happy.

JASPER

. . . And he was really happy.

Pause. KJ and Jasper giggle.

EVAN

Um. That's kinda weird.

The sound of a distant, muffled explosion. The sky is significantly darker at this point.

EVAN

   (forgetting to be cool)
Oh wow.

A pause.

EVAN

I like forgot it was the Fourth of July for a second.

Another pause. Jasper looks at his watch.

JASPER

They won't happen for at least another ten minutes.

No one knows what to say.

KJ

Music!

JASPER

Already?

KJ

Frogmen.

KJ runs over to the corner and unbuckles the guitar case. He removes an acoustic guitar.

> JASPER

Lemme eat a brownie first.

Jasper grabs a brownie out of Evan's Tupperware, stuffs it in his mouth, and swallows it.

> JASPER

Okay.

KJ hands him the guitar and sits down next to him in a chair.

> JASPER
>
> *(to KJ)*

Do you want to give some kind of introduction? Explanation?

KJ shakes his head. Jasper nods and starts playing the opening chords to the song. He underscores the following monologue/dialogue with the opening chords. He speaks in that rhythmic way people speak over guitar chords. It opens him up a little.

> JASPER
>
> *(to Evan)*

This is a very old song. Actually our oldest song.
Vintage Kevin Jano.
So.
When was this.
Shortly after we met.
KJ was a recent UVM dropout
and I never graduated from high school.

> EVAN

Did you go to SHS, too?

> JASPER

Fuck no. I grew up in Alstead. You know where that is?

Evan shakes his head.

Annie Baker

JASPER

New Hampshire. It's a shithole.

There's nothing. There's a fucking war memorial and a soda fountain and that's it. Trailer trash.

I am a living piece of trailer trash.

Anyway

Moving on

KJ's a college dropout, I'm a street urchin, and:

we meet.

in Vermont.

in this town.

and two weeks later

KJ writes this song

and comes to me

and says:

you make up the music.

you make up the chords.

(after a pause, to KJ)

you want to sing this alone?

KJ

Frogmen sing together.

Jasper nods, plays the opening chords a few more times, and then they sing. During the song the sun sets completely, and by the end they are in the dark, lit only by the moon and perhaps a dim outdoor light on the patio.

JASPER AND KJ

FROM SAGAMORE TO OGDEN

COME THE SLIMY FROGMEN

THEY JIGGLE AND JANGLE THROUGH THE ANGLE

FROM THE BRIDGE TO THE RIDGE AND UNDER THE FRIDGE

THE FROGMEN COME WITH BOTTLES OF RUM

KJ

(MMM RUM)

JASPER AND KJ

MACHO COMACHO THREW THE FIRST SHINDIG
WHERE THE FAT LADY ATE ALL THE RING DINGS
THE YOUNG ONES ATE LIKE RABBITS
AND DREAMT OF LAKE PLACID
(THE FROGMEN ATE FROG STICKS FROG CAKE AND
FROG ACID)
FROM UNDER A LANDING CAME BUTCH AND HIS
BANDMATES
THEY PLAYED MULTIPLE SETS OF
BENNY AND THE JETS
AND WE ALL PLACED BETS
YEAH
WITH PURPLE CIGARETTES
AND THE PARTY WAS FINE TILL QUARTER PAST NINE
FROM UP IN MAINE TO DOWN IN SPAIN
THE FROGMEN CREW BLEW THEIR BRAINS
FROM FRICK TO FRACK
I FLICK MY ASH
FROM DUST TO DUST
I EAT YOUR CRUST
FROGMEN, FROGMEN
NO MATTER WHERE THEY GO
THEY LEAVE TIME FOR THE WILDLIFE
FROGMEN, FROGMEN
THEY MARCH TO AND FRO TO THE DRUM AND THE FIFE
YEAH
FROM SAGAMORE TO OGDEN—

The fireworks interrupt them. The noise is powerful, despite the fact that it's coming from a distance. They all sit and listen, in silence. The explosions build over the next minute or so the way that fireworks do, rising to some sort of climax, then fizzling out, then rising again, then working up to a series of short and manic bursts.

At some point, probably about twenty seconds in, KJ gets up and starts dancing. He dances in weird little circles around the patio. Jasper and Evan watch him. The fireworks continue.

JASPER

You got any friends at SHS, Shelmerdine?

Evan shakes his head peacefully.

EVAN

No.

They watch KJ dance to the fireworks. After a while:

KJ

(*still dancing*)
I NEED A SPARKLER!

Evan gets a sparkler out of the box. Jasper lights it and hands it to KJ. They flinch and move back as it rains down light.
KJ dances with the sparkler.
They watch him.
After a little while, quietly:

JASPER

Don't forget to come back from band camp, Shelmerdine.

EVAN

Um. It's not technically band camp.

The fireworks reach their climax.

KJ

(*referring to the sparkler*)
It's going out it's going out it's going out!

The sparkler goes out.
Darkness.
End of Act One.

Act Two

Scene One

The same set. KJ is sitting by himself, with a cup of tea.
He sits by himself, thinking.
He sits by himself for a long time.
This should be at least twenty seconds.
Finally he says:

KJ

If P then Q.

More silence. More sitting by himself. Then Evan comes out the back door, radiant.

EVAN

Hey!

KJ

. . . Hey!

Pause.

> KJ

Welcome back from band camp!

> EVAN

Thanks.
Yeah.

Another pause that goes on a little too long.

> KJ

Did you have a good time?

> EVAN

Yeah. Actually.
It was pretty cool. I, like, I don't know. It was cool. The kids were cute or whatever. And I like—yeah. The other CITs were cool.
  (pause)
I met a girl, actually.

> KJ

Excellent.

> EVAN

Yeah. I mean, whatever. It was just like a week. But she was pretty cool.
  (pause)
Nicole.

> KJ

Nic*ole.*

> EVAN

Yeah. She's like a violist.
I don't know.
She lives in Boston.
So if I wanted to visit her I'd have to like drive three hours. So I don't know.
It was cool, though.
  (pause)

I mean, it's kind of humiliating that it's taken me this long, but . . .
It's kind of humiliating.

> KJ

No. That's beautiful, man.
> (pause)

Did you finger her pussy?

Evan blanches a little.

> KJ

Oh. Sorry. Is that inappropriate?

> EVAN

No. Um. I mean. Yeah. I did.
Yeah.

> KJ

. . . Great!

> EVAN

Seventeen is like kind of pathetic, though, right? I mean, that it's
happening for the first time, like, now?

> KJ

There are no rules, man.

> EVAN

Yeah.
I mean.
When was your first . . . whatever? Kiss. / Or—

> KJ

Ah . . . let's see. My first kiss I was, like, fourteen?

Evan nods.

> KJ

It was with this like sixteen-year-old chick at an Allman Brothers
show. And I was totally tweaked out just to like kiss her but then

she tried to give me a blow job in a Porto Potty and my like little hairless dick like didn't respond and I was totally humiliated.

EVAN

Oh man.

KJ

And then I dated this like younger girl when I was in high school, she was like a freshman and I was a senior and I think I kind of fucked with her head. We had sex and like now looking back I'm not sure that she was like totally ready, you know? Then I fuckin' cheated on her with this girl at a Chess Championship and we like had mindblowing sex or whatever, me and the Chess girl, and then I made the mistake of like coming back home and like TELLING her or whatever to like get it off my chest and right after I told her she like crumpled in this little like . . .

(he makes a vague gesture and waits for the word to come)

. . . *heap* on the ground and she like cried and cried but she stayed with me and then I broke up with her anyway right before I went off to UVM.

So yeah.

EVAN

Wow.

KJ

Bleak, man. It was bleak.

EVAN

When did you have your like first serious girlfriend?

KJ

Ah . . .

KJ shrugs uncomfortably.

EVAN

At UVM?

KJ

Well. Sophomore year I fucked this girl in my interdisciplinary seminar but then I dropped out at the beginning of junior year.

A weird pause.

KJ

Yeah. I'm not really interested in, like . . . I don't know. Serious shit or whatever.

Another weird pause.

EVAN

Um. Cool. Well. I should probably go inside. I'm workin' the three to ten.

KJ

Awesome.

EVAN

Maybe I'll see you guys tomorrow.

KJ

Wanna hear a song?

Evan looks at his watch.

EVAN

Um. Sure. Yeah. I should go inside in like, a / minute, but—

KJ starts singing.

KJ

DRAWING ON THE STRENGTH OF THE COMMUNITY
A PERIOD OF SPIRITUAL ACTIVITY
ANGO
A JAPANESE WORD
THAT LITERALLY MEANS
A PEACEFUL DWELLING
INCREASING IN VIGOR AND CLARITY

> UNFOLDING NEW SECTIONS
>   OF OUR NEIGHBORHOOD
> AMONG A SMALL BAND OF STUDENTS
> COLLECTIVE COMMITMENT
> TO REALIZATION
> RELAXATION
> TRANSLATING INTO STIMULATION
> PRACTICING ZAZEN IN OUR ZENDO
> UPON AN ALTAR IN MY DOJO
> I AM A SENSEI
> I AM A SENSEI

                                EVAN

(edging toward the door)
That's awesome.

                                 KJ

It's not over.

> IN OUR CITY OF HARMONY
> THIS INCREDIBLE NATION
> CIRCLED OVER THE WORLD AROUND US
> RETURNS HOME WITH US
> THE FIRST TIME I ASKED THE INCENSE
> SUSTAIN THE ONGOING DELUSION
> SOCIAL STATUS QUO
> INTUITIVE ENERGY FLOW
> I AM A SENSEI.

A pause.

                                EVAN

Cool.

                                 KJ

Thanks.

                                EVAN

Are you, like, a Buddhist?

KJ

You could say that.
You could say that.

Pause.

EVAN

Um. See ya later, KJ.

Evan exits into the coffee shop.
KJ sits by himself. He thinks hard about something, and then, upon
realizing something else, smiles. Then he goes back to thinking again.
Blackout.

Scene Two

KJ is standing next to the back door, leaning up against the wall.
He is humming quietly to himself. It looks a little like he's waiting
to surprise someone.
After a while, Evan comes out through the back door in his white
apron, lugging a full garbage bag. He starts when he sees KJ.

EVAN

Oh. Wow!

KJ giggles.

EVAN

You scared me. Kind of.

They stand there for a second, and then Evan walks over to the
garbage bin, opens it, and throws the garbage bag in. Then he tries
leaning casually against the garbage bin, but it's too uncomfortable.
He stands up straight, stuffs his hands in his pockets, and stands
there while KJ gazes at him, smiling.

EVAN

I have a five-minute break.

KJ claps his hands.

KJ

Yay!!!

EVAN

Where's Jasper?

KJ

He's sick.

EVAN

Oh man. That sucks.

KJ

Yeah.

EVAN

Does he have like a cold? Or / like—

KJ

Yup.

A long pause. They are both at a loss. Evan decides to try sitting in one of the plastic chairs. KJ stays by the door. Silence for a while.

KJ
(with exaggerated excitement)
So are you gonna go to college?!

EVAN

Um. Yeah. Next year? Yeah. I think so.

KJ

Where?

EVAN

Um. I don't know. I mean, wherever I get in I guess? I don't know. I'm kind of interested in Bates?

KJ

Never heard of it.

EVAN

Yeah. It's kind of small. It's in Maine.

Pause.

EVAN

You dropped out, right?

KJ nods.

EVAN

Why? Um. If it's not rude to ask.

KJ

I had a breakdown. I don't know. I wouldn't really call it a breakdown.

A pause.

EVAN

Okay. Cool.

KJ

College is bullshit, though.
If you're like . . . I mean, if you've like . . . if you're the real thing, or if you've got like . . . college is just like pointless.

Evan nods.

KJ

Jasper didn't go to college.

EVAN

Yeah.

Pause.

> EVAN

Did you have like a major?

> KJ

Double Major. Math and Philosophy.

> EVAN

Oh cool! Philosophy is cool. I mean, I don't know anything about it.

> KJ

Ever heard of propositional calculus?

> EVAN

No. I mean. I haven't—I'm taking pre-calc next year.

> KJ

Propositional calculus is different from regular calculus, my little friend. It's Logic.

Evan nods, confused.

> KJ

I was gonna write my thesis on it.
You woulda loved it.

> EVAN

What was it . . . what is it, / like—

> KJ

You know about truth tables?

Evan shakes his head.

> KJ

No? Okay. Well.

KJ scratches his beard thoughtfully.

> ### KJ
>
> It's like: If P then Q, then, you know, Truth.
> Or it's like: If P then *not* Q.
> Or it's like: P and Q. Or P *or* Q.
> But when it gets interesting is when you try to figure out what can
> be a P and Q in the first place.

A pause.

> ### KJ
>
> So okay. Let's say P is: "I'm a wizard." And Q is: "The wizard is
> yellow." Then, uh . . .
> You have to figure out if there's even such thing as a . . .

KJ trying to think. A long pause. Evan is starting to feel uncomfortable.

> ### EVAN
>
> Um—

> ### KJ
>
> Or:
> Let's say you're feeling sad, right? You're feeling sad.

> ### EVAN
>
> Okay.

> ### KJ
>
> And you like look at your own sadness. From like above. And
> that's how you're able to say, you know: "I feel sad."

> ### EVAN
>
> Okay.

> ### KJ
>
> But like: what do you—which of your senses like—how do you
> *do* that?

Pause.

KJ

Or like: or: or:
J, right? Picture the letter J. As in Jasper.

EVAN

. . . Okay.

KJ

And then picture another J. Sitting next to it.

Evan nods.

KJ

And I say to you: J is the same thing as J.

EVAN

Okay.

KJ

But *how do you prove that?*

A pause.

EVAN

Um.
   (*a short pause*)
Because they look like each other?

KJ

EXACTLY!
That was my point.
That was the gist of my thesis.

Pause.

EVAN

Um. I should probably go back inside.

Evan starts to head back inside.

                              KJ

I love you, Shelmerdine.

Evan stops in his tracks, terrified. Is he supposed to say it back? A long pause while KJ gazes at him. Finally:

                              EVAN

Um. I love you too.

                              KJ

Just kidding.

Another pause.

                              KJ

Just kidding!

                              EVAN

Yeah. Um. Me too.

Evan hesitates, then goes back inside the coffee shop. KJ doesn't move. Blackout.

Scene Three

The same day. Evening.
KJ has not left. He is lying across two plastic chairs, sleeping.
There are a couple of tiny liquor bottles at his feet.
Evan comes out with his backpack on. He is closing up the coffee shop.

                              EVAN

Oh shit.

Evan stands there looking at KJ for a while. He approaches him and tries poking him very lightly. Nothing happens. He tries poking him harder. After a few seconds, KJ opens his eyes but does not move.

KJ

Was I snoring?

EVAN

No.

A pause.

EVAN

Is. Um. Is everything okay?

KJ

Do you like Jasper more than me?

EVAN

Um.
No.
No!

KJ

Every time I see you you want to know if Jasper's here.

EVAN

That's because Jasper is usually / here.

KJ

He's sick!

EVAN

I know. I'm sorry.

Pause.

KJ

I wanna kill myself.

EVAN

Oh shit.

Evan sits down near KJ on a chair, takes out his cell phone and dials.

EVAN

Mom.

I'm gonna be late for dinner.

   (*a short pause*)

Um . . . this guy I work with is upset.

   (*a short pause*)

He broke up with his girlfriend.

   (*pause*)

Please don't ask me that. Please don't ask me that. Please don't ask me that.

   (*a short pause*)

Please don't ask me that.

I don't care.

I don't care.

Okay.

Evan hangs up. KJ is still lying across the chairs.

EVAN

I hate her.

KJ

Whoa.

EVAN

She like—she does this thing? She does this thing where she like asks what kind of—like if I want cauliflower or carrots with dinner and then if I like tell her carrots she's like well your father doesn't—and it's just like whatever I say she like contradicts me and I'm just like—

Never mind. It's stupid.

KJ nods understandingly.

KJ

Yeah.

This one time . . .

This one time I couldn't stop saying this one word? I was like obsessed with this word. I would just walk around whispering it to myself.

I was a little kid. I was like five.

I would walk around all day saying:

(*he whispers softly*)

Ladder. Ladder. Ladder.

EVAN

Ladder? Like what you climb on?

KJ nods.

KJ

I couldn't stop saying it. I started like whispering it to myself at night and I wouldn't be able to fall asleep. And finally one night my mom got into my bed with me and she was like: you can say it for as long and as loud as you want and I'll hold your hand the whole time.

And I was like: okay.

And I just went:

Ladder.

Ladder.

Ladder.

Ladder.

Ladder.

Ladder.

Ladder. Ladder. Ladder. Ladder. Ladder. Ladder. Ladder. Ladder.
Ladder. Ladder. Ladder. Ladder. Ladder. Ladder. Ladder. Ladder.
Ladder. Ladder. Ladder. Ladder. Ladder. Ladder. Ladder. Ladder.
Ladder. Ladder. Ladder. Ladder. Ladder. Ladder. Ladder. Ladder.
Ladder. Ladder. Ladder. Ladder. Ladder. Ladder. Ladder. Ladder.
Ladder. Ladder. Ladder. Ladder. Ladder. Ladder. Ladder. Ladder.
Ladder. Ladder. Ladder. Ladder. Ladder. Ladder. Ladder. Ladder.
Ladder. Ladder. Ladder. Ladder. Ladder. Ladder. Ladder. Ladder.
Ladder. Ladder. Ladder. Ladder. Ladder. Ladder. Ladder. Ladder.
Ladder. Ladder. Ladder. Ladder. Ladder. Ladder. Ladder. Ladder.
Ladder. Ladder. Ladder. Ladder. Ladder. Ladder.

(he has begun to cry by this point)
Ladder. Ladder. Ladder. Ladder. Ladder. Ladder. Ladder. Ladder.
Ladder. Ladder. Ladder. Ladder. Ladder. Ladder. Ladder. Ladder.
Ladder. Ladder. Ladder. Ladder. Ladder. Ladder. Ladder. Ladder.
Ladder. Ladder. Ladder. Ladder. Ladder. Ladder. Ladder. Ladder.
Ladder. Ladder. Ladder.
   (a pause)
. . . And then I stopped.

Pause. Evan is frozen in place.

EVAN

Um.

A long pause.

KJ

He died.

Evan looks at him uncomprehendingly. Pause.

KJ

Jasper died.

Pause.

EVAN

. . . No he didn't.

KJ

He died a week ago.

Pause.

EVAN

No.

KJ nods.

EVAN

Come on. Stop it.

A pause.

                              EVAN

No he didn't.

Silence.

                              EVAN

Why are you . . . stop fucking with me.
     (*pause*)
You just said he was sick!

                               KJ

I'm sorry.
I'm really really sorry.

                              EVAN

Why are you saying that?!

KJ shrugs. Silence.

                               KJ

Isn't that weird?
That he died?
I just think it's so weird.

*Evan walks over to the big recycling bin and tries to knock it over.
But this is hard to do. The recycling bin is very, very heavy. It takes
Evan a long time. For a while, it seems like he's not going to be able
to do it. Then, finally, he tips it over. The sound of glass bottles fall-
ing. Maybe a few roll out onto the ground.
Evan walks inside.
KJ is alone.
After a long time Evan walks out again. He is holding an oatmeal
raisin cookie.*

                              EVAN

What did he die of.

                               KJ

He died.

> EVAN

What did he die of?!
(*pause*)
Are you fucking with me? You can't . . . you have to tell me if
you're fucking with me!

> KJ

He died in his sleep. I think. He died in his room. He was shooting
up. He died.

> EVAN

He was *what*?

> KJ

He wasn't like . . . he'd only done it a couple of times before. He
was just . . . it was an accident.

> EVAN

Were you *there*?

KJ shakes his head.

> EVAN

That doesn't make any sense!

Pause.

> KJ

It's okay if you can't cry.

Evan begins to cry.

> EVAN

Oh my god.
I have to go home.
I have to go home.

> KJ

Okay.

EVAN

I have to go home. I'm sorry. I don't know why I have this cookie.
I have to go home.

Evan puts his cookie down on the table and leaves.
KJ is alone.
Eventually he starts singing, softly and slowly.

KJ

ZANE
SITS
BY A BROOK
A LITTLE STREAM
IN A NOOK
IN A CRANNY WITH HIS KRAMMY
HE SITS BY A BROOK
AND HE LOOOOKS
IN THE WATER
THAT FALLS DOWN THE ROCKS—

KJ notices the fallen recycling bin. He stops singing and walks over
to it. He tries to right it. It takes a very long time, but he succeeds.
He stares at it for a while, then lays his hand on top of it.
Blackout.

Scene Four

The next day.
Evan is standing outside by himself, on a break. He wears his white
apron. He looks around furtively, and then takes a pack of cigarettes
out of his pocket. He tries tapping the pack of cigarettes against his
palm, a little unsure of what direction to tap it in. Then he unwraps
it, with some difficulty. Then he takes out a cigarette. Then he takes
out a book of matches from his pocket. He lights the cigarette.
This is the first time in his life he has ever bought a pack of ciga-
rettes and this is the first time in his life that he has ever smoked a
cigarette by himself.

There is a certain bittersweet joy in it.
While he smokes, he gazes around, looking for KJ.
After a little while, Evan takes out his cell phone and dials. He
waits, then:

EVAN

Hey.
It's Evan.
How are you.
Um.
I'm smoking a cigarette.
   (*pause*)
I'm calling because I want to know how your recital thing went
and if they gave you the first part for Pachelbel's or if you had to
play the other part.
I bet you were good. Either way.
Um.
   (*pause*)
I'm also calling because my friend died? Um. I know that sounds
really dramatic but um. My friend died. I don't know. Um. He was
like a genius and like a novelist and he died of a drug overdose.
He was like one of my best friends.
I'm um . . .
I'd like to come visit you in Boston.
He's the only person I um . . .
My grandparents died when I was a baby.
Okay. Sorry this message is ramble-y.

Evan hangs up.
He stubs out his cigarette.
He waits for KJ, in vain.
A minute passes.
Blackout.

Scene Five

The set is empty.
After a few seconds KJ enters, with Jasper's guitar case on his back.
It's a bit startling to see him enter because we have only seen him
attached to the picnic table and plastic chairs up until this point.
KJ puts his guitar case down and sits in one of the plastic chairs.
He is wearing shorts and sneakers and sunglasses. He sits there for
a while, in the sunlight, and then he bends down and unlaces his
shoe. He turns his shoe upside down.
A pebble falls out onto the ground and makes a small noise.
KJ doesn't put his shoe back on.
He takes a paperback book out of his bag. He flips through it and
opens to a page and starts reading it.
Evan appears at the back door, peeks out, and sees KJ. He opens
the door and walks out. He is wearing his white apron. KJ keeps
reading. Evan doesn't know what to do. He takes out his pack of
cigarettes and lights one. He is much better at smoking by this
point. Evan smokes while KJ reads.
Eventually:

EVAN

Hey.

KJ

Hey.

EVAN

I haven't seen you for a few days.

KJ

Yeah.
  (pause)
I might be moving.

EVAN

Oh. Wow. Um. Really?

KJ

I might be. I'm thinking about it.

EVAN

Where?

KJ

I have a list of places.
I'm trying to decide.
 (*a short pause*)
Wanna hear?

EVAN

Yeah.

KJ wrenches a small, wrinkled, soggy piece of paper out of his pocket.

KJ

These are just some ideas.
Okay.
 (*he reads:*)
Austin Texas.

EVAN

Oh cool. It's supposed to be cool down there.

KJ

It's high on the list.
Iowa City.
Olympia Washington.
Taos. I don't know if I said that right.
Amherst Massachusetts.
Orion's wind farm.
Seattle.

EVAN

What's Orion's wind farm?

KJ

Oh. Uh. This guy? Jasper's old weed dealer? He lives on like a wind farm in Marshfield.

EVAN

What's a wind farm?

KJ

It's like . . . it's like the white windmill things by the side of the road. The big uh . . . like the / spinny—

EVAN

Oh yeah.

KJ

(going back to the paper:)
Eureka California.

EVAN

How does he *live* there?

KJ

(ignoring him)
Eureka California.
Asheville. Question mark.
Commune in Virginia where they make hammocks find out name.
. . . Can't read my own handwriting. Resnick? Redding?
This one's a stretch: Winnipeg?

EVAN

Where's that?

KJ

It's in the Canadian province of Manitoba? I believe.

Pause.

KJ

That's it.

EVAN

Those all sound cool.

KJ

Yeah.

I'm thinkin' about it. I don't know. Sandy Jano is against the idea. But.

Evan stubs out his cigarette on the ground.

KJ

. . . Smoker.

EVAN

Yeah. I guess. I mean, hopefully. Not.

Pause.

EVAN

Um. I'm sorry I um. Ran away. Or whatever. On Wednesday.

KJ nods.

EVAN

Is there gonna be a funeral? Cause I'd really / like—

KJ

It was last week.

Evan nods. A long pause.

EVAN

He was so. um. cool.

A self-conscious pause.

EVAN

I kind of feel like a completely different . . .

Evan shakes his head tearily and can't finish his sentence.
KJ looks at him for a little while.

KJ

Come here.

Evan walks over to him.

KJ

Kneel down.

Evan tentatively kneels down.

KJ

I'm going to bless you. I'm going to remove your toxins.

KJ puts his fingers together and touches Evan's cheek.

KJ

   (quietly)
Zhoop.
   (a pause)
That's it.
You can stand up again.

Evan stands up again.

EVAN

Um. KJ? I should / tell you—

KJ

I'm sending his novel out. It was almost finished so I thought they could publish it as like. You know. An unfinished thing.

EVAN

Oh. Cool.

KJ

Yeah. I'm just like looking in the like book jackets of all my mom's books and I'm like: all right. Farrar Stroose and Geeroosh. Union Square. I'll send it to you.

EVAN

Don't you like need an agent or something?

KJ shrugs and lifts up the book in his lap. It is Bukowski's The Last Night of the Earth.

KJ

Did *Bukowski* have an agent?

EVAN

Yeah. I don't know.
  (*a short pause*)
I'm reading some of his . . . I took out um . . . I'm reading *Ham on Rye*? And um—yeah. *Love Is a Dog from Hell*.

KJ

You like it?

EVAN

Yeah. Yeah. He like. It's um. It's great. He says "cunt" a lot.

KJ

Yeah!

EVAN

. . . Yeah.

Pause.

EVAN

Um.
KJ?

KJ

Yes.

EVAN

Rahna came back yesterday.
I guess she was on vacation?

KJ

Uh-huh.

EVAN

And she said you guys, um . . . she said that you can't be back
here. And she was really, um, mad. And I explained to her about
um . . . about what, um, happened while I was gone—

KJ slowly starts putting his shoe back on.

EVAN

—but she was really pissed at me and she told the manager which
was really stupid of her but she told him and he said that um: that
you guys, that um, you, can't be here anymore. I mean, nobody's
supposed to be back here except for staff.

KJ nods.

EVAN

. . . And I got really mad and I like argued with him and I was
like: he's not *doing* anything, but um they found um those liquor
bottles I guess and apparently Jasper once um *peed* out here or
something so they um . . .

His voice fades out. KJ nods.

EVAN

He's coming back tomorrow and he's gonna be check / ing all the—

KJ

It's cool.

EVAN

You can start coming inside if you want.
I can make you free tea.

KJ

Yeah. I don't know. They always play that Ani DiFranco shit inside.

> EVAN

. . . Yeah.

> KJ

Uh.

> EVAN

You can stay as late as you want today! I mean. Nobody's gonna check.
　(*pause*)
I should probably go back inside in a minute.

> KJ

Yeah.

A pause.

> KJ

I have a present for you.

KJ points to the guitar case.

> KJ

I don't know how to play, so.
It's his guitar.

> EVAN

I can't take that.

> KJ

It's for you. His roommates didn't want it.

> EVAN

. . . I don't know.

> KJ

Do you already have one?

EVAN

Um. No. I mean, my mom has a really crappy one and I play that sometimes.

KJ

Take it. It's pretty good. He stole it from some yuppie asshole in Burlington.

Evan looks at it. He bends down and unbuckles the case. He takes out the guitar. He looks at it. He holds it.

KJ

Try it.

EVAN

I'm not very good.

Evan plays a few halting chords.

KJ

Yeah!!
Yes.

Evan smiles a little.

EVAN

I feel weird taking it.

Pause.

EVAN

Okay. I mean. Thank you.

KJ

Thank Joseph Yoseph. Thank the Limp Handshakes.

EVAN

Okay.

                          KJ
Thank The Aliens.

                          EVAN
Okay.

                          KJ
Play something!

                          EVAN
I should go back inside.

                          KJ
Play something first!

                          EVAN
Um.

Evan thinks.

                          KJ
Don't think!

                          EVAN
Um.

Evan hesitates, and then messily starts playing the first few chords of "If I Had a Hammer."

                          EVAN
   (*singing softly*)
   If I had a hammer, I'd hammer / in—

                          KJ
No covers!

Evan stops playing.

EVAN

Oh. Um. Sorry.

I don't know any, um . . . I don't have any, like, originals. I don't write music.

KJ

Why not?

EVAN

Um. I don't know. I don't think I'm good enough. I don't know. I'm not like a genius musically or anything.

KJ

How do you know?

Evan shrugs.

KJ

I'm a genius. *Jasper* was a genius.

EVAN

. . . Yeah.

KJ

Maybe you're a genius too!

Pause.

EVAN

Yeah.

Pause.

EVAN

Um. I should probably go back inside.

KJ

Play The Hammer Song.

Pause.

KJ

Play The Hammer Song!

EVAN

Really?

KJ

Play it.

Evan looks anxiously toward the back door, and then starts playing "If I Had a Hammer." He's not great. He strums haltingly and botches the chords a couple of times, but gets better as he goes on. He has a thin, slightly out-of-tune voice.

EVAN

IF I HAD A HAMMER, I'D HAMMER IN THE MORNING
I'D HAMMER IN THE EVENING, ALL OVER THIS LAND
I'D HAMMER OUT DANGER, I'D HAMMER OUT
   WARNING
I'D HAMMER OUT LOVE BETWEEN MY BROTHERS
   AND MY SISTERS
ALL OVER THIS LAND.

Evan takes in a long, shaky breath.

EVAN

IF I HAD A BELL, I'D RING IT IN THE MORNING
I'D RING IT IN THE EVENING, ALL OVER THIS LAND
I'D RING OUT DANGER, I'D RING OUT WARNING
I'D RING OUT LOVE BETWEEN MY BROTHERS AND
   MY SISTERS
ALL OVER THIS LAND.

IF I HAD A SONG, I'D SING IT IN THE MORNING
I'D SING IT IN THE EVENING, ALL OVER THIS LAND

I'D SING OUT DANGER, I'D SING OUT WARNING
I'D SING OUT LOVE BETWEEN MY BROTHERS AND
   MY SISTERS
ALL OVER THIS LAND.

A pause. Evan puts down the guitar, crimson-faced.

EVAN

Um. Yeah.
It's kind of a stupid song. I don't even know what it means.

KJ

. . . That was awesome.

EVAN

I kind of fucked it up.

KJ

You're gonna go far, man.

EVAN

Come on.

KJ

I'm not kidding.
You're gonna go far.

EVAN

. . . Yeah?

KJ

Yeah.

Evan tries not to smile. But then he does.
They stand there.
Blackout.

END OF PLAY

Circle Mirror Transformation

Production History

Circle Mirror Transformation was developed, in part, with the assistance of the Sundance Institute Theatre Program, with additional support from the Sundance Institute's Time Warner Storytelling Fellowship. *Circle Mirror Transformation* received its world premiere at Playwrights Horizons (Tim Sanford, Artistic Director; Leslie Marcus, Managing Director; Carol Fishman, General Manager) on October 13, 2009. The production was directed by Sam Gold; the scenic and costume design were by David Zinn, the lighting design was by Mark Barton, the sound design was by Leah Gelpe and the production stage manager was Alaina Taylor. It was performed by:

MARTY	Deirdre O'Connell
JAMES	Peter Friedman
SCHULTZ	Reed Birney
THERESA	Heidi Schreck
LAUREN	Tracee Chimo

Characters

MARTY, fifty-five
JAMES, sixty
SCHULTZ, forty-eight
THERESA, thirty-five
LAUREN, sixteen

Setting

A windowless dance studio in the town of Shirley, Vermont.
There is a wall of mirrors. There is a big blue yoga ball.
Summertime.

Note

The week titles ("Week One," "Week Two," etc.) should somehow
be projected and/or displayed onstage, but not the scene numbers
("I," "II," etc.).
A slash (/) indicates where the next speech begins.

Prologue

Lights up.
Marty, James, Theresa, Lauren and Schultz are all lying on the
floor, in various positions.
After at least fifteen seconds of silence:

THERESA

One.

A long silence.

JAMES

Two.

Silence.

LAUREN/SCHULTZ

Three.

MARTY

Start again.

Silence.

SCHULTZ

One.

MARTY

Two.

JAMES

Three.

Another long silence.

LAUREN

Four.

MARTY

. . . Five.

JAMES

Six.

Silence.

THERESA/SCHULTZ

Seven.

SCHULTZ

Shoot.

MARTY

Start again.

Silence.

SCHULTZ/JAMES

One.

LAUREN

. . . Oh my god.

MARTY

Okay. Wait.
We're not getting it.
   (*pause*)
Let's all . . . everyone take a deep breath.
   (*pause*)
Okay.

About five seconds go by.

JAMES

One.

Silence.

THERESA/LAUREN

Two.

MARTY

Start again.

Blackout.

Week One

————

I

James is standing center stage, facing the audience. The rest of the class sits downstage, facing James.

JAMES

Hi.

My name is Marty Kreisberg. Short for Martha, but they've been calling me Marty since I was born.

Ah . . .

   (he scratches his head, then grins)

My husband is supposed to do this, ah, monologue about me but he doesn't really know what to—

   (Marty is trying to signal something to him)

Why can't I do that?

   (he shakes his head)

Allrightallright.

I'm fifty-five and I'm, ah . . . I live in Shirley, Vermont. I'm co-executive director here at the community center and I also teach a bunch of classes . . . ah . . . pottery, jewelry-making, Creative Drama for youth . . . I've been pushing for an adult Creative

Drama class for a while and I'm . . . I'm really glad they let me
do it.
   (*pause*)
Okay.
Ah . . . I'm from New Jersey. Originally. I don't have any kids, but
I'm a great stepmother.
My husband is named James. He's in the class too.
Ah . . . let's see. I'm really into nontraditional healing and sort of
. . . unconventional, ah . . .
   (*he scratches his head again*)
I'm fifty-five years old. I really love the Southwest. I hope to move
there some day.
Did I already say that?
Okay.

Blackout.

II

*Theresa, Schultz, Lauren and James are all walking around the
room in different directions, sock-footed. This should last at least
thirty seconds. Everyone is taking this seriously. Marty is sitting on
her yoga ball, watching.*

MARTY

. . . Faster.

They all walk a little faster, still going in different directions.

MARTY

. . . Even faster.

*They start zooming around the room, except for Lauren, who tries
to keep a safe distance away from everyone.*

MARTY

Now . . . I want you to slow down.

(pause)
Start noticing everyone around you.

They all keep walking while making an effort to notice everyone around them. About twenty seconds pass.

> MARTY

. . . And I want you to find people and shake their hand.

They obey. About twenty more seconds pass.

> MARTY

Now say your name when you shake hands!

About thirty seconds of walking/shaking hands/saying your own name.

> MARTY

Okay! Good.
Great.
Stop.

They stop and look at her. She smiles at them.

> MARTY

How'd that feel?

An awkward silence.

THERESA	SCHULTZ
Great.	Weird.
	. . . Good.

> MARTY

Okay.
    (she gets up off her ball)
Um.
Well.
Welcome.
    (pause)

I just . . . I'm so excited to get to know all of you.
   (*an even longer pause*)
I um . . . I don't want to talk too much, because that's . . .
   (*she makes a vague gesture with her hands*)
But. Um. I just hope that you all feel, um, safe here. And open.
And willing to *go* with it.
Ah . . . okay.
Let's keep going!

Blackout.

III

Marty, Theresa, Lauren, James and Schultz are sitting in a circle.

MARTY

I

THERESA

Took

LAUREN

This

JAMES

Class

SCHULTZ

Because

MARTY

It

THERESA

Was

LAUREN

In

JAMES

The

SCHULTZ

. . . Paper.

A weird pause.

MARTY

Love

THERESA

. . . Truth!

LAUREN

Um . . . discovery

JAMES

Self-Actualization

SCHULTZ

. . . Friends

MARTY

Were

THERESA

Part

LAUREN

Of

JAMES

All

SCHULTZ

The

MARTY

Mess!

Annie Baker

THERESA

And

LAUREN

(pause)

Stuff.

JAMES

. . . Enormous.

A confused pause.

SCHULTZ

I

MARTY

Feel

THERESA

Fantastic!

LAUREN

Period.

MARTY

Oh. Hey. Yeah. I forgot to—we don't have to . . . you don't have to say "period." You can just / keep—

JAMES

Pain

SCHULTZ

Um . . . ah . . . Loneliness

MARTY

Are

THERESA

Feeding

98

LAUREN

Me

JAMES

. . . Sky.

Pause.

SCHULTZ

Evil

MARTY

. . . Blue

THERESA

Birds

LAUREN

Fly

JAMES

Over

SCHULTZ

Head.

Pause.

MARTY

Green

THERESA

Wondrous

LAUREN

Um . . . sunshine

JAMES

Washes

SCHULTZ

Over

MARTY

My

THERESA

Little

LAUREN

Tiny

JAMES

Face

Pause.

SCHULTZ

. . . Hopefully.

Pause.

MARTY

Okay.
Great.
   (pause)
Maybe next week we'll try to make it a little more like a real story.

Blackout.

IV

Breaktime.
Schultz and Theresa are the only people in the room. Theresa is squat-
ting in the corner next to her hula hoop, listening to a cell phone
message. Schultz is drinking from a bottle of water and eyeing her.

SCHULTZ

How long did she say?

Theresa holds up one finger and mouths, "Sorry." After a few seconds she snaps her phone shut.

THERESA

Sorry. What?

SCHULTZ

How long did she . . .
(*a pause while he tries to reformulate his thoughts*)
Ah . . .
How long is the break?

THERESA

I think she said ten minutes?

Schultz nods, embarrassed, and goes back to drinking water. Theresa watches him drink and smiles at him. He puts down the water and smiles back at her.

SCHULTZ

I'm sorry. You have . . .
Sorry. Do you / ah—

THERESA

What?

SCHULTZ

I just ah . . .
I was going to say that you have very . . . you have very alive *eyes*.

THERESA

Oh. Wow. I—

SCHULTZ

But that sounds / kind of—

THERESA

No! Thank you.

SCHULTZ

I don't mean it in a, uh . . . in a weird way.

> THERESA

No. It's a—it's a compliment.

They smile at each other. A pause.

> SCHULTZ

What's your deal?

> THERESA

Oh. God. I / um—

> SCHULTZ

I just mean . . . I haven't seen you around. It's a small town, / so—

> THERESA

I moved here like five months ago.

> SCHULTZ

All right.

A pause.

> THERESA

Do you live near here? Or do / you—

> SCHULTZ

I live in the Brook.

> THERESA

I'm . . . what? Sorry. / The—

> SCHULTZ

They're condos. The Brook. It's on Hitchcock? Right off 7. Across from / the—

> THERESA

Oh yeah. I know where that is.

A silence, during which Theresa notices his wedding ring.

THERESA

So do you live there alone or do / you—

SCHULTZ

I live there alone.
   (*pause*)
My wife and I recently . . . we're divorced. That's why I live in the,
uh . . . I moved out about a year ago.

THERESA

Oh. Okay.

SCHULTZ

She lives in our house. It's a great house. With a . . . I spent years
working on the garden.

THERESA

Huh.

SCHULTZ

The Brook is . . . it's very corporate. Very corporate-feeling.

Theresa smiles sympathetically at him. Another silence.

THERESA

I was just confused because you um . . . you're still wearing your
wedding ring.

Schultz looks down at his hand.

SCHULTZ

Yes. Yes I am.

*Lauren enters, her cell phone pressed to her ear. She eyes them
suspiciously, then goes over to her bag, rummages through it, removes
something, slips it into her pocket, then leaves. They watch her.*

SCHULTZ

I should probably take it off.

THERESA

Yeah. I don't know. What's the rush, I guess.

Pause.

SCHULTZ

Would you be interested / in—

Marty and James enter, in the middle of talking.

JAMES

So *she* called *you.*

MARTY

Yeah. We / just—

JAMES

What'd you talk about?

MARTY

Nothing really.
    (*she looks up and smiles at Theresa and James*)
We've got about three more minutes, you guys.

James walks out of the room and heads to the bathroom. A weird silence. Marty's cell phone rings. She takes it out and looks at it, then puts it back in her pocket.

SCHULTZ

    (*to Theresa*)
So you're a . . . you like to hula hoop!

THERESA

Um. The correct term is actually hooping.

SCHULTZ

Oh god. I'm sorry.

> THERESA

No, no. It's a common, um . . . but "hula hooping" is, actually, um
. . . it's a misnaming.

> SCHULTZ

Ah.

*Schultz keeps staring at the hoop. James reenters and stands near
the doorway, watching Schultz and Theresa.*

> SCHULTZ

It's big.

> THERESA

The big ones are actually easier to use.
Wanna see?

> MARTY

We're about to start. Whenever Lauren gets back.

> THERESA

It'll take two seconds.

*Theresa runs over to the corner, gets the hoop, and runs back to the
center of the room. Schultz stands aside while she raises the hoop to
her hips and then, with a few small, deft tilts of her pelvis, begins
hooping.*

> SCHULTZ

. . . Wow.

Theresa continues hooping. After a while:

> THERESA

The key is actually less movement.

> SCHULTZ

Uh-huh.

> THERESA

As opposed to more movement.

Now Marty and James are watching, too. Everyone is a little hypnotized.

> SCHULTZ

Jesus.

Theresa stops and gracefully catches the hoop before it falls to the ground.

> THERESA

(*to Schultz*)
Try it.

> SCHULTZ

Oh. No. I can't. / I ah—

> THERESA

It's actually really easy.

Schultz shakes his head.

> THERESA

Schultz.

> SCHULTZ

Nope.

Lauren reenters, turning off her cell phone.

> MARTY

Oop! You know what? Everyone's back. Let's get / started.

> JAMES

(*suddenly*)
I'll try it.

THERESA

Yeah James!

James walks over to Theresa. She hands him the hoop.

JAMES

What do I do?

THERESA

Okay. Just um . . . put one foot forward.

James puts one foot forward.

JAMES

Uh-huh.

THERESA

Now just . . . try it. Don't think too much.

James throws his pelvis forward and sends the hoop aloft. It crashes to the ground in about three seconds.

JAMES

(*shaking his head*)
Ah.

THERESA

Try again. It's just a little motion. Like a little . . . spin.

James tries again. He sends the hoop aloft, awkwardly swinging his hips back and forth.

THERESA

Good! Oh my god! That's awesome!

Everyone watches James, half impressed, half aghast. The hoop crashes to the ground. Schultz and Theresa and Lauren all applaud. James hands the hoop back to Theresa.

MARTY

. . . That was amazing.

Blackout.

V

They are all sitting in a circle. Marty is in the middle of a story. Everyone is rapt.

MARTY

And it was at this . . . this wedding was like . . . it was a real hippie wedding. We were all sleeping on the floor of . . . we were sleeping in the lobby of this old abandoned hotel in Eureka. And I spread out my little straw mat . . . this was at the end of the night, and we were all a little drunk, and we'd been dancing, and singing, and I was about to go to sleep, but then I looked over . . . and next to me, lying on his little straw mat, was this, um, this *guy*.

(*pause*)

This really cute guy. I'd seen him earlier that night dancing with all . . . I mean, he was constantly surrounded by women.

And I hadn't gotten a chance to talk to him, but I'd noticed him.

(*pause*)

So we were all lying in the dark, so I couldn't quite tell if . . . but then my eyes started adjusting and I said: holy . . . this guy lying next to me is . . . this adorable guy is just staring at me and smiling at me.

And we just lay there smiling at each other for the next couple of hours.

Not touching or . . .

I don't even remember when we fell asleep.

And the next morning we woke up, smiled at each other again, and he said: I'm James.

SCHULTZ

(*softly*)
I knew it.

MARTY

And I said: I'm Marty.
And he said . . . I couldn't believe the . . . without any kind of . . . he
just said, with total . . . "Wanna go camping with me tomorrow?
I'm driving north to Arcata."
I couldn't believe the nerve of this guy! And I had all these obliga-
tions back in . . .
But I found myself saying . . . I just said:
"Sure. Why not."

James grins, embarrassed. Schultz applauds a little. A pause.

THERESA

That is really really cute.

Another pause.

MARTY

Okay. Who else has a story? And don't forget to really listen, you
guys. We're gonna have to remember these.

A long pause.

THERESA

I'll go.

MARTY

Perfect.

Theresa stands up, somewhat unnecessarily.

THERESA

Okay. Well. This one time when I was still living in New York? I was
on the . . . there was this old Jewish guy in my subway car. I knew
he was Jewish because . . . well, he was stereotypically Jewish.
I mean, not that all Jews look this way, obviously, but he had
this humongous nose and this long like white beard with these

big glasses and he had this accent like an old Jewish Yiddish-y Brooklyn accent and these . . . um . . . suspenders kind of pants. Anyway.

The point is he was very clearly Jewish and he was sitting there talking to these old black guys. Who seemed kind of crazy. They all seemed crazy. But he was holding these pamphlets and he was yelling at them not angry just kind of yelling all this stuff and they were nodding and saying like Totally Man or like You're So Right and I started listening and he was talking about this Jewish Conspiracy and he used the phrase "Jew S.A." And then he was like: "Do you think the World Trade Towers came down by themselves?" And then he was talking about how, you know, the Jews killed Christ, and then . . . ah . . . what else. Oh. Something about World War II. How that happened because Jews were running Wall Street and Wall Street paid for Germany or something?

A very long, weird silence. No one knows what to do.

THERESA

I guess that's it.

She sits down.

MARTY

What made you think of that story?

THERESA

Um. I don't know. I think about it when . . . you know. The issue of self-hate or whatever.

Silence.

MARTY

That man may not have been Jewish.

THERESA

Oh. Um. I'm pretty sure he was.

MARTY

He may have fit your stereo . . . he may have fit your stereotype of a Jewish person but he may not have been Jewish.

Another silence. Finally Marty looks at her watch.

MARTY

Okay. It looks like we're out of time!

Everyone starts getting up.

MARTY

Thanks, you guys.
I think this was a really really great start.

They all start going over the corner to get their bags, put on their shoes, turn on their cell phones, etc.

MARTY

Hey—Lauren? I almost forgot. Just before you—I think you still owe me a check?

LAUREN

My mom was supposed to mail it to you.

MARTY

I don't think I . . . would you be willing to remind her?

LAUREN

Um. Yeah. Sure.

Blackout.

Week Two

I

Lauren is standing center stage, facing the audience. Everyone else sits downstage, facing Lauren.

LAUREN

Hi.

My name is Schultz.

I'm a carpenter.

And I don't just . . . I mean, I do regular carpenter things but I also make these amazing chairs that are like . . . this one chair has, like . . . like the headrest is the sun and the whole thing is gold?

(*Lauren looks at Schultz*)

It's kind of hard to explain.

There's this other chair that looks like a cloud.

Um . . . I'm forty-eight-years old.

I grew up in Maryland and my mom died when I was really little. She was an elementary school teacher. I always wanted to be a baseball player.

Um . . .

I'm really nice to everyone.

(*pause*)

I met my wife Becky right out of college and we . . .

(*Schultz is trying to subtly indicate something to her*)

Yeah. I know. I was gonna—

We just separated. Divorced.

I'm in a lot of pain about it.

But, um, to look on the bright side, I have more time now to work on my chairs and maybe find a way for them to um, spread out to um, more people.

(*pause*)

I am an artist.

I am a really good artist.

Blackout.

II

Schultz, James, Theresa and Lauren are playing a particularly confusing and chaotic version of Explosion Tag while Marty stands in the corner and watches. Explosion Tag is basically regular tag except you're supposed to "explode" when tagged. When you're tagged you also become It, and as It you're supposed to be exploding constantly. When the lights come up Lauren is It. Everyone is awkwardly darting around the room. Lauren is exploding vocally, not physically (she keeps saying "Powccchrrrpowpow"), and half-heartedly scurrying after people. Everyone has a different way of eluding her, although it is not very difficult. This can last up to a minute. Finally Lauren tags Theresa on the elbow. It is unclear whether or not Theresa purposely let this happen.

LAUREN

You're it.

Theresa explodes balletically for a while, and then tags Schultz, who is thrilled to be touched by her. Schultz makes a melodic falling-bomb sound ("NEEEEEEEeeeeeerrrr") while sinking to his knees. There is a long pause while he remains there, still. Everyone stops and watches.

Finally Schultz explodes: silently, beautifully, atomically. His arms are thrust out, his eyes are wide open, his mouth is gaping open in a silent scream.

MARTY

. . . Gorgeous.

Schultz falls backward onto the floor and lies on his back. There is a long silence while everyone remains standing, watching him.

MARTY

You're It now, Schultz.

SCHULTZ

(sitting up)
Oh. Sorry.

Schultz reaches out, quick as a snake, and grabs James's ankle.

JAMES

Ah! Jesus.

SCHULTZ

You're it.

Blackout.

III

Breaktime.
Marty and Theresa are squatting by their bags in the corner, talking quietly. Schultz is lurking in the other corner, drinking from his water bottle.

THERESA

It's natural.

MARTY

It *is*?

THERESA

Weird, right?

MARTY

Well. It's beautiful.

THERESA

Thanks.

MARTY

Have you . . .
   (*a pause*)
. . . I just . . . I saw them in CVS the other day, and I . . . have you
seen these things?

THERESA

Wait, what are you talking about?

MARTY

These um . . . they're like these little packets of dye, but they're . . .
   (*she giggles, then whispers*)
. . . they're for . . . it's for *pubic* hair.

THERESA

Oh my god.

MARTY

They were in their own little section, and I was: I said: Oh. My.
God. and I called James over and he said: what's the big deal?

THERESA

Well. Of / course. He—

MARTY

And I was in a huff about it, I was in this big huff, and then I thought . . .

Marty stops talking and glances over at Schultz.

THERESA

(*giggling*)
Can you hear us, Schultz?

Schultz lowers his water bottle.

SCHULTZ

What? No.

Marty and Theresa dissolve into more giggles. Schultz looks tormented.

SCHULTZ

I have to check my uh . . . my phone messages.

Schultz takes his cell phone out of his pocket, crosses to the front corner of the room, and pretends (convincingly) to listen to a message.

THERESA

So you were really angry—

MARTY

I was in a big huff about it, but then I . . . oh god. You probably don't have to worry about this. You're too young. But my um . . . that hair is half-*gray* now and it drives me crazy . . . and I / thought—

THERESA

Did you buy it?

MARTY

I'm thinking about it.

THERESA

Oh my god. Awesome.

MARTY

But then James will . . . I know he's going to accuse me of being a hypocrite.

THERESA

I bet he'll like it.

MARTY

Theresa.

THERESA

I bet he will.

Marty shakes her head.

MARTY

I have to pee.

Marty gets up and exits. Silence. Schultz is still listening to the imaginary message. Theresa smiles at him.

THERESA

Hey.

Schultz snaps his phone shut.

SCHULTZ

Hi.

THERESA

How was your week?

SCHULTZ

It was okay.

Pause.

SCHULTZ

How was your week?

THERESA

It was good.
(*pause*)
I bought a plant!

SCHULTZ

Oh yeah? What kind?

THERESA

Um . . . I don't know. The tag says that it's a "money plant"? Like if you put it under—if you put it in the window you'll make a lot of money or something.

SCHULTZ

Wow.

Silence.

THERESA

Who called you?

SCHULTZ

My friend.

THERESA

Oh.

Another silence. Theresa looks at the door, then back at Schultz.

THERESA

So what do you think?

SCHULTZ

I ah . . . ?

THERESA

About the class.

SCHULTZ

Huh. Well . . .
(he glances nervously toward the door)
Uh . . . I like it. I don't feel . . . I guess I'm having a little trouble feeling totally comfortable?

THERESA

Yeah.

SCHULTZ

I feel pretty self-conscious.

THERESA

You'll get the hang of it.

SCHULTZ

You seem so . . . you're so good at everything.

THERESA

Well. I'm / actually—

SCHULTZ

You do everything in such a . . . you're so graceful.

THERESA

Oh god. That's . . .

She shakes her head and grins. They look at each other. A long silence.

THERESA

Schultz.

SCHULTZ

What.

THERESA

Do you maybe wanna get a cup of coffee after class? Or um . . . .

Schultz stands there, speechless. Theresa is confused. After a pause:

THERESA

I'm sorry. Did I do something wrong?

SCHULTZ

No.
I mean yes.
Didn't I say yes?

THERESA

You didn't say anything.

SCHULTZ

Oh god. Yes.
I'm sorry. I thought I said yes.
Yes!

Blackout.

IV

James, Schultz, Theresa and Lauren are sitting up against the stage right wall. Marty is in the center of the room, facing them.

MARTY

Okay. So I'm going to use myself as an example.

They all nod. Marty taps her chin thoughtfully.

MARTY

Schultz.

SCHULTZ

Yes.

MARTY

Will you be my father?

SCHULTZ

Gladly.

He stands up. She takes hold of his arm and leads him into the center of the room.

MARTY

   (to the group)
Don't be afraid to physically take hold of people and guide them. That's the point. Okay.
   (pause; to Schultz)
All right. Um . . . let's see. You are . . . you're . . . you're a very condescending . . .
You're always kind of quietly Looking Down on everyone. So maybe . . .
   (Marty manipulates Schultz's arms until they're folded across his chest. Schultz is thoroughly enjoying himself)
And also . . . you have this certain . . .
   (she reaches up and pushes his eyebrows)
You have a condescending sort of . . .
   (Schultz raises his eyebrows in exaggerated contempt)
Perfect.
Okay. Stay that way.
   (she turns back to the group)
Now. Theresa. I want you to be my mother.

THERESA

Awesome.

Theresa leaps up. Marty guides her toward the center of the room and puts her next to Schultz.

MARTY

Okay. You are . . . you're very angry. You're this very aggressive, very dominating woman . . . people have always asked so much of you and not respected your intelligence and so you're really . . .

(*manipulates Theresa's hands so that she's clutching her own hair*)

And if you could turn toward Schultz . . . your husband . . .

(*Theresa turns toward Schultz*)

And . . .

(*Marty takes hold of Theresa's mouth; this surprises Theresa a little*)

And just . . . you're screaming at him.

Good. Good.

And Lauren?

LAUREN

(*not getting up*)

Yeah.

MARTY

You're me.

A pause.

MARTY

Can you get up?

Lauren gets up. This time Marty doesn't go over and take her arm. Instead Lauren slowly walks toward the center of the room.

MARTY

I want you to sit on the ground.

Lauren sits cross-legged on the ground.

MARTY

Except I want you to hug your knees.

Lauren obeys.

                              MARTY

Yep. And kind of bury your head in . . .
Yep.

Marty observes for a while.

                              MARTY

That looks great.

She looks over at James, who is still seated against the wall.

                              MARTY

Don't they look great?

He nods. Silence.

                              MARTY

Wow.
Okay. You can relax.

Theresa and Schultz exhale and let their arms drop to their sides, laughing. Lauren lifts her head up a little but doesn't move otherwise.

                              SCHULTZ

Can I go next?

                              MARTY

Of course! Yes. Everyone back at the wall.

Everyone starts heading back to the wall.

                              MARTY

And this is just the beginning! Next week we start reenactments.

Blackout.

V

They are all lying on the floor again. The lights are dimmed.

SCHULTZ

One.

MARTY

Two.

THERESA

Three.

Long silence.

THERESA

Four.

Silence.

SCHULTZ

FIVE.

Silence.

JAMES

Six.

Silence.

SCHULTZ/LAUREN

Seven.

MARTY

Start again.

Blackout.

Week Three

I

Schultz, center stage, facing the audience. Everyone else sits down-stage, facing Schultz.

SCHULTZ

My name is Theresa.

Ah . . . I am a very special person.

  (*he looks tenderly in Theresa's direction*)

I am thirty-five years old.

I'm very passionate. About all things. I care about things very deeply.

  (*pause*)

I grew up in a small town in New Hampshire. I have a younger brother named Brendan. He's getting married next summer.

Ah . . . I lived in New York for about . . . for many years. I was . . . I am an actress. The decision to move to Vermont was a difficult but I think ultimately positive one. There was a competitiveness and a claustrophobia that was very difficult for me in New York . . . also this sense that people didn't really care about each other.

  (*he shoots another tender look at Theresa*)

I have always wanted to make a difference. I have an amazing soul, an amazing warmth, that, that, that people can sense the minute they meet me. I had hoped to reach people through theater, but the realization that maybe this was impossible caused me to reevaluate and try living in a, a smaller place, where I could work, uh, directly with people. I'm studying for a certificate in acupressure and, ah . . .

Shoot.

Rolfing.

Rolfing.

About six months before I left New York I broke up with my boyfriend, Mark. He was not very good to me. Sometimes I guilt myself out and convince myself that I ruined something and that I made a mistake, but those, uh, my friends and people who are close to me know that I did the right thing. That was a toxic relationship. My father has prostate cancer. It's a, ah, blessing to be only a few hours away from him and to be able to see him on the weekends. I'm also worried about my mother.

I don't want my parents to die.

(a long pause while he thinks deeply about this)

Yeah. Okay. That's it.

Blackout.

II

Theresa, James and Lauren are standing against the wall. Schultz is standing in the center of the room, whispering to Marty. She nods, smiling.

MARTY

. . . Okay.

Yeah.

Yes. Beautiful.

He thinks, then whispers something again.

MARTY

Sure.

She turns and smiles at Theresa, James and Lauren.

MARTY

We're just figuring this out.

Schultz whispers something to her again.

MARTY

Well. Either way.

Schultz nods. Marty walks back to the wall and stands against it with Lauren, Theresa, and James. A long silence while Schultz stands there, looking around the room, troubled.

MARTY

Why don't you start with your bed.

SCHULTZ

(*to James*)
Will you be my bed?

JAMES

Ah . . .
(*he looks at Marty*)
Sure.

James steps forward.

MARTY

What did your bed look like?

SCHULTZ

. . . It was small.
(*pause*)
It was next to my window.

MARTY

Can you describe some of the . . . some of its special qualities to James?

A silence.

SCHULTZ

Small.
  (*pause*)
Soft.

Marty looks at James. Slowly, a little creakily, James gets on his hands and knees. They all watch him.

MARTY

Great. What's next?

SCHULTZ

Ah—

MARTY

What's something you loved about your childhood bedroom?

SCHULTZ

. . . The tree outside my window.

MARTY

Perfect.

SCHULTZ

  (*to Theresa*)
Will you be the tree?

THERESA

Of course.

Theresa steps forward.

THERESA

What kind of tree?

SCHULTZ

Ah . . . maple.

THERESA

Am I large or small?

SCHULTZ

Large.

Theresa stands near James and strikes a beautiful Tree pose.

SCHULTZ

Oh. Yeah.

Schultz and Theresa smile at each other.

SCHULTZ

(*to Lauren*)
Ah . . . will you be my baseball glove?

LAUREN

Um . . .

MARTY

What are some of the qualities of your baseball glove that you'd
like Lauren to embody?

SCHULTZ

Uh . . .

Lauren plops down on the ground, cross-legged.

SCHULTZ

Yeah. Okay.

MARTY

What else, Schultz? What else did you love about your bedroom?

SCHULTZ

Ah . . .
(pause)
My stuffed snake.

MARTY

Your—

SCHULTZ

Right before she died my mother, uh . . . she gave me this stuffed
animal. A, ah . . . a stuffed snake.

Silence.

MARTY

Do you want me / to—

SCHULTZ

Yeah.

MARTY

Where do you want me to go?

SCHULTZ

Will you sit on my bed?

*Marty nods. She sits on James's back, and mimes, as best she can,
the position of a stuffed snake.*

MARTY

(still in stuffed snake position)
Okay. Now . . . take a step back . . . and look at your bedroom.

*Schultz takes a step back. They all freeze in their positions. He
looks at them for a while.*

MARTY

What are you feeling?

SCHULTZ

Ah . . .
(pause)
It doesn't really . . .
I'm sorry.
(pause)
I ah . . .
It doesn't really look like my bedroom.

MARTY

Does it feel like your bedroom?

Schultz shakes his head. A sad silence.

MARTY

. . . Well. Okay.

SCHULTZ

Sorry.

MARTY

No. No. It's fine.

She gets off James's back, a little embarrassed.

MARTY

Let's um . . . we can all . . . everybody can relax.

James and Lauren get up immediately. Schultz smiles at Theresa.

SCHULTZ

You were great.

Blackout.

III

Breaktime.
Theresa is by herself, sitting by her bag, listening to her messages.
Schultz enters. He walks over to her, touches her hair, then kneels
down and tries to kiss her.

THERESA

Hold on. I have to finish listening to my—

Schultz keeps trying to kiss her.

THERESA

Schultz. Hold on a second.

Schultz stops and waits. After a second she snaps her phone shut.
They look at each other. After a second, he leans in again and they
kiss. She stops and looks nervously around the room.

SCHULTZ

They're out feeding the meter.

THERESA

What about Lauren?

SCHULTZ

(*softly*)
I thought about you this morning.
In the shower.

They begin to kiss again. After a few seconds Lauren walks in, sees
them, freezes, and walks out. They don't notice her.

THERESA

. . . Oh god.
Okay.
We have to stop.

Schultz looks at his watch.

SCHULTZ

We have three more minutes.

THERESA

Schultz.

SCHULTZ

Come into the bathroom with me.

THERESA

I think that's probably a bad / id—

SCHULTZ

Just for a minute.
Just for a minute.

He starts walking out the door. Reluctantly, Theresa follows. The room is empty for a full thirty seconds. Then Lauren reenters, looking a little traumatized. She puts her bag down. She isn't sure what to do. She stands facing the mirrors, looking at herself. She frowns, then walks closer and inspects a pimple on her chin. After a little while Marty enters, looking at her phone. She sees Lauren and smiles.

MARTY

Hey Lauren.

LAUREN

. . . Hey.

MARTY

Are you excited about school starting in a few weeks?

LAUREN

Um.
I'm not sure.

Marty laughs a little.

MARTY

That's understandable. I guess school is a mixed bag.

A long pause while Marty smiles at Lauren. Then Marty walks over to her bag in the corner and starts rummaging through it.

LAUREN

(suddenly)
Hey.
Um.
I have a question.

MARTY

(looking up)
Yes.

LAUREN

Um . . .

A long silence.

LAUREN

Are we going to be doing any real acting?

Another silence.

MARTY

. . . What do you mean by Real Acting?

LAUREN

Um . . .
(pause)
Like acting out a play. Or something. I don't know.
(pause)
Like reading from a . . .
(she trails off)

MARTY

Um. Well. Honestly? I don't think so.

Another silence.

LAUREN

Okay.

MARTY

Did you . . . were you looking forward to that?

LAUREN

Um . . . I signed up for this class because I thought we were gonna act.

MARTY

We are acting.

LAUREN

. . . Yeah.
  (*pause; she sighs*)
Okay. Thanks.

Lauren exits. Marty watches her go. After a few seconds James enters.

JAMES

She won't pick up. Her phone is on. She just won't pick up.

MARTY

Do you want me to call her?

JAMES

No. That's absurd.
  (*pause*)
She's so fucking *ungrateful.*

MARTY

I don't know if I agree with that assessment.

JAMES

Okay. Could you please—

Schultz and Theresa enter holding hands. Theresa drops Schultz's hand the second she sees other people in the room, then goes over to her bag and starts looking through it. Schultz is smiling. James looks at Schultz.

JAMES

What.

SCHULTZ

Sorry?

JAMES

You're smiling like something . . . like something hilarious just happened.

SCHULTZ

Oh. Ah . . . no. Sorry.

Blackout.

IV

James and Theresa, standing, facing each other. Schultz and Lauren and Marty watch.

JAMES

(hello)
Ak Mak.

THERESA

(hello)
Goulash.

JAMES

Ak Mak?

THERESA

Ah . . . goulash. Goulash.

JAMES

Ak. Mak.

James giggles.

MARTY

Stay in it.

THERESA

(becoming serious: "I have something to tell you")
Goulash . . . goulash goulash goulash.

JAMES

(what is it)
Ak Mak.

THERESA

(sometimes, at night, I feel incredibly lonely)
Goulash, goulash, goulash goulash goulash.

JAMES

(I don't understand what you're saying)
Ak mak, Ak mak.

THERESA

(I lie in bed staring at the ceiling, and I think about couples and families, like you and Marty)
Goulash goulash goulash goulash, goulash goulash goulash goulash, goulash goulash goulash goulash.

JAMES

(you are very beautiful)
Ak mak, ak mak ak mak ak mak.

THERESA

(are you sad too)
Goulash?

JAMES

(I am attracted to you)
Ak mak.

THERESA

(you're sad, too. I knew it)
Goulash goulash goulash. Goulash.

JAMES

(I feel really guilty when I think about how attracted I am to you)
Ak mak ak mak ak mak ak mak.

A long silence.

THERESA

(I feel like you understand me)
Goulash goulash.

JAMES

(I feel like you actually understand me)
Ak mak ak mak.

They gaze at each other.

MARTY

Okay. Good. Stop. What were they communicating?

SCHULTZ

. . . They seemed very connected.

MARTY

Uh-huh. Good.

LAUREN

They were in love.

A silence.

LAUREN

It seemed like they were in love.

Another silence.

MARTY

Huh.

Okay.

Um . . . what was actually happening, though? What was being sad? Sorry. Said. What was being said?

Silence.

SCHULTZ

Uh . . . well . . . I mean, the sentiment / was—

LAUREN

At first she seemed upset.

SCHULTZ

It seemed like she was sharing a secret.

LAUREN

Yeah. Like a . . .

SCHULTZ

But I thought that . . . it felt like James understood her.

THERESA

(softly)

I'm sorry. Excuse me.

She quickly walks out of the room and shuts the door. Silence.

JAMES

Should / someone—

SCHULTZ

I will.

MARTY

No. That's okay.
I'll be right back.

She walks out of the room and shuts the door.
Blackout.

V

The group stands in a circle. Theresa starts swinging her arms back
and forth and making a corresponding sound.

THERESA

WOOP.
WOOP.
WOOP.
WOOP.

MARTY

Let's all mirror it back to her!

Everyone mirrors the gesture/sound back to Theresa, in unison.
After a few seconds of this:

MARTY

Now Lauren! Transform it!

Lauren, after a second of hesitation, transforms the gesture/sound
into a different gesture/sound. The whole group mirrors it back to
her. They go around the circle, twice, playing Circle Mirror Trans-
formation. This is the only improvised part of the play. Except: the
exercise should end with Schultz transforming someone else's ges-
ture into a form of solemn and silent davening. Everyone silently
davens on their knees for a while.
Blackout.

Week Four

———

I

Schultz enters the room, in darkness. He is the first one there. He switches on the lights. He puts his backpack down, drinks some water, gives himself a long look in the mirror, then starts doing knee bends and touching his toes.
Theresa enters, carrying her hula hoop. She starts a little when she sees Schultz.

THERESA

Hey.

SCHULTZ

Hey.

A long, terrible silence.

THERESA

I'm sorry I didn't / call you last—

SCHULTZ

You don't need to apologize.

Silence.

THERESA

I know I don't.

Silence.

THERESA

But I'm sorry I didn't call you back.

SCHULTZ

Twice.

THERESA

What?

SCHULTZ

You didn't call me back twice.

THERESA

. . . I'm sorry.

Schultz shrugs and takes a long drink of water. Theresa watches him for a while.

THERESA

You seem angry.

Schultz lowers the water and sighs.

SCHULTZ

Um . . . I think I'm . . . I think I'm a little disappointed.
In you.
But. Uh. I'm not *angry*.

Silence.

THERESA

Well. You shouldn't be disappointed in me.
  (*pause*)
Because I've made it . . . I've made it really, really clear that I /
can't—

SCHULTZ

Yes. Thank you. Okay.

THERESA

Schultz.

SCHULTZ

It's just . . . it's funny. The not-calling.
Because a week and a half ago you were calling me every day.

Pause.

THERESA

Yeah.

SCHULTZ

So . . . it's just . . .
  (*pause*)
I'm at a really vulnerable place in my life right / now, and—

THERESA

So am I!

SCHULTZ

—and the, uh, I really don't need someone who—someone who's
going to be inconsistent?

Silence.

THERESA

I'm sorry.

Schultz convulses in horrible, strained, silent laughter.

THERESA

I won't be . . . I won't be inconsistent anymore.
I think we . . . I think the best thing might be for . . . maybe we
should take a break from seeing each other. Outside of . . . and
then I won't have to—

*The door opens. It's Marty and James and Lauren. They all come in
together, with their purses, backpacks, etc. Lauren and Marty are
in the middle of a tense exchange.*

LAUREN

She said she mailed it to you three weeks ago.

MARTY

Okay. Sure. But I never got it.

LAUREN

Maybe it got lost in the mail.

MARTY

All right. Fine. But then she has to cancel it and . . .

Marty notices Theresa and Schultz.

MARTY

Is everything okay?

THERESA

    (after a pause)
Mm-hm.

Blackout.

II

Theresa, center stage, beaming, facing the audience. Everyone else sits downstage, facing Theresa.

THERESA

I'm James.

I grew up in a lot of different places because my father was in the army. Um . . . Germany. Chicago. Florida. I spent the last, um, three years of high school in Long Beach, California, so that was nice cause I got to graduate with people I knew and make real friends.

I went to school at UC Santa Barbara, which was pretty crazy in the late sixties! I learned a lot about myself during college. One, it was pretty hard to break away from my father and all his expectations for me. I also learned a lot about women and men and sexual politics.

Um . . . I have a really funny story about avoiding the draft . . .

(she glances briefly at James and grins)

. . . but, um, okay.

I traveled around a lot after college. I lived in Monterey. I lived at this crazy campground and I had to um, when I did my laundry I would hang my clothes out on the tree branches. Um . . . I went to law school. That was a really different world. But I got really interested on my own in, um, Marxist philosophy, and, um, oh . . . I met my first wife there. Her name was Sylvia. We got married a couple of years later. Um . . . what else. Oh god.

There's just a lot of good stuff.

I'm really interesting.

(she giggles)

Um. Okay. I got through law school and I landed myself this really like great job at a firm in Berkeley and then the day of the bar exam came and I went there and I sat down at the desk and I looked down at the paper in front of me and then I just, like, put down my pencil and I walked out.

Because I realized at that moment that I didn't want to participate in that. In the system. I didn't want to contribute to like a fundamentally flawed . . .

(a pause; she glances at Marty)

Oh god. Okay. Sorry. I'll stop um . . .

I have a daughter! Her name is Erin. She's my only child but I wish we were a little closer . . .

(Theresa sobers up a little)

. . . and that's hard for me.

She's close with Marty. Marty is my wife.

(she grins)

Marty is *awesome.*

We live in this amazing house near the center of town painted these really amazing colors. It's like purple and orange and yellow and people stop their cars and take pictures of it. We have a cat named Coltrane.

Coltrane only has three legs.

(she giggles again)

Um . . . okay.

I am . . .

(she sobers up and thinks again)

I am a very strong man. By strong I don't mean physically strong, although, um, that too. I've been through a lot. My first wife was an alcoholic. My whole family is alcoholics. Alcoholic. My father was emotionally abusive to my mother and although I'm not that way I feel a lot of his anger inside of me. I feel it and I think instead of dealing with it I push it, um, I push it deep down inside me and repress it.

(a pause)

But the truth is . . . I mean, I haven't said this. But . . .

I think the problem is not my father so much as my fear of being my father. Like if I run away too hard from him I will become something else that is also problematic.

Because actually?

I'm an amazing person.

(she grins)

Okay. Thank you.

Blackout.

III

Lights up. Theresa, Marty, Schultz and James stand in a line. Lauren is facing them.

LAUREN

Um.

Silence. Lauren steps forward. She taps James on the shoulder.

LAUREN

You're my dad. Neil. You're Neil.

JAMES

Okay.

LAUREN

Just . . . um . . .

She takes him by the arm and leads him over to a different spot in the room.

LAUREN

This is um. You're . . . um. You're in an armchair. You're reading.

James nods and pretends to be studying an invisible newspaper. Lauren walks back over to Theresa and Marty and Schultz.

LAUREN

Um.

Lauren taps Marty on the shoulder.

LAUREN

Will you be my mom?

Marty nods, smiling. Lauren leads her to a spot in the room across from James.

LAUREN

(to Marty)
You're um . . .
You're angry.

MARTY

Why am I angry?

LAUREN

Um . . . because he's angry?

A confused pause.

JAMES

Should I just . . .

LAUREN

You should / just—

JAMES

Wait—what you said before? About / the—

LAUREN

Yeah.

MARTY

Why don't we start? And Lauren . . . you can stop us at any time.

Lauren nods, then steps back. Silence.

MARTY

Neil.

James continues reading his invisible newspaper.

MARTY

Neil. I need to talk to you about something.

A pause while James studies his invisible newspaper. Then he looks up.

JAMES
(to Marty and Lauren)
I'm sorry. I'm having a little—I'm kind of drawing a blank.

MARTY
Can you just go off what Lauren told you?

JAMES
I don't really . . . I don't really know who this guy is.

MARTY
. . . Can you try?

JAMES
Can I try to *what*?

Marty sighs. A pause.

JAMES
Never mind.
Start again.

He goes back to reading his newspaper.

MARTY
James. I mean Neil.
Neil.
I need to talk to you.

JAMES
I'm busy.

MARTY
You're reading the newspaper.

JAMES

The newspaper is important to me.

MARTY

Please pay attention to me, Neil.

After a second, James puts down his newspaper.

JAMES

What is it?

MARTY

I'm lonely.

JAMES

Well, fine. I'm lonely too. We're all lonely.

MARTY

Then why do you ignore us? Why do you insist on . . . why are you always reading at the dinner table? Or watching TV when you should be talking to Lauren?

A pause.

MARTY

Why don't you engage with me anymore?

JAMES

You're too neurotic.

LAUREN

(from the corner)
He wouldn't say that. I mean, he wouldn't think that.

MARTY

What would he think / was—

LAUREN

He would say that she's always nagging him.

JAMES

(to Marty)
You're always nagging me.

MARTY

Maybe I'm nagging you because you're ignoring me!

James stands up.

JAMES

Maybe I'm ignoring you because you're driving me crazy!

A pause.

MARTY

Then leave, Neil.
Why don't you just leave?

Another pause.

JAMES

I'm stuck.

MARTY

Well, I'm stuck, too.

JAMES

And I, uh . . .

He is in pain. A long pause.

MARTY

But what about Lauren? Just because you're mad at me doesn't
mean you should . . . you can still be nice to your daughter!

Another pause.

JAMES

(softly)
I'm worried she's going to judge me.

MARTY

She's not going to judge you. She loves you.

JAMES

I'm worried she's going to . . .

James starts rubbing the spot between his eyes. It's unclear whether or not he's going to start crying.

JAMES

I, uh . . .

MARTY

What? Be straightforward for once!

JAMES

. . . I feel ashamed.

MARTY

Of what?

JAMES

Of what I've . . .
   (a long pause)
. . . Of my life.

MARTY

But Lauren isn't judging you, Neil.
   (pause)
She just wants you to love her.
Neil. Look at me.

James looks up, tears in his eyes.

MARTY

Lauren just wants you to love her and pay attention to her.
   (pause)
That's all you need to do.

After a while, James nods. He and Marty look at each other sadly.
After a while Marty breaks and looks at Lauren.

MARTY

Well?

Lauren purses her lips, thinking. Everyone waits nervously for her
response. After a long silence:

LAUREN

That was pretty good.

Blackout.

IV

Breaktime.
Theresa is alone, drinking from her water bottle. The door opens.
It's Schultz. He sees her, sees that she's the only one in the room,
then darts away, shutting the door behind him. Theresa sighs. The
door opens again. It's James.

THERESA

Hi.

JAMES

Hi.

James steps into the room and shuts the door behind him.

JAMES

. . . That was intense.

THERESA

Yeah.

A pause.

THERESA

You got / pretty—

JAMES

I got kind of worked up.

THERESA

I mean, I think that's great. Maybe that's what Lauren needed.

JAMES

Yeah.

THERESA

She's a really sweet kid.

JAMES

Yeah.
She reminds me of my daughter. In some . . . in certain ways.

THERESA

Erin?

JAMES

Yeah. Good memory.

THERESA

Oh god. I never forget stuff like that. I mean, about people that
I . . . people that I find interesting.
    (*pause*)
My ex-boyfriend . . . I like totally memorized his entire life. I'd
bring up some girl he kissed in high school and he'd be like:
"Who?" and I'd be like: "Lopie Grossman, you made out with her
twenty years ago" and he'd be like—
Jesus. That's actually her name.
See? I still remember.

JAMES

That's amazing.

THERESA

It's actually horrible.
(*pause*)
I'm like haunted by these . . .

A *pause.*

JAMES

So are you and Schultz . . . ?

THERESA

Oh. No.
Yeah. No.

JAMES

Huh.

Pause.

THERESA

We were. For a little while. I mean, we went out on a / couple of—

JAMES

Yeah. I mean, I knew that.

Pause.

THERESA

That was a . . . I feel like such an asshole. It was a mistake and now . . . and now things are really weird. I shouldn't be talking to you about it.

Theresa glances toward the door.

JAMES

He said that you were still hung up on Mark?

THERESA

Schultz said that?

155

                                    JAMES

Yeah.

                                    THERESA

So / he—

                                    JAMES

He called me and Marty the other night. He was really upset. He
hadn't heard back from you and / he—

                                    THERESA

Oh god. That's . . .
Oh god. Poor Schultz. I'm such a . . .

She shakes her head.

                                    JAMES

What?

                                    THERESA

It's just . . . I mean, I *am* really screwed-up about Mark. But it's
like . . . I mean . . . I would . . . I would like to be, to try being in
a relationship right now, you know?
     (*pause*)
Just not with Schultz.
Oh god. I hate myself.

                                    JAMES

You shouldn't hate yourself.
     (*pause*)
Was it . . . did you feel like he was too old for you?

                                    THERESA

Oh. God. No. I always date older guys.

*An awkward silence. Theresa goes back to drinking from her water
bottle. James watches her.*

JAMES

You shouldn't hate yourself.

Theresa smiles at him.

THERESA

Aw. James. Well . . . thanks.
You're really cool.

James looks down.

THERESA

You and Marty are like the coolest couple ever. I loved hearing all
your . . . your stories and . . . it made me really happy. I was just
like: this couple is so cool!

JAMES

Yeah. She—

Lauren enters.

LAUREN

Hi.

THERESA

Hey, Lauren.

*James nods. Lauren goes over to the corner, sits down, riffles through
her backpack, and pulls out a wrapped sandwich. She opens the
sandwich and begins eating it, while curiously looking over at James
and Theresa. They are self-conscious. After a while:*

THERESA

So tell me about Erin!

JAMES

Oh. Ah . . .

James rubs his forehead.

THERESA

How old is she?

JAMES

She's twenty-three.

THERESA

Okay. Cool.

JAMES

She actually ah . . . she refuses . . . she's refusing to, ah, *speak* to me right now.

Lauren stops chewing. James clears his throat.

THERESA

Oh no. Um . . . can I ask / why—

JAMES

Marty ah . . .
    (he shakes his head)
I guess it's not really Marty's fault.

THERESA

Uh-huh.

JAMES

Ah . . .
    (he lowers his voice)
About two months ago, she—Marty—told her something I wish she hadn't . . . Marty didn't—I don't know *why* she—but Marty didn't realize that Erin . . .
That I hadn't told Erin about, ah . . . this ah . . . this, ah . . .
    (his voice drops even lower and quieter)
. . . very minor infidelity that I, ah, committed during my marriage to, ah, Erin's mother—

THERESA

Oh. Okay.

JAMES

—And ah . . . anyway Marty sort of brought it up on the phone in this sort of casual—I don't know *why* she—but that's beside the—and Erin said: Who's Luisa?

THERESA

Oh. God.

JAMES

And now she's not speaking to me.

THERESA

Oh James.

JAMES

She is speaking to Marty.

THERESA

Well. That makes sense.

JAMES

Yeah. Ah . . . does it?

THERESA

I'm sorry.

JAMES

Yeah. I just ah . . .

THERESA

It'll get better.

James nods. Lauren chews her sandwich and stares at them from her spot in the corner.
Blackout.

V

They are all lying on the floor again. The lights are dimmed.

THERESA

One.

JAMES

Two.

Silence.

MARTY

Three.

SCHULTZ

Four.

Silence.

SCHULTZ

Five.

Silence.

LAUREN

Six.

MARTY

Seven.

Silence.

JAMES

Eight.

THERESA/SCHULTZ

Nine.

A very long, disappointed silence.

JAMES

One.

Silence.

LAUREN

Two.

Silence.

SCHULTZ

Three.

Silence.

MARTY

Four.

LAUREN
  (still lying on her back)
I don't get it. I don't get what the point is.

MARTY

Lauren, maybe you should wait until after class to talk to me about this.

Lauren sits up abruptly.

LAUREN
  (to Theresa)
You were like a real actress. Why aren't you the teacher?

Still lying down, Theresa shuts her eyes and shakes her head.

LAUREN

What's the point of counting to ten?!

MARTY

The point is being able to be totally present. To not get in your head and second-guess yourself. Or the people around you.

LAUREN

I want to know how to become a good *actress*.

MARTY

That is how you become a good actress.

THERESA

She's right, Lauren.

Lauren looks at Theresa, wounded. After a few seconds she lies back down. A long silence.

THERESA

One.

JAMES

Two.

Silence.

LAUREN

Three.

MARTY/SCHULTZ

Four.

Blackout.

Week Five

I

Marty, center stage, facing the audience. She has a tiny Band-Aid on her forehead. Everyone else sits downstage, facing Marty.

MARTY

My name is Lauren Zadick-White.

I'm sixteen.

I was born right before midnight, on October 24th. Um . . . I'm a Scorpio, and my mother says that accounts for why I'm such a hard worker.

Also why I'm so stubborn!

Ah . . . this fall I'll be a junior at Shirley High. School is okay, but I can't wait to go to college and start doing what I love, which is theater and dance. I'm also really interested in going to veterinary school. We'll see. I don't have to make any decisions right now, even though I think I do.

   (*she gazes pointedly at Lauren*)

I don't enjoy talking that much about my family and my, um, background, but it's actually fascinating and just . . . really, really interesting.

My mother is Lebanese, and my father is Irish. Both of them were born outside of the States and they met at the University of Iowa. Um . . . my grandmother lives with us. We call her "Sitti." That's Lebanese for "grandma." I'm really close with her. Everyone says we look alike.

(*pause*)

I have agreed to let all of you know that in the past couple of years my father has had some problems with the, um, law. I hope that this will remain strictly confidential. It has been really hard for my whole family, especially my mother and grandmother, who have always had such high expectations. My grandmother thinks my mother should leave my father. They fight about it.

(*pause*)

I'm not going to go into any more detail.

(*pause*)

It is really hard for me to talk about it and I should be so proud of myself for sharing it with all of you.

(*pause*)

Oh. Also. This fall they're doing *West Side Story* at the high school and I would really like to get the part of Maria. It's my dream role. I signed up for this class so I would be, um, better prepared for it.

(*pause*)

I hope that I . . .

Maybe one day I can stop putting so much pressure on myself.

Blackout.

II

James and Lauren and Marty are watching Theresa and Schultz, who stand in the center of the room facing each other.

THERESA

I want it.

SCHULTZ

You can't have it.

Silence.

THERESA

I want it.

SCHULTZ

You can't have it.

THERESA

I WANT IT.

SCHULTZ

You can't have it.

THERESA

I WANT IT.

SCHULTZ

You can't have it.

MARTY

Come on, Schultz. Really get into it.

THERESA

I want it.

SCHULTZ

Well, you can't have it.

THERESA

But I want it.

SCHULTZ

You can't have it.

THERESA

I FUCKING WANT IT!

Silence.

SCHULTZ

Jesus.

Schultz wipes his mouth with his sleeve, a little upset. He puts his hands on his hips.

SCHULTZ

(*shaking his head*)
You can't have it.

MARTY

Switch phrases.

THERESA

I want to go.

SCHULTZ

. . . Wait, what do I say?

MARTY

"I need you to stay."

SCHULTZ

I need you to stay.

THERESA

Well, I want to go.

Schultz regards Theresa sadly.

SCHULTZ

I need you to stay.

THERESA

I want to go.

SCHULTZ

I need you to stay.

THERESA

But I / want to—

SCHULTZ

I need you to stay.
   (*after a short pause*)
I need you to stay.

MARTY

Good.

THERESA

I want to go.

SCHULTZ

I. Need. You. To. Stay.

THERESA

I want to go.

Schultz runs forward and grabs Theresa by the shoulders.

SCHULTZ

I NEED YOU TO STAY.

MARTY

Okay, no touching.

THERESA

I want to go.
   (*to Marty*)
I'm sorry. I need to go the bathroom.
   (*to James*)
Will you step in for me?

JAMES

. . . Sure.

Theresa exits quickly. Schultz and James stand facing each other. Blackout.

III

Lauren and James are standing, facing each other. Theresa is hovering nearby, watching them. Schultz and Marty are leaning against the mirrors.

LAUREN

Stop haunting me, Mark.

A pause.

JAMES

You shouldn't have broken up with me.
You made a mistake.

LAUREN

No I didn't.

JAMES

Yes you did.

LAUREN

No I didn't. You were domineering and you made me feel . . . you
made me forget Who I Am.

JAMES

Who cares? Now you're going to be alone forever.

LAUREN

No I'm not.

JAMES

Yes you are.

LAUREN

No I'm not.

JAMES

Yes you are.

LAUREN

No I'm not.

JAMES

Yes you are.

Silence.

LAUREN

No I'm not.

MARTY

(from the corner)
Okay. Let's make it a little / more—

LAUREN

I'm not going to be alone forever.

JAMES

I'm the best guy you'll ever have, Theresa. I was the best guy you'll ever have.

LAUREN

You don't know that. Have you . . . have you, like, met all the guys in the world?

Pleased with herself, Lauren glances over at Theresa.

JAMES

No one will ever love you the way that I do.

LAUREN

You were too possessive.

JAMES

That was one of the things you secretly liked about me.

LAUREN

(*glancing over at Theresa*)
No it wasn't?

Theresa shakes her head no.

LAUREN

Yes it was. Okay, yes it was, but that doesn't mean it was good for me. I am a beautiful um really cool woman and I'm really attractive and there are lots of men out there who will like me and be nice to me.

JAMES

You're fooling yourself.

A pause. Lauren sighs.

LAUREN

I don't know what I'm supposed to say.

Theresa speaks up from the corner.

THERESA

I don't want to be with a man who threatens me.

JAMES

I'm not threatening you. I'm telling you the truth.

THERESA

(*stepping forward*)
No. That's not . . . it's because you're insecure, Mark. You could never just let me love you and be free. You were so . . . you were so judgmental and moralistic. You were always lecturing me. If you really love someone, you don't make them feel bad about

themselves! All this negative stuff you're saying . . . it's just . . . it's just further proof that you don't really care about me the way that you say you do. If you really loved me, you'd want me to feel okay about the future. You'd want me to be optimistic.

Silence. Then James smiles.

JAMES

I'm speechless.

Theresa grins.

THERESA

Whew!

MARTY

That was great.

LAUREN

(*to Theresa*)
Sorry.

THERESA

No! You were awesome.

LAUREN

(*to Marty*)
He was starting to make me feel really bad.

Theresa gives James a high five.

THERESA

That was so crazy, man! You totally reminded me of him!

James beams. Schultz watches all of this, expressionless. Blackout.

IV

Breaktime.

Marty is alone in the room, standing in front of the mirrors, look-ing at her reflection and fussing a little with the Band-Aid on her forehead. After a while Schultz enters. He looks at her.

SCHULTZ

What happened?

MARTY

Oh. God. Yeah. It's . . . I fell out of bed. Two nights ago. If you can believe it.

SCHULTZ

Why?

MARTY

. . . Why what?

SCHULTZ

Why did you fall out of bed?

MARTY

Oh. Um . . . I don't know. I'm not sure what happened. I just woke up and I was on the floor. It's happened to me a bunch of times in the past couple of years.

SCHULTZ

Are you a restless sleeper?

MARTY

Um—

SCHULTZ

Do you talk a lot? Wake up screaming?

MARTY

Well, James says I do. And the other week / I—

SCHULTZ

Night terrors.

MARTY

What?

SCHULTZ

You probably have night terrors.

Marty smiles.

SCHULTZ

It's a real thing, Marty.

MARTY

What is it?

SCHULTZ

Becky used to get them. They're uh . . . they're different from dreams because they're just . . . they're just fear. And they can make you have these like, these little seizures. And sometimes you fall out of bed.

MARTY

Huh.

SCHULTZ

Were you abused as a child?

MARTY

I'm sorry?

SCHULTZ

Were you abused as a child?

MARTY

. . . No. Um. No. I don't think so.

SCHULTZ

Okay. Cause it's a common symptom among abuse survivors.

MARTY

Huh.

Pause.

SCHULTZ

Night terrors.

MARTY

Huh. Yeah. Maybe. I don't know what it was.

SCHULTZ

It was night terrors.

MARTY

Yeah.

SCHULTZ

Becky went on medications for . . . she went on some kind of epilepsy medication. It helped her.

MARTY

Huh.

Pause.

MARTY

And it's a real—

SCHULTZ

It's a real thing. It's a real thing. Look it up online.

MARTY

Okay. Yeah. Thanks.

Silence.

MARTY

How're you doing, Schultz? Are you okay?

Pause.

SCHULTZ

Uh . . . I don't know.
  (pause)
How are you?

James suddenly enters, exuberant, with a bottle of water.

JAMES

I hooped.
I hooped for over a minute.

MARTY

. . . Wow.
Great.

JAMES

Now Theresa is giving Lauren a massage. In the parking lot. It's
hilarious. You guys should go take a look.

Marty and Schultz both attempt to smile.

MARTY

. . . That's great.

*James suddenly grabs Marty in his arms and gives her a kiss. It's a
little awkward. Marty smiles at Schultz, embarrassed.*
Blackout.

V

The entire group is sitting in a circle.

MARTY

When I go to India . . . I'm going to bring my purple shawl.

LAUREN

Wait. I've played this before. Isn't it California? "When I go to California"? We played this in fifth grade.

MARTY

This time we're playing it with India.
When I go to India I will bring my purple shawl. Schultz?

SCHULTZ

I don't understand / what—

LAUREN

Say what she said and then add something.
    (after a pause)
"When I go to India I'm gonna bring my purple shawl and a" like another object. Then the next person lists all the other things and adds on something new.

SCHULTZ

Ah . . . when I go to India I'm gonna bring my purple shawl and ah . . .

A long silence.

MARTY

Whatever you want.

Another long silence.

SCHULTZ

Phillips head screwdriver.

MARTY

Okay.

LAUREN

When I go to India I'm gonna bring a purple shawl and a Phillips head screwdriver and a . . . a toothbrush.

MARTY

Theresa! Quick! And get creative!

THERESA

When I go to India I'm going to bring a purple shawl and a Phillips head screwdriver and a toothbrush and . . . a tiny velvet cape.

LAUREN

What?

THERESA

Sorry. Just a cape. A velvet cape.

MARTY

Good! Keep going! James!

JAMES

When I go to India I'm gonna bring a . . . a . . . a purple shawl and a Phillips head screwdriver and a toothbrush and a velvet cape and . . . ah . . .
The Bible.

MARTY

WhenIgotoIndiaI'mgonnabringapurpleshawlandaphillipsheadscrew driverandatoothbrushandavelvetcapeandacopyoftheBibleand . . .
a bottle of red wine!
   (pause)
Schultz!

SCHULTZ

Okay.
I can do this.

(*pause*)

When I go to India I'm gonna bring a purple shawl and a Phillips head screwdriver and a toothbrush and a and a and a and a copy of the Bible and a . . . and a big ol' bottle of red wine! Yes! Oh. And a battle-axe!

A long pause.

LAUREN

You forgot the velvet cape.

SCHULTZ

. . . I did?

A pause.

MARTY

Did he?
Who remembers?

LAUREN

He forgot.

JAMES

I didn't notice.

MARTY

Me neither.

A silence, during which Theresa grapples with an ethical dilemma. Finally:

THERESA

Um . . . I think he forgot.

A wounded silence.

MARTY

Okay. Um. Schultz, you're out.

SCHULTZ

What does that mean?

MARTY

You're just . . .
You have to leave the circle.

After a while Schultz gets up. He stands there for a few seconds, then walks away from the circle. He wavers on his feet, clenching and unclenching his fists.

MARTY

Whose turn is it?

LAUREN

Me.
Um . . . When I go to India I'm gonna bring a purple ca—a purple shawl, a Phillips head screwdriver, a toothbrush . . .

While Lauren is talking Schultz walks over to the wall of mirrors and stands there, making direct eye contact with his own reflection. He remains there, unmoving.

LAUREN

. . . a velvet cape, a copy of the Bible . . . a bottle of red wine . . . and um . . . .a battle-axe.
And a calico kitten.
   (*pause*)
I did it! Right? I did it!

Marty, who has been glancing over in Schultz's direction, clears her throat.

MARTY

You know what? I want us to try something different.

LAUREN

But—

SCHULTZ

(*still facing his reflection, not moving*)
It's fine, Marty.

MARTY

No. No. I . . . I just forgot how competitive this game is. And
it's . . . this . . . what we're doing in this class is really not about
competition.

Silence.

MARTY

Schultz.
Please come back and join us in the circle.

Schultz slowly turns around and rejoins the circle.

MARTY

Great. So this next exercise is . . . hm. Wait. We need paper.

*Marty gets up and hurries over to her backpack. She takes out a
flier and hurries back into the circle. She begins tearing the flier
into five strips.*

MARTY

Okay. We're going to . . . uhp. You know what? We also need
pencils.

*She gets up again and hurries back over to her backpack, then
rummages through it. They all watch her.*

MARTY

I've got one . . . two . . . three . . . this is usable, I guess . . . four . . .

JAMES

I've got a pen.

> MARTY

Okay. Perfect.

She returns to the circle.

> MARTY

So. Everyone take a . . .

Marty hands out the pencils/pens.

> MARTY

Okay. So I want everyone to take your scrap of paper and write on it . . . I want you to write down a secret that you've never, ever told *anyone*.

> LAUREN

Whoa.

> MARTY

And . . . you don't have to be specific. We don't need to know it's you. In fact, we *shouldn't* know it's you. This is an opportunity to have people . . . to be able to air a secret in front of a group without feeling like you have to . . . like you have to answer to it. Or someone.

Silence.

> THERESA

What if we don't have any secrets?

> MARTY

You must have *one*.

> THERESA

I don't know. I've been pretty open in all my relationships. I basic-ally tell my partners everything.

> MARTY

Okay. Well, if you can't—just try to think of something that . . . something that's hard for you to talk about.

Theresa nods.

> MARTY

Okay. So. Just . . . don't take too long. Write down the first big thing that comes into your mind. Even if it's scary.

They all nod.

> MARTY

All right. Go for it.

Everyone (including Marty) starts writing/thinking/chewing on their pens/scootching away to a different part of the floor to have the right amount of privacy to write/think/chew on their pens. Silence, and then the sound of scribbling for about forty-five seconds.

> MARTY

Is everyone done?

> LAUREN

Just . . . hold on.

> SCHULTZ

Yeah. I need a few more seconds.

Mary waits for about ten more seconds.

> MARTY

Okay. Now fold up your paper into four—fold it twice into a little square and give it back to me.

They all obey.

MARTY

And let's all sit together again.

They return to the circle.

MARTY

Okay.
> (*she takes the little pieces of paper and shakes them in her cupped hands*)

. . . We're each gonna pick one. And we're gonna stand in front of the group and read it silently to ourselves, and then we're gonna read it out loud to the group. In a very sincere . . . in a meaningful way.

SCHULTZ

What if you pick your own?

MARTY

Just read it anyway. We won't know.
> (*pause*)

Okay?
Trust me, guys.
Lauren.
Pick one.

Lauren picks a square of paper.

MARTY

Okay . . . now . . .
> (*she hands the rest of the papers out*)

Schultz . . .
James . . .
Theresa . . .
Okay.
And I guess this one is for me.
> (*pause*)

Um . . . Schultz. Can you stand up?

Schultz stands up.

MARTY

Will you deliver your secret, please?

Schultz opens his piece of paper, reads it silently, and then looks up.

SCHULTZ

My father may have molested me.

A slightly shocked silence.

MARTY

Okay. Thank you.

Schultz sits down.

MARTY

Theresa?

Theresa stands up. She unfolds and looks at her piece of paper.

THERESA

I secretly think I am smarter than everyone else in the world.

A pause. Lauren giggles.

MARTY

Lauren.
Great, Theresa. Good job.

Theresa sits back down.

MARTY

James?

James slowly stands up, unfolds, and then reads directly from his paper.

JAMES

I have a problempossibleaddiction
   (*he looks up*)
. . . that's written as one word . . .
. . . with internet pornography.

Lauren covers her mouth with her hand.

MARTY

Great. Thank you.

James sits back down.

MARTY

Lauren?

Lauren stands up. She reads her paper, then stuffs it into her pocket. She looks out at the group.

LAUREN

I think I might be in love with Theresa.

A very long silence. Lauren is still standing.

LAUREN

Um . . .

MARTY

You can sit down. Thank you.

Lauren sits down. Another horrible ten-second silence. Schultz frowns, then looks traumatized, then glares at James, then looks traumatized again.

MARTY

Okay. Ah . . .
I guess it's my turn.

Marty stands up. She unfolds her piece of paper and reads it out loud, not taking her eyes off the paper. Her voice is shaky.

MARTY

Sometimes I think that everything I do is propelled by my fear of being alone.

A very long silence. Marty finally crumples the paper in her fist. She refuses to make eye contact with anyone.

MARTY

Great job, you guys.

Blackout.

VI

They are all lying on their backs in the semi-darkness. Silence for a while.

MARTY
(*dully*)
Okay. Next week is our last class. So let's really try to . . .

A long silence.

LAUREN

One.

Silence.

JAMES

Two.

Silence.

LAUREN

Three.

Silence.

THERESA

Four.

JAMES

Five.

A long silence.

SCHULTZ

Six.

Silence.

JAMES

Seven.

THERESA

Eight.

MARTY

Nine.

A very very long silence.

LAUREN

Ten.

No one moves.
Blackout.

Week Six

———

I

The room, in darkness. The sound of footsteps in the hallway. Marty enters the room, her bag over her shoulder, and turns on the lights. She stands there for a while, tired. She walks over to the corner of the room and puts her bag down.
She walks over to the yoga ball, and sits down. She bounces there, sadly, for about fifteen seconds.
The door opens. James enters.
Marty stops bouncing.
James walks over to the corner and puts his bag down. He stands there in the corner, looking at her. She stays on the ball and looks at him. They look at each other for a while.

MARTY

You came.

JAMES

Of course.

She nods. Silence for a while.

JAMES

I talked to Erin the other night. Finally.

Marty nods.

JAMES

She said you didn't call her back this week. That she left you / five—

MARTY

So that's good. So you talked to each other.

He nods. More silence.

JAMES

How's Phyllis?

MARTY

Fine.

Silence.

JAMES

So what are you . . .
Are you on the *couch* / or—

MARTY

There's an air mattress.

More silence.

JAMES

Come home, Marty.

MARTY

No fucking way.

Another silence.

JAMES

You . . . did you want this to happen or something?

MARTY

Did I *what*?

JAMES

Having us write out—
Did you *want* me / to—

MARTY

Okay. See. That's exactly. That's exactly the problem.
That right there.

The door opens. It's Schultz, with his backpack.

SCHULTZ

Hi, guys.

JAMES

Hey, Schultz.

*Schultz steps inside and starts putting his backpack down in the
corner.*

SCHULTZ

How were your—did you guys have a good week?

*Marty and James both nod. Schultz unzips his backpack and takes
out a little box.*

SCHULTZ

Ah . . . Marty?

MARTY

Mm-hm?

SCHULTZ

I wanted to, uh . . .

Schultz walks over to Marty and hands her the little box.

SCHULTZ

. . . Thanks.

MARTY

Oh Schultz.

SCHULTZ

For everything. It's been a great class.

Marty looks down at the box.

MARTY

Should I—

SCHULTZ

Yeah. Open it.

Marty rips off the paper and takes the lid off the box.

MARTY

Oh wow.

She stares at the box's contents.

SCHULTZ

Yep.

MARTY

This is really great.

SCHULTZ

Do you already have one?

MARTY

Um . . . well, yes, I do, but it's bigger, and not as nice. It's in the living room.

JAMES

(*from across the room*)
What is it?

SCHULTZ

It's a dream catcher.

MARTY

We can put this one . . .
I can put this one in the . . .

Marty trails off. She lifts the dream catcher out of the box and holds it up to the light.

MARTY

I love the little purple—

SCHULTZ

Ah man. I was hoping you didn't already have one.

MARTY

No. No. I love it. I love it.

Marty puts it back in the box.

SCHULTZ

The Native Americans used them to uh . . .

An awkward silence. He has forgotten.

MARTY

Thank you so much, Schultz.

SCHULTZ

Maybe it'll help with the night terrors.

MARTY

Mm-hm.

SCHULTZ

Night terror catcher.

Schultz looks at James.

SCHULTZ

Did she tell you about those?

James shakes his head.
Blackout.

II

They are all sitting in a circle.

MARTY

If

LAUREN

I

SCHULTZ

Wanted

THERESA

To

JAMES

Become

Annie Baker

MARTY

A

LAUREN

. . . Actress

SCHULTZ

I

THERESA

Would

JAMES

Just

MARTY

Go

LAUREN

(pause)
Home.

SCHULTZ

. . . I

THERESA

Have

JAMES

Learned

MARTY

So

LAUREN

Um . . . .Much.

SCHULTZ

(pause)

I

THERESA

Will

JAMES

Try

MARTY

To

LAUREN

Realize

SCHULTZ

The

THERESA

Gigantic-ness!

JAMES

Of

MARTY

Capabilities!

LAUREN

And

SCHULTZ

The

THERESA

Way

195

JAMES

I

MARTY

Express

LAUREN

Anger

SCHULTZ

Is

THERESA

. . . Indescribable.

JAMES

Peace

MARTY

Is

LAUREN

Just

SCHULTZ

Okay

THERESA

For

JAMES

Everybody

MARTY

But

LAUREN

We

SCHULTZ

Will

THERESA

Succeed

JAMES

Always

MARTY

If

LAUREN

We

SCHULTZ

Try

THERESA

And

JAMES

Become

MARTY

. . . Flowers.

Silence.

MARTY

That was perfect.

Blackout.

III

They are all sitting in a circle.

LAUREN

Okay. Um.
I was on the subway. In New York. And there was this old guy.
Who was . . . who was maybe Jewish.
He had a beard.
A—and . . .
   (a pause)
He was totally anti-Semitic.

Lauren sighs.

MARTY

It's okay, Lauren.

LAUREN

I don't remember anything else.

Lauren sits back down.

MARTY

Does anyone else remember something from the first day?

A pause. No one says anything.

MARTY

Okay. Well. I think maybe we'll do one more exercise and then /
call it a—

SCHULTZ

Wait! I do.

Schultz stands up. He clears his throat.

SCHULTZ

Uh . . . okay.

I was at a wedding. In, ah . . . Eureka, California.

Right near the Oregon border. Where there are a lot of redwoods. It's really beautiful up there.

This is 1980 . . . something.

There was this big wedding. Two of my friends were getting married in this big old hotel. And we . . . uh . . . we were all sleeping on straw mats. In the lobby. Of the hotel.

We were all drunk. And we'd been dancing.

And uh . . . there was this guy. I'd been looking at this guy all night. This really attractive, really beautiful guy who just . . . who caught my attention. But I didn't think anything would happen because he was just surrounded by women. All the women liked him.

(pause)

He was one of those guys. Those guys that get all the women. `

(pause)

Then I was getting ready to go to sleep on my straw mat and I noticed that he was sitting . . . that he was lying next to me. On his straw mat. And even though they'd turned off all the lights I could tell that he was looking at me.

And I felt . . .

I felt seen.

And he smiled at me. I could feel him smiling in the dark.

And then I smiled back.

And neither of us had to say anything, because we knew that we would spend the / rest—

MARTY

Schultz?

SCHULTZ

—of our lives together.

MARTY

That was great. Thank you.

SCHULTZ

I'm not finished.

MARTY

The thing is . . . it's quarter till, and I want to make sure we can squeeze in the last exercise.

SCHULTZ

. . . Oh. Okay.

Silence.

THERESA

That was beautiful, Schultz.

Schultz can't quite bear to look at Theresa, but he nods.

SCHULTZ

Yeah. Thanks.

Blackout.

IV

Schultz and Lauren stand in the center of the stage, facing each other. Marty, James and Theresa watch from the wall.

SCHULTZ

(to Marty)
Five years?

MARTY

Ten years. Ten years from now.

Schultz takes a deep breath.

SCHULTZ

Okay.

Schultz walks away from Lauren, then turns around and feigns surprise.

SCHULTZ

Lauren?

LAUREN

Yeah?

SCHULTZ

Is that you?!!

LAUREN

Yeah. Hi, Schultz.

SCHULTZ

Hey!

Silence.

SCHULTZ

What are you doing here in . . . Burlington?

LAUREN

Um . . . I live here now.

SCHULTZ

Weird. So do I!
    (*pause*)
I live here with my wife.

LAUREN

You got married again?

SCHULTZ

Yeah. Yeah. She's fantastic.

LAUREN

That's so cool.
  (*pause*)
What's her name?

SCHULTZ

Ah . . . Susan.
Yeah.
She's a, uh . . .
She's a seamstress.

LAUREN

Wow.

Silence.

SCHULTZ

How are you?

LAUREN

I'm, um, I'm okay.

SCHULTZ

How old are you now?

LAUREN

I'm . . .
  (*a pause while she calculates*)
. . . twenty-six.

SCHULTZ

Oh. Man. That's awesome.

Silence.

LAUREN

I live here with my boyfriend.

SCHULTZ

Aw. Great.

LAUREN

Todd.

SCHULTZ

That's great.

LAUREN

He's a, um . . . he's a doctor. Veterinarian.
We run a veterinary clinic together.

SCHULTZ

What happened to acting?

LAUREN

Oh. Yeah.

SCHULTZ

I thought you wanted to be an actress.

LAUREN

No. I . . . I did a lot of acting in college. I was, like . . . I starred in
a lot of . . . but now I'm a veterinarian.

SCHULTZ

That's great.

LAUREN

I really like it.

Silence.

SCHULTZ

So you're happy?

LAUREN

Yeah. I think so.

SCHULTZ

Yeah.

LAUREN

Are you happy?

SCHULTZ

I am. I am. I'm very happy. Susan is just . . . she's changed my life
around. And business is going really well.

LAUREN

Are you still making your chairs?

SCHULTZ

Oh yeah. Oh yeah.
  (pause)
Have you heard from any of the others?

LAUREN

Oh. Um—

SCHULTZ

Do you know how Theresa is doing?

*Marty opens her mouth and starts to step forward to interrupt them,
but Theresa stops her.*

LAUREN

Um. Yeah.
  (she glances over at Theresa)
She's like a really successful massage therapist. In Putney.

SCHULTZ

Oh, that's good.

LAUREN

Yeah. And she married this like actor. He's kind of famous.

Theresa giggles from the wall.

LAUREN

I forget his name. He's really good-looking.

SCHULTZ

Huh. That's good.
   (*pause*)
Man. She really screwed with my head.

LAUREN

. . . Yeah.

SCHULTZ

But ah . . . I don't really think about her that much anymore.

LAUREN

Yeah.

SCHULTZ

Have you heard from Marty or James?

Over the next minute, the lights fade so that Marty, James and Theresa eventually disappear, and only Lauren and Schultz remain, in a spotlight.

LAUREN

Um . . . yeah. A couple of years ago. I got um . . . I got like a Christmas card from Marty.

SCHULTZ

What'd she say?

LAUREN

Oh. She um. She moved to New Mexico.

SCHULTZ

Oh wow.

LAUREN

Yeah. She started some kind of like arts program? For poor kids? Some kind of like drama thing?

SCHULTZ

Huh.

LAUREN

Yeah. She lives in Taos. In this really beautiful, um, adobe hut. She sent me a picture.

SCHULTZ

So you two kept in touch.

LAUREN

Yeah. A little. I got . . . it's funny. I didn't get the lead in *West Side Story* that fall, but I got the um . . . I got the part of Anita? Which was actually—

SCHULTZ

Aw. I wish I'd known.

LAUREN

Yeah. I called Marty and told her. She came to see it.

Silence.

SCHULTZ

So she and James aren't together anymore?

Lauren shakes her head.

SCHULTZ

Do you know where / he—

LAUREN

I think he's still in Shirley. At the college. Teaching economics.

SCHULTZ

Huh.

Silence.

SCHULTZ

How's your family?

LAUREN

Oh. Um . . . my parents got divorced this past fall.
Yeah.
After um . . . after thirty years of marriage.

SCHULTZ

I'm so sorry.

LAUREN

Yeah. No. I mean, I think it was a good decision.

An awkward silence.

LAUREN

Hey. Um. This is kind of a weird—but do you ever wonder how many times your life is gonna end?

A pause.

SCHULTZ

Uh . . . I'm not sure I know what / you—

LAUREN

Like how many people you're . . . like how many times your life is gonna totally change and then, like, start all over again? And you'll feel like what happened before wasn't real and what's happening now is actually . . . (*she trails off*)

SCHULTZ

Uh . . . I don't know.
I guess I feel like my life is pretty real.

LAUREN

. . . Yeah.

Silence.

SCHULTZ

Well. Uh. It's great seeing you.

LAUREN

Yeah.
You too.

SCHULTZ

I always really liked you, Lauren.

LAUREN

Yeah. I liked you too.

They smile awkwardly at each other and do not move. Then, perhaps, very very faintly, we hear the sounds of a street in Burlington: people talking, a car honking, plates clinking at an outdoor restaurant. The spotlight goes out.

END OF PLAY

Nocturama

———

Production History

Nocturama was developed at the Soho Rep Writer/Director Lab and was workshopped at The Cape Cod Theatre Project.

Characters

SKAGGS, disheveled, twenty-six
AMANDA, bespectacled, twenty-seven
JUDY, a small woman, fifty-eight
GARY, a large man, sixty

Setting

Two houses: one old, one new. Ideally the sets would overlap and occupy the same space. When Amanda is giving her tour she is walking around the historical house; when Skaggs and Judy and Gary are at home they are in the newer house.

In both houses there is a bay window with lots of flowerpots resting on its sill and there is a living room and two bedrooms and a kitchen and a study and a front door and a hallway.

When the audience comes in Amanda is sitting on a bench in the hallway, reading *Harry Potter and the Order of the Phoenix.* Shortly before the play begins she exits.

Time

2007

Note

A slash (/) indicates where the next speech begins.

Act One

—

Scene One

Skaggs and Judy enter through the front door, loaded down with duffel bags. They walk into the spare bedroom, which is right off the hallway, and throw the bags down on the floor. Then Judy walks into the kitchen, opens the refrigerator, and smells a carton of milk. Skaggs sits down on the guest bed in the spare bedroom and stares into space. After a few seconds he gets up, walks into the kitchen, sits down, and rests his head on the table. Judy pours the carton of milk into the sink then crushes it beneath her foot with some difficulty. Skaggs slowly lifts his head up.

SKAGGS

I just remembered my dream from last night.

JUDY

Are you hungry?

SKAGGS

Meghan died.

JUDY

Mm.

SKAGGS

Then there were like three funerals and I missed the first one cause I thought it was just for relatives but then it turned out I should've gone and everyone was pissed at me. Then you were there and you were like holding her ashes in this little folded sheet of paper and I screamed at you, like, "GIVE ME THE ASHES," and you wouldn't, and then I just, uh, grabbed them and ran around and cried.

JUDY

Well, that's pretty self-explanatory.

SKAGGS

Yeah.

JUDY

I might go into town to get a salad. Or some kind of soup? Wanna come?

SKAGGS

No.

JUDY

It might make you feel better. We can have a cup of tea, take it easy . . .

SKAGGS

Just the thought of it makes me nauseous.

JUDY

We'll sit. We don't even have to talk.

SKAGGS

It's freezing out there.

JUDY

You can borrow Gary's parka.

SKAGGS

(*burying his face in his hands*)
Oh my god.

JUDY

What?

SKAGGS

Something about that. "Gary's parka."

Judy washes her hands, then walks behind Skaggs and puts her hands on his shoulders.

SKAGGS

Your hands are cold.

JUDY

You made it back.

SKAGGS

Ha.

JUDY

Welcome.

Skaggs shakes his head ruefully. Car lights fill up the room.

JUDY

I think that's Gary. He's really excited / to see—

SKAGGS

(*standing up*)
I'm gonna go to bed.

JUDY

It's only seven.

SKAGGS

Yeah. I'm weirdly tired.

JUDY

We wanted to give you a little tour.

SKAGGS

Can we do it in the morning?

JUDY

Sure.

Skaggs starts to walk out of the room, then stops.

SKAGGS

Is my laptop still in the car?

JUDY

I put it next to your nightstand.

Skaggs nods and walks into the spare bedroom. Blackout. Lights up on Amanda. She is standing next to the bed.

AMANDA

This is . . . this is the spare bedroom. We've kept it pretty much intact . . . this is not the original bed, but the desk and the arm-chair have been here since the 1840s. Pretty incredible! So. This is the room where one of Vermont's most beloved poets composed the majority of her work. It's also the room where she, um, ended her life.
  (*she points out the window*)
If you look out this south window . . . past the Cumberland Farms . . . past the highway . . . you can get a sense of what Elizabeth Collins saw when she sat here at her desk. Rolling hills. Freedom! Open . . . openness. And this other window, over here . . . faced . . . um . . .
  (*she walks over to the other window*)
. . . It still faces the old Shirley cemetery. Okay. Moving on. Oh. First. You might want to take a closer look at the desk. How small

it is? Desks were *tiny* back in the mid-nineteenth century. That's because people were using oil lamps, mostly, um, whale oil lamps, and the light only covered a small area of space. Okay. Everyone please follow me into the hallway and then we're gonna stop underneath the portrait of Edward Vandevoort—he's the sort of stern-looking guy with the beard right next to the staircase. Thanks!

Blackout.

Scene Two

The next morning. The kitchen. Skaggs is wearing blue boxer shorts and a T-shirt. Judy is fully dressed and giving him a tour of the kitchen cabinets and their contents.

JUDY
(*pointing inside a cabinet*)
Cereal. Crackers. Oatmeal. Pasta.
(*she opens another cabinet*)
Canned stuff. Also baking supplies . . .

SKAGGS
Why are the cans labeled?

Judy shuts the cabinet. Skaggs steps in front of her and opens it.

SKAGGS
"Judy." You put your name on a can of garbanzo beans.

JUDY
I have to.

SKAGGS
Why?

Judy looks around furtively.

SKAGGS

Are you looking for Gary?

JUDY

Shhh.

SKAGGS

He's at his office. He left like two hours ago.

JUDY

(*whispering*)
He eats *everything*.

SKAGGS

Well, he's bigger than you.

JUDY

No. You don't . . .
   (*she sighs*)
I'll go out and I'll . . . last Wednesday I bought this really expensive cheese with, uh, little green things in it? I was really excited about just having a tiny bit every night before dinner. By Thursday morning it was completely gone.

SKAGGS

Big deal.

JUDY

He *binges*. He wakes up in the middle of the night and everything in the kitchen disappears. I can't buy desserts anymore. I have to label everything else.

SKAGGS

Are you sorry you moved in?

JUDY

No.

                        SKAGGS
Do you miss the condo?

                        JUDY
No. That has nothing to do with anything.

                        SKAGGS
I kind of miss the condo.
    (pause)
This house is drafty, man.

                        JUDY
It's beautiful.

                        SKAGGS
Am *I* allowed to eat food that's labeled "Judy"?

                        JUDY
Absolutely.

Skaggs walks out of the kitchen and into his bedroom. Calling out:

                        SKAGGS
Why doesn't he go on a diet?

                        JUDY
It's an addiction!

Skaggs comes back with a duffel bag.

                        SKAGGS
Eating? That's not an addiction.

                        JUDY
Yes it is. It's a clinically diagnosed . . . it's a clinical condition!

Skaggs unzips the bag, takes out an enormous multitiered bong, and sets it on the table.

JUDY

Oh my god. Skaggs.

SKAGGS

I know, right? It's kind of ostentatious.

JUDY

I don't understand.

SKAGGS

Elijah gave it to me.

Judy goes around shutting all the blinds.

JUDY

We should . . . I don't want the neighbors to see.

Skaggs takes the bong over to the sink and fills it with water. Then he puts it back on the kitchen table and starts packing it. Judy watches, mesmerized.

JUDY

How often do you um smoke . . . do you smoke that?

SKAGGS

Uh . . . I actually just decided. None of your business.

JUDY

It is if / you're—

SKAGGS

You're just gonna get worried and give me shit. And I'm not dependent on it, like, at all. You could take this away from me and throw it in the trash. Seriously.

JUDY

Then why are / you—

SKAGGS

Because I don't want to fucking kill myself?
  (*after a long pause*)
Shit. I shouldn't have come home. I don't . . . it's like dread, man.
It's like horrible horrible dread.

JUDY

You know that pot is a depressant, right?

SKAGGS

Pleasepleasepleasepleaseplease do not give me shit about it.

JUDY

Have you thought about going on medication?

SKAGGS

I find antidepressants to be extremely creepy. *Extremely* creepy.

JUDY

They helped me after the divorce.

SKAGGS

Going on antidepressants would actually depress me.

JUDY

Okay, okay.

SKAGGS

I will become depressed if I go on antidepressants!

JUDY

You already are depressed.

SKAGGS

I'm like . . . heartbroken or whatever.

JUDY

You seem depressed.

SKAGGS

Well, I'm nauseous. And I sort of feel like a repulsive sea serpent
. . . monster thing.

JUDY

That's depressed.

SKAGGS

Huh. Yeah. Maybe.

*Skaggs sits down and takes a long hit from the bong. Judy watches.
Blackout. We hear Amanda's voice somewhere on the pitch-black
stage.*

AMANDA

Okaaay . . . here we are in the . . . hold on. I'm having a little
trouble um . . .
    (she struggles around in the darkness)
. . . Hold on . . .
    *(she finally finds the string and pulls it. The kitchen light goes
    on above her)*
Whoops. Sorry. I always have trouble finding that string.
Okay. So. Here we are in the kitchen. Low ceiling, right? People
were a lot shorter back in the nineteenth century.
Um. Okay. When she wasn't writing, Elizabeth Collins spent a lot
of time in this room. Married women in rural Vermont didn't just
have to *cook* . . . they also had to . . . well, they had to pluck their
own chickens, grow their own yeast . . . um . . . shell nuts, soak
grains . . . anyway. If you all come a little closer . . .
    (she beckons the audience, then squats down on the floor)
Elizabeth had this, um, very strange habit, I find it kind of fascinating . . . she would write certain phrases in Latin over and over
again? In her notebooks . . . on the backs of recipes, and receipts
. . . and after she died they kept finding certain phrases written on
the walls and um scribbled into the floorboards.
Anyway. What's so cool . . . if you look down here . . .
    (she points to a spot on the floor)
You can see these tiny tiny little . . . Very tiny. In black ink. The

letters were almost faded, so we've . . . we reapplied the ink ourselves, but . . . look. Unmistakably her handwriting.
"Cadere Animis."
Which is one of her two most common, um, refrains. It means
"to lose heart."

Blackout.

Scene Three

*Lights up on Skaggs and Judy sitting at the kitchen table, a few
hours later. The bong has been pushed aside. Skaggs is tipping
backward in his chair. Judy is sipping a cup of tea.*

JUDY

It was incredible. She was just . . . she had this way about her.

SKAGGS

Like she was blessed or something?

JUDY

Yeah.

SKAGGS

I don't get that. I don't get when people say other people are like
"holy" or something. It always sounds like bullshit.

JUDY

I know, I know. But honestly. I want you to meet this woman . . .
Something in her eyes. This, um, warmth. And / this—

SKAGGS

I've never met anyone who made me say, like: "Whoa. That guy
is holy."

JUDY

You should meet her.

SKAGGS

I'd probably be like: oh, yeah, she seems like a nice lady.

JUDY

(after a pause)
She hugged me.

SKAGGS

When you met her?

JUDY

I went up to her after the seminar to thank her, and we made eye contact, and then she opened her arms and just . . . we stood there holding each other for I think over a minute.

SKAGGS

Maybe she's a pervert.

JUDY

She did this . . . we did this visualization?

SKAGGS

Oh god. I feel like I'm gonna throw up.

JUDY

Is it the pot?

SKAGGS

No. The pot is making me feel better. Otherwise I'd be slicing my wrists open.

JUDY

Okay. Your language is really starting to concern me.

SKAGGS

Why?

JUDY

I mean, if you're contemplating suicide, if you're contemplating it at all—

SKAGGS

I'm probably not going to kill myself.

JUDY

—you need to go on medication or see someone or check in somewhere where they / can—

SKAGGS

Mom! Listen to me! Most likely I am not going to kill myself!
(after a pause)
Although one appealing thing about it is Meghan.

JUDY

What about Meghan?

SKAGGS

Her reaction.

JUDY

You would want to put her through that?

SKAGGS

No, I mean . . . she would just . . . I don't know.
(pause)
I miss her.
I mean, I want to rip her fucking head off but I also just miss her. I know this is technically not about her, like technically it's projection or something? But I actually really miss *her*. Her stupid face next to me in bed.

Judy reaches over and touches his hair, but then gets self-conscious and pretends to pick a piece of lint off his shirt.

SKAGGS

Do you think it would be weird if I called? Just to let her know I'm in Vermont?

JUDY

Is she still seeing that guy?

225

SKAGGS

Uh. I don't know. Yes. Maybe. I just have this weird feeling that if I called right now she'd pick up.

JUDY

Would it be a productive conversation?

SKAGGS

Yeah. It's possible she's like in the middle of fucking someone *this second.*

Judy winces.

SKAGGS

What?

JUDY

. . . I don't know. I've never been comfortable with that word when it relates to sex, / or—

SKAGGS

Fucking?

JUDY

Yes.

SKAGGS

Huh. I think it's kind of expressive.

JUDY

Gary said it to me once.

SKAGGS

He what?

JUDY

He said it to me once, and I got very upset, but then I felt like . . . I don't know . . . a prude or something. Uptight.

SKAGGS

Gary said he wanted to *fuck* you?

JUDY

Just . . . when we first started dating. Once. And—

SKAGGS

That is like the most repulsive thing I've ever heard.

JUDY

Don't repeat that.

SKAGGS

That is truly disgusting, man.

JUDY

I think maybe I'm affected by the, um . . . secondhand smoke.

Pause.

JUDY

Hey. I have some really great dark chocolate from this place in Putney. Wanna try a piece?

SKAGGS

I thought you didn't keep any desserts in the house.

JUDY

(*getting up*)

Well. I just . . . I always keep a bar in my sock drawer. Just to nibble on. It lasts me for weeks.

Judy heads into the bedroom.

JUDY

Don't tell Gary.

Judy opens her drawer, finds the chocolate bar, breaks off two small chunks, then returns to the kitchen and sits back down at the table. She gives Skaggs a piece. He tastes it.

227

SKAGGS

Whoa. Dark.

JUDY

It has antioxidants.

They both chew thoughtfully. A pause.

JUDY

. . . So she did this Forgiveness Ritual.

SKAGGS

The Buddhist nun?

JUDY

(*nodding*)
Or . . . I guess it was more of a visualization. It was amazing. And
. . . are you interested?

SKAGGS

(*shrugging*)
Sure.

JUDY

We were all sitting on the floor with our eyes closed, and she said:
You're standing in a hallway, in front of a big set of doors. And
then you look down and you see that you're wearing a black robe.

SKAGGS

Like a bathrobe?

JUDY

No. Just. Wait a minute. Then the doors open and you walk down
this long aisle . . . and you sit behind a . . . like a podium. And you
look out, and you see everyone you've ever known sitting there
in the audience facing you. And then you realize that you're in a
courtroom. And *then* you realize that you're a judge.

SKAGGS

That kind of robe.

JUDY

That kind of robe. And you're there, and you have, um, the thing. The hammer. What's it called?

SKAGGS

Oh yeah.

JUDY

What's it called?

SKAGGS

The THING!

JUDY

The thing you—

SKAGGS

The bang-y thing! Oh man! It's on the tip of my tongue. It is literally on the tip of my tongue.

JUDY

I can't believe I forgot that word.

SKAGGS

What's that fucking word? Oh my god!

JUDY

It's the—

SKAGGS

It's the thing. It's the Pebble. It's the . . . Loomer. The thing you hit the thing with.

JUDY

Yes!

SKAGGS

The banger. The . . . navel. The—

Gary appears in the doorway. He has just come in from the cold.

GARY

Gavel.

They look up, disappointed.

JUDY

Oh yeah.

GARY

What are you guys talking about?

JUDY

Sumi's seminar.

Gary hangs up his coat.

JUDY

I told you about the Forgiveness part, right?

GARY

You told me about the breathing.

JUDY

Yeah. No. This part was . . . this was in the afternoon.

GARY

(folding his arms)
That's some contraption you've got there, Skaggs.

Skaggs avoids eye contact. An awkward pause.

JUDY

So you're a judge! Everyone you've ever known is out there. And you realize that everyone is there to ask for your forgiveness. So then someone steps up to the podium. The first person. They look very nervous, and scared, and . . . vulnerable.

SKAGGS

Who's the first person?

JUDY

First person who comes into your head.

SKAGGS

Dad. FUCK. That's so obvious.

JUDY

So that person comes up and they look at you, very scared, and you say . . . you really have to picture saying this to them . . . you say: "I release and forgive you."

SKAGGS

I'm not saying that to Dad.

JUDY

Well, you're not really in the visualization. If you were doing it you'd say: "I release and forgive you. I . . ." Wait. I have to remember. "I release and forgive you, because when I look into your heart I see that you are innocent." And then that person walks away and a new person steps up.

SKAGGS

What if they're not innocent?

JUDY

That's the point of the visualization.

SKAGGS

What is?

JUDY

Everyone is innocent.

SKAGGS

Uh . . . I beg to differ.

JUDY

Okay, that's . . . that's the point of her teachings. Expanding your Core Heart. Touching on your own . . . your own points of tenderness.

SKAGGS

Your Core Heart? What the hell is that?

JUDY

She means that beneath anger is forgiveness.

SKAGGS

But some people don't deserve to be forgiven.

JUDY

She would say you're wrong.

SKAGGS

That's—she's an idiot.

JUDY

Okay, see, I actually don't want to hear you say that.

SKAGGS

Fine. Jesus.
    (standing up)
I'm gonna go take a nap. I feel like shit.

Skaggs starts dismantling the bong.

GARY

    (to Judy)
Who did you picture?

JUDY

When?

GARY

When you did the exercise. Who was the first person?

JUDY

Oh. My mother.

GARY

Huh.

JUDY

What about you? Just now?

GARY

Uh . . . I don't know why. But I pictured you.

Skaggs grins broadly. Blackout. Lights up on Amanda in the middle of the living room.

AMANDA

Did you know that most New England Puritans kept a diary? They always had to be introspecting and evaluating everything because, literally, the day of reckoning could come at any time. This compulsive self-analysis is what is often referred to as the, um . . .
     (she makes quotation marks with her fingers)
. . . "Puritan Drama of the Soul." And we can look at this tendency in Elizabeth's family, this tendency to worry and talk about everything . . . what Winnie Rosebath called the "Collins Instability" . . . and we can see how it was clearly in many ways a sort of *dying Puritanism* inherited from Elizabeth's father Samuel and his father Josiah, who was actually a great orator and minister in Boston before he moved the family up to Vermont in 1810. To call Elizabeth herself Puritanical would be a stretch . . . she stopped attending church in her young adulthood. But we can see from her poems that she's always looking for redemptive meaning in the world. And yet she's always unable to find enough of it! Her poems aren't so much spiritual quests, as endless, um, *disputations.* Um . . . okay. Let's move onto the parlor.

Blackout.

Scene Four

Lights up on Judy doing Salutes to the Sun on a purple yoga mat in the middle of the living room. Skaggs is lying underneath a nearby coffee table staring at a little green nightlight plugged into the wall. After a pause, panting a little:

JUDY

Wanna join me?

Skaggs does not respond.

JUDY

Getting your heart rate up might be helpful.

SKAGGS

In what sense.

JUDY

Endorphins.

SKAGGS

I don't believe in endorphins.

JUDY

They exist. It's not . . . it's been proven.

SKAGGS

Yeah. Whatever. Doing yoga with my mother will not make me feel better.

Judy keeps doing Salutes. She is quite good. She begins to pant more and more while they're talking.

SKAGGS

This nightlight is insane.

JUDY

Why?

SKAGGS

I think it's death.

JUDY

I got it at Walgreens.

SKAGGS

It's death.

JUDY

You know . . . you haven't left the house in three days. Fresh air might help you feel better. Or exercise.

She launches herself into a Downward Dog pose.

JUDY

Nana's NordicTrack is in the basement.

SKAGGS

Oh man. I remember her doing that. Watching some like fucking Pat Sajak show and doing her NordicTrack.

Judy continues her Salutes. Skaggs rolls onto his stomach and stares directly into the nightlight.

SKAGGS

It's death, and it's kind of throbbing out at me. It's saying:
   (*he pauses*)
"hello."
   (*pause*)
I see this very clearly.

JUDY

Tell me if you start feeling suicidal.

SKAGGS

Yeahyeahyeah. Where's Gary?

JUDY

At his office.

Annie Baker

SKAGGS

It's Christmas break.

JUDY

He's still doing final grades. Also . . . he likes to play video games on the, um, desktop computer at the college. Whenever he plays them at home I get on his case.

SKAGGS

He plays *video* games?

JUDY

Well. He likes this one particular game. I forget what it's called. Sometimes he'll play until four in the morning.

SKAGGS

That's humiliating.

JUDY

It's part of his addictive . . . he shouldn't feel humiliated.
    (*after a pause*)
He should just try to change.

SKAGGS

Did you know Gary was addicted to video games when you started dating him?

JUDY

No. / But—

SKAGGS

Weird. At what point do you like admit to your new girlfriend that you're a middle-aged man addicted to video games?

JUDY

At least he's not addicted to something else.

SKAGGS

Eating.

JUDY

He's in therapy. And Skaggs? He has worked through so, so much
in the past few years. I can't even tell you.

SKAGGS

Like what?

JUDY

You can ask him yourself.

SKAGGS

I'm not going to ask Gary about his fucking addictive issues.

JUDY

You should. He's trying to be more open.

SKAGGS

Was he an alcoholic?

JUDY

No.

SKAGGS

Was he a, uh, a child molester?

JUDY

Stop it.

SKAGGS

Okay. What. Coke? Was he a cokehead?
  (*after a pause*)
I'm not gonna feel comfortable asking him. I mean, I don't . . . I
don't even know how to bring up Nick.

JUDY

What about Nick?

SKAGGS

Like, "Hey Gary, how's your son?"

JUDY

Just say that.

SKAGGS

It feels weird.

JUDY

Why?

SKAGGS

I could say "how's Nick" and that wouldn't be weird?
  (*after a pause*)
Is he a nice guy?

JUDY

Nick?

SKAGGS

Yeah.

JUDY

He'll be back in the summer. He's very sweet.

SKAGGS

Is he . . . is he *over* there right now?

JUDY

No . . . he's in Georgia. He leaves again in like a month.

SKAGGS

Yeah.
  (*pause*)
Man. I feel, like, *particularly* terrible today.

Judy ends her final Salute, puts her hands together, and bows. Skaggs keeps staring at the nightlight.

SKAGGS

I think Meghan was probably smart not to get back together. I think I might be a horrible person.

JUDY

You're not.

SKAGGS

I don't know.
   (*after a pause*)
Do you ever feel that way? Like you might *morally* be like a really
bad person?

JUDY

. . . No.

Blackout.

Scene Five

*Lights up on Amanda sitting on her bench in the hallway reading
the* Order of the Phoenix. *The door opens. Skaggs walks in wearing
Gary's parka, soaked. Amanda slams her book shut.*

SKAGGS

Hi.

AMANDA

Hi!
   (*after a pause, anxiously*)
Could you . . . um . . .

SKAGGS

Sorry?

AMANDA

It's just . . . um . . . that wallpaper is a hundred and twenty-five
years old.
   (*a confused pause*)
You're wet.
   (*an even longer confused pause*)

Could you just . . . step away . . . just kind of step away from the wallpaper?

SKAGGS

Oh.
   (he steps away)
It's like *slushing* out there.

At the same time:

SKAGGS	AMANDA
What are you reading?	Are you interested in taking a tour? Um . . .

SKAGGS

(peering at her book)
Harry Potter and the what?

AMANDA

Order of the Phoenix.

SKAGGS

Is that like the third or something?

AMANDA

It's the fifth.

SKAGGS

Cool. I, um, I only read the first one. My girlfriend . . . my, uh, ex-girlfriend and I read it together and then we were like: oookay. We'll stop now.

AMANDA

(standing up)
Are you interested in taking a tour?

SKAGGS

Yes. Yes I am.

AMANDA

It's ten for adults and seven if you're a student.

Skaggs takes out his wallet.

SKAGGS

I . . . I have a student ID.

Skaggs digs through his wallet. A bunch of cards fall out onto the ground.

SKAGGS

Fuck.

He bends down and gathers them up.

SKAGGS

For some reason I'm, like, unable to throw away my Metrocards.

AMANDA

Your what?

SKAGGS

Oh. Ha. That's funny.

AMANDA

What? Why?

SKAGGS

No. Nothing. It's like the . . . it's the subway card for New York.

AMANDA

I thought they used tokens.

SKAGGS

Whoa. Was the last time you went to New York in like *1987*?

AMANDA

. . . Yes.

SKAGGS

Jesus.

AMANDA

I actually saved . . .

Amanda gets out her change purse from underneath the chair. She fishes through it, then holds something out to him in her palm.

AMANDA

I still have this.

SKAGGS

Oh my god.

Skaggs holds the token up to the light.

SKAGGS

This is like an *ancient relic*.

AMANDA

Really?

SKAGGS

You could probably get like a hundred bucks for this now.

AMANDA

Yeah?

SKAGGS

Uh . . . actually, I don't know.

He hands it back to her. She puts it back in her change purse.

AMANDA

I wouldn't want to sell it anyway.

SKAGGS

Oh. Right. Here's my ID.

Skaggs hands her his ID. She looks at it, nods, and hands it back to him.

AMANDA

Seven dollars.

Skaggs starts counting out dollar bills from his wallet, then hesitates.

SKAGGS

Um. Wow. I'm actually . . . I suddenly feel obligated to tell you that I'm not a student.

AMANDA

You have a student ID.

SKAGGS

It's from, like, five years ago. I graduated five years ago. Sorry. I'm, like, attempting to be a better person or something.

AMANDA

It's not a big deal.

SKAGGS

No, but I might like at least attempt to not like swindle the owner of a historical house in / rural—

AMANDA

I'm not the owner.

SKAGGS

Whatever. I just . . . it's not like this is like some AMC 500 movie theater or something. I just . . . I felt like a douchebag. Just now.
   (*pause*)
I'm going to pay adult. Adult price.

He takes out a ten-dollar bill and gives it to her. She pockets it.

AMANDA

Thanks.

SKAGGS

Um . . . so . . . do we sit around and wait for other people to show up?

AMANDA

Uh. No. I don't . . . I don't think anyone else is . . . fall is actually our busiest time, so—

SKAGGS

Because of / the fo—

AMANDA

Because of the foliage.

SKAGGS

Yeah.

AMANDA

Winter is a little slow.

SKAGGS

Yeah.

AMANDA

Summer's okay.

SKAGGS

What about spring?

AMANDA

It's—

SKAGGS

I don't know why I just asked that.

AMANDA

Spring is okay. I mean, April, May is okay. March is kind of . . .

A pause.

SKAGGS

So you just sit here all day and wait for someone to walk in?

AMANDA

That's my job.

SKAGGS

You have this like little tour running through your head and you're like waiting for someone to walk in so you can make it come out of your mouth?

AMANDA

Wait. Make the / tour—

SKAGGS

It's just . . . wow. Everybody has, like, the saddest life of all time.
    (*pause*)
Not in a bad way.

Amanda stares at him.

SKAGGS

You're like . . . I wouldn't have come up with that. I mean, I grew up here and it never occurred to me to, like . . . I think I like skipped class when we were supposed to come in seventh grade. And it's just . . . the whole time you were in this house, puttering around giving your little tour, leading this totally particular like / tragic—

AMANDA

I've only been here eighteen months.

SKAGGS

But another you. Another little puttery you.

AMANDA

I actually love this job.

SKAGGS

Well, yeah. Exactly.

An uncomfortable pause.

AMANDA

Um . . . I'm gonna start. How much do you know about Elizabeth Collins?

SKAGGS

Nothing.

AMANDA

Is there a reason you . . . um . . . what piqued your—

SKAGGS

My mother said she was going to kick me out if I didn't leave the house this morning?

AMANDA

Oh.

SKAGGS

I was gonna see a movie in Bellows Falls but everything there was playing in New York like six months ago. It's kind of amazing. They were really bad anyway. Bad movies.

AMANDA

Are you on vacation?

SKAGGS

I had a nervous breakdown. I think. I don't actually know the technical definition for nervous breakdown.

AMANDA

It's when / you—

SKAGGS

I lay in bed for a week and I didn't speak or go to my job or like notify them or anything and then I called my mother and was like: come pick me up.

(pause)

Number one most humiliating moment of my life.

AMANDA

Why did you . . . what made / you—

SKAGGS

My girlfriend broke up with me. Or . . . not really. I kind of . . . whatever.

(*he sighs*)

Then like a week later I was hailing a cab . . . whatever . . . I'm a drummer. I put down my set for like two seconds and some fucker . . . I honestly have no idea how it happened. Someone just like picked up my shit and *absconded* with it. I turned around and . . . I mean, it's fucking *heavy equipment*. And there was no way I could afford to . . . anyway, I lost my set and the next day Meghan ceased all contact with me and, uh . . .

(*pause. He repeatedly pushes his hand through his hair*)

I don't know.

(*pause*)

I am convalescing. And . . . I don't know. I guess I'm trying to be open about it.

(*he looks closely at her*)

Whoa. Um . . .

AMANDA

I'm not crying.

SKAGGS

You have these like little tears in the corner of your eyes.

AMANDA

No. It's um . . . my eyes just do that sometimes.

SKAGGS

You can tell me if you're crying, man.

AMANDA

Why would I be crying?

SKAGGS

I have no idea. But there are these / little—

AMANDA

I just . . . I have this weird response to . . . like if it's really cold outside?

SKAGGS

We're inside.

AMANDA

No, but . . . or like if people . . . like if I'm watching TV and someone is crying onscreen? If it's supposed to be sad or something? I'll feel no like emotion but then my eyes will tear up. Even if it's a really stupid show. I'm not crying. I swear to god.

(she takes a deep breath)

Have you ever read any of her poems?

SKAGGS

Oh, god. They made me . . . there's that stupid thing they always quote? We had to read it like a million times in elementary school. It's so cheesy. The line about the kid?

AMANDA

What line?

SKAGGS

With the toy? There's like this kid playing with a toy?

AMANDA

At last you've come, said I to he—

SKAGGS

Jesus.

AMANDA

He turned and walked away—
As if distracted by a toy—
With which to pass the day.

SKAGGS

Weird. Yeah. I don't know why they were always talking about that poem. I guess cause it's about a little kid.

AMANDA

It's about death. "The hands of that cold child, *death*"?

SKAGGS

Huh. I forgot about that part.

AMANDA

(*flushing*)
Um . . . I'm gonna start.

SKAGGS

I'm Skaggs.

AMANDA

I'm Amanda.

SKAGGS

Excellent.

AMANDA

Um. I'm just gonna give the tour like . . . I kind of have it memorized in a certain way?
(*pause*)
I'm gonna pretend there are more people here. Just cause that's what . . . that's how the language is.

SKAGGS

Sure. Whatever.

AMANDA

Okay. Um. I don't know why I feel nervous.

Amanda clears her throat and walks into the living room. Skaggs follows her.

> AMANDA

This is the parlor. Elizabeth Collins and her husband Alfred would, um, congregate in this parlor nightly to, uh, read, and talk, and occasionally play music.

(pointing)

The piano in the corner is called a "square grand." Has anyone here ever heard of a square grand?

Skaggs looks around, then shakes his head no.

> AMANDA

The square grand was a, ah, short-lived style of piano from the 1840s, when there was this new, um, affluent middle-class in New England that was concerned with buying objects that connoted this idea, of, um, Culture. The piano was as much a decorative item as it was a functional one. This particular square grand did not actually belong to the Collinses, but it is extremely similar to the one they owned, and, actually, the stool—

(she pauses for a second and wipes her eyes)

—the stool did belong to Elizabeth Collins herself, and we know . . . um, this has been confirmed by the Houghton Library at Harvard, this was definitely hers, and you can see the, uh, distinctive animal feet at its base, which were in fashion at the time. I like to refer to them as "raptor claws."

Amanda walks over to the coat closet next to the front door.

> AMANDA

If you could just follow me over to the . . .

Skaggs follows her. Amanda opens the coat closet and takes out a long blue dress, encased in plastic.

> AMANDA

This is . . . well, this was her nightgown, but in the last few years of her life it sort of became her uniform. Elizabeth was famous in the 1860s for standing out on her balcony in this nightgown and watching all the funeral services in Shirley cemetery take place below.

(*she fingers the dress*)

. . . She was wearing this nightgown when she killed herself. She was . . . she was also buried in it, so obviously this is . . . obviously this is a re-creation.

SKAGGS

She killed herself?

Amanda nods.

SKAGGS

They never told us that. Was she like really depressed?

AMANDA

Well. It's a long story. Her husband met this woman named Winnie Rosebath and they eventually ran away to California and—

(*she stops herself*)

Um . . . I actually go into more detail about this later in the tour.

SKAGGS

Oh. Okay.

AMANDA

I mean, Elizabeth was always pretty sad. People didn't call it depression back then.

SKAGGS

So she was depressed *before* her husband left her?

AMANDA

Well, I mean . . . her mother and sister always described her as having a "melancholy temperament." Also her dad died when she was nine and she was always kind of obsessed with him.

SKAGGS

Huh.

AMANDA

She also . . . she had this thing when she was a teenager where she was convinced that all these household objects were alive and, um, out to get her? She wrote about that a lot in her diary. "The rocking horse is crushing me." "The heliotrope in the garden are crushing me."

SKAGGS

Cool, man.

AMANDA

Well. I wouldn't really use the word *cool*.
  (*after an awkward pause*)
Okay. Let's move onto the master bedroom.

Blackout.

Scene Six

Nighttime. Judy and Gary's room. Judy and Gary are lying in their bed, reading. Skaggs walks into the room in his blue boxer shorts and stands in front of them.

SKAGGS

Would it be weird if I got into bed with you guys?

GARY

A little.

SKAGGS

I'll just . . . perch.

Skaggs perches on the edge of the bed and watches them read. After a while:

SKAGGS

I spent an hour and a half outside today.

JUDY

Hey. Great.

SKAGGS

I took that tour.

JUDY

Ooh. Fun.

SKAGGS

Unbelievably boring.

GARY

She's the one who killed herself, right?

SKAGGS

Yeah. She, like, stabbed herself in the chest with a knife.

JUDY

(*wincing*)
Ach.

SKAGGS

It's crazy. Her husband . . . she was like married to this Shirley State nineteenth-century astronomy guy? He cheated on her for like a decade with this woman named like Rose Hooverfish or something and when he finally left her she went completely berserk and like wrote all these poems and killed herself.

JUDY

I've always had a hard time getting into her poetry.

SKAGGS

The, uh . . . the girl who gave the tour?
She was black.
Which is kind of interesting.

GARY

Why?

SKAGGS

Cause there are like no black people here?

GARY

There's a black guy in the economics department. James. His office is across the hall from mine.

SKAGGS

Okay, well, there wasn't a single kid at our high school.

JUDY

There are definitely a couple now. At The Green Sheep? We saw a woman there last week. (*to Gary*) Remember?

GARY

She wasn't black.

JUDY

The woman I'm talking about was black.

GARY

I know who you're talking about and she wasn't black.

JUDY

We're probably talking about different people.

GARY

She was . . .
     (*he sighs, exasperated*)
She wasn't black.

JUDY

Then what was she?

GARY

I don't know.

JUDY

Why are you the expert?

SKAGGS

(after a pause)
She was kind of interesting. She seemed depressed.

JUDY

Did you like her?

SKAGGS

In / what—

JUDY

Were you interested in her?

SKAGGS

I am way way way too fucked up about Meghan.

JUDY

It might be nice to just go out on a date or something.

SKAGGS

Yeah. No.
(after a short pause)
This girl was *extremely* dweeby.

Skaggs lies down between them and stares at the ceiling. After a minute he bolts upright to a sitting position.

SKAGGS

Don't you guys feel like you're going crazy?

GARY

Don't *you* feel like you're going crazy?

SKAGGS

Yes. *(pause)* Don't you?

GARY

Because / of—

SKAGGS

Because of your *lives?*

GARY

No, I don't. I do feel like I'm doing constant work to not fall back into my old, unproductive patterns. Which is hard work. Your mother has helped me . . . she's helped me do a lot of it.

Skaggs and Judy make eye contact.

SKAGGS

Uh . . . what unproductive patterns?

GARY

You know, it's funny. I've been trying to be more open about it.

SKAGGS

That's what Mom said.

Gary turns and stares at Judy.

GARY

Huh.

JUDY

I said that you *were* open. Not that you were *trying* to be.

GARY

No . . . I . . . what did you tell him?

JUDY

I said that you were a very open person. That's all.

Gary looks at Skaggs and takes a deep breath.

GARY

My family has a history of alcoholism.

SKAGGS

Uh-huh.

GARY

But I . . . it's interesting. I'm the one who never had a full-blown
. . . I've always acted out in other ways.

SKAGGS

Uh-huh.

Gary looks at Judy. She nods encouragingly.

GARY

Well, uh . . . through promiscuous behavior. Um . . .

SKAGGS

What / does—

GARY

. . . uh . . . infidelity problems, mostly? Both my first and my second
wife . . . I, uh, had a lot of extramarital affairs? Sort of compulsively.
It was my way of . . . in general I have a lot of trouble asserting my
needs. This is what I've been working through in—anyway, I have
trouble asserting my needs, I grow resentful, and in the past I've
acted it out in these incredibly unproductive ways.
  (Skaggs stares at him. A pause)
Anyway. I'm working on it.

Gary goes back to his Patrick O'Brian novel.

SKAGGS

Meghan cheated on me.

GARY

Your mom said.

SKAGGS

And she just like made *out* with someone. But it was . . . it was the
worst thing that ever happened to me, man.

GARY

Well, I hope that continues to be true.

SKAGGS

Excuse me?

GARY

(to Judy)
Are you hungry?

JUDY

No.

GARY

I might go have a bowl of cereal.

JUDY

You're hungry?

GARY

Uh . . . yes.

JUDY

We just had dinner. Are you sure you're not just feeling anxious?
(they stare at each other. After a long silence . . .)
. . . Because if you're *actually* hungry, you should go have a bowl
of cereal.

GARY

Never mind.

JUDY

I'm serious.

GARY

Forget it.

SKAGGS

. . . Jesus.

GARY

What?

SKAGGS

We're all just . . . we're these walking corpses. I'm looking at you guys, at, like, myself, and we're just . . . we're basically dead.

Judy puts down her copy of Psychotherapy Networker.

JUDY

Live in the moment, Skaggs.

SKAGGS

Oh my god, Mom. Are you kidding me?

JUDY

Really try it, though.

SKAGGS

You . . . it's . . . you grow cheesier with age. You really do. It's terrifying.

JUDY

Take a step back and just . . . stay in the moment.

SKAGGS

Like this moment. This one right now.

JUDY

Yup.

SKAGGS

I'm supposed to look at you and Gary and be like: this is it. This is a beautiful moment.

JUDY

Yes.

Skaggs looks at Judy for a long time. She smiles at him. Slowly, Skaggs turns and looks at Gary. Gary continues to read his Patrick O'Brian novel but, after a few seconds, he looks up, waves briefly at Skaggs, as if for a camera, and then goes back to reading. Skaggs looks at Gary for a while. It seems like Skaggs might cry. He buries his face between his knees. Judy reaches out and touches his hair.

JUDY

Are you inside the moment?

SKAGGS

(shakily)
I don't know.

JUDY

Sumi . . . the one I was telling you about?

SKAGGS

I don't know if I can hear about the Buddhist nun right now, Mom.

JUDY

She says the most important thing is realizing that you have to Abandon Hope.

Skaggs looks up at her, his eyes filled with tears.

JUDY

Abandon all hope.

GARY

That seems a little extreme.

JUDY

It's not extreme, Gary.

GARY

It seems extreme to me.

JUDY

Well you have no idea what you're talking about.

Blackout. Spotlight on Amanda, standing in Judy and Gary's bedroom.

AMANDA

Here we are in the master bedroom. And this . . .

Amanda slowly eases open Judy's sock drawer and takes out a little wooden box.

AMANDA

(hushed)

. . . This is the box. This is one of the few items . . . you can all actually hold the box, if you want to, hold it in your hands.

(a dramatic pause)

This is the box they found in Elizabeth's chest of drawers a week after she died. It contained exactly twenty hand-bound, dated fascicles of poems. We know from these dates that Elizabeth wrote seven volumes of poetry in 1864, her most productive year, um, ever. What's interesting is that 1864 was *also* the bloodiest year of the Civil War. But nowhere in Elizabeth's poems, in the, I think in the more than three hundred poems she produced in that year, is there any mention of the war itself. Not that . . . I mean, one of her primary obsessions is death . . . in her most famous poem she's actually asking death to come lie in the grass with her! But Elizabeth is never explicitly writing about actual, um, violence, or the war itself. Pretty interesting, huh? I always think of this one quote by Nathaniel Hawthorne . . . when he was writing about the Civil War . . . it goes, um: "There is no remoteness of life and thought, no hermetically sealed seclusion, except perhaps that of the grave, which the disturbing influences of this war do not penetrate."

(she grins)

Whew! Heavy stuff.

Let's move on to Alfred's study.

Blackout.

Scene Seven

Gary is up late in the study, sitting in front of his laptop. It casts a sickly glow across his face. Skaggs appears out of the darkness in his blue boxer shorts.

SKAGGS

Hi Gary.

GARY

Oh god. You scared me.

SKAGGS

You're up late.

GARY

So are you.

SKAGGS

What are you doing?

GARY

Playing Nocturama.

SKAGGS

Is that / a—

GARY

It's a game.

SKAGGS

Do you get internet access on that computer?

GARY

Sorry. I'm really tired. What?

SKAGGS

I asked if you got internet access on that computer.

Gary yawns.

SKAGGS

Internet access.

GARY

Uh, yeah, sometimes. If we pick up a signal from the neighbors. We don't pay for it or anything. It just kind of blips in and out.

SKAGGS

So, uh . . . what do you look at? When you're not playing video games.

GARY

What do you mean?

SKAGGS

Like, do you just use the internet for email, or . . . ?

GARY

Uh . . . I also really enjoy Google Earth . . .

SKAGGS

Huh.

GARY

When you were in Brooklyn, your mom gave me your address and I actually went and floated above your apartment building and I saw this, uh, green car in your driveway, and the trees and / the—

SKAGGS

Oh man! That was totally my landlord's car!

GARY

Yeah. This little blurry car. And / uh—

SKAGGS

He was such a fucking madman!

GARY

—I really enjoyed that. I really enjoyed seeing where you lived.

SKAGGS

From above.

GARY

Yeah.

SKAGGS

I miss that place.

GARY

Your apartment?

SKAGGS

No. That apartment is a shithole. I miss Brooklyn.

GARY

Are you in touch with any of your friends?

SKAGGS

I mean, Elijah and I shoot each other emails.
   (*after a pause*)
Was that your stomach?

GARY

Ah . . . I think so.

SKAGGS

Wow.

Gary goes back to looking at his computer.

SKAGGS

Do you ever Google yourself?

GARY

I have.

SKAGGS

And?

                              GARY

Well, there are a lot of Gary Millers, but there's this one site that's
. . . Nancy . . . my ex-wife and I used to take tango lessons and
we participated in this workshop and our names are still up there
in the, uh, dance studio archives? It's kind of funny to see that.

                            SKAGGS

Google me.

                              GARY

Really?

                            SKAGGS

Yeah. I mean, put me in quotes.

                              GARY

I know.

Gary types away at the computer. He waits.

                              GARY

It's a little slow.
    (*pause*)
Uh . . . your search did not match any documents.

Skaggs raises his eyebrows significantly.

                              GARY

You knew that.

                            SKAGGS

There is no record of my existence.

                              GARY

Well. Skaggs Bernstein is a pretty unusual name.

                            SKAGGS

What's weird is . . . I drummed for this lesbian chick, Julie Schil-
ler, like two years ago? She made this demo and then we played

out a little bit and there was actually Googleable evidence of it for a while. Like listings and stuff. But a month ago it just . . . disappeared. Like *right* after Meghan and I broke up.

GARY

Hmm.

SKAGGS

I lose like half of my *soul* and then all evidence of me and my accomplishments like vanishes from the face of Google.

GARY

You know, Skaggs . . . *I* had a really difficult time right after college.

SKAGGS

This isn't right after college. I'm twenty-six. It's much more pathetic.

GARY

I don't know. I was, what, twenty-three, twenty-four . . . and I remember feeling very, uh, discouraged. I also briefly dated this woman and she, uh, she completely destroyed my heart.

SKAGGS

But / you—

GARY

She completely broke my heart and I just . . . I remember hating myself. And thinking there was no point. To anything.

SKAGGS

(*after a pause*)
Are you telling me all this to, like, belittle my experience?

GARY

No. I just . . . I hope that you find a passion, Skaggs. I hope that for you.

SKAGGS

Um . . . I do have a passion, Gary.

GARY

I hope you find a passion that you can pursue wholeheartedly / without—

SKAGGS

I *can* pursue it wholeheartedly!

GARY

But you're not.

SKAGGS

Oh my god. Gary. You are not my father. You are not allowed to—

GARY

I'm your friend, though, Skaggs, and I / think—

SKAGGS

That is a questionable statement!

A long, hurt pause.

SKAGGS

I lost my set, man.

GARY

But you can buy a new one. You can get a job and you / can—

SKAGGS

Okay, ah . . . Gary? I'm having a hard time *standing* these days— and I do not think it would be responsible for me to go get some part-time job working with kids or something and then I fuck them over because I'm too sad to get out of bed / and—

GARY

You don't have to get a job working with kids. My point / is—

SKAGGS

—and I don't want to like fail at something, especially if I knew before I started that I was going to fail at it. My plan is to like stay here and recuperate and abandon hope or something and then when I feel better I'll move back to New York and start working at Le Cherche again—

GARY

Is that appealing to you?

SKAGGS

No, it's not appealing to me, but obviously if I lull myself into some kind of positive-thinking state I'll think it sounds fine and I'll be totally content with some pathetic like waiter existence, but right now the veil has been, um, pulled aside, and I'm seeing the world for what it is, and it's pathetic, and we're all like these painful pathetic people trotting around in little circles and like jerking off all over each other.

GARY

Do you think I'm pathetic?

SKAGGS

I think everyone is pathetic.
   (*pause*)
No. Okay. Not everyone. Like certain, um, great artists. I exempt them.

GARY

Who?

SKAGGS

Um. I don't know. Like that Elizabeth Collins woman? She was like a crazy hermit genius person or whatever. Or, uh, Picasso?

GARY

You're a big fan of Picasso?

SKAGGS

Ah. I don't know. He's a genius, though, right?

Gary shrugs.

SKAGGS

And people like . . . definitely Elliott Smith. And / def—

GARY

Who's that?

Skaggs stares at Gary in exaggerated disbelief.

GARY

Okay, okay.

SKAGGS

Even Mom knows who Elliott Smith is. I put a bunch of his songs on her Hanukkah Mix CD and she fucking *loved* them.

GARY

Great.

SKAGGS

Oh my god. Gary.

GARY

Well, this might be a generational difference. Have you heard of "Captain Beefheart"?

SKAGGS

YES I have heard of Captain Beefheart. Are you comparing CAPTAIN BEEFHEART to ELLIOTT SMITH? . . .

GARY

No I was trying to show you how / certain generations . . .

SKAGGS

. . . because then I would have to challenge you to a *duel*. In the snow. With, like, pistols.

Skaggs goes over to the bookshelf and hauls out his gigantic book of CDs.

GARY

You know what, Skaggs? I'm really concerned about something.

SKAGGS

Hold on hold on. I'm gonna play you his stuff.

GARY

Skaggs.

Skaggs riffles through the book of CDs.

SKAGGS

Question is: what song. Whoa. Actually. This is really really hard. Oh Gary. There are so many options. And this is big. I have like a moral responsibility here to play you the, um, *perfect* Elliott Smith song, the song that will—

GARY

I'm concerned that you care too much about whether you appear Cool.

SKAGGS

(*looking up*)
Cool.

GARY

Yes. You seem very concerned with it.

SKAGGS

I'm not concerned with seeming . . . with being Cool. At all.

GARY

Mm-hm.

SKAGGS

(*after a pause*)
You know what, Gary? I think *you're* worried about whether you seem Cool.

GARY

Well, no. I don't spend a lot of time worrying about that stuff.

SKAGGS

Okay. Hold on. We haven't even *defined* Cool. What we even *mean* by Cool.

GARY

I think you expend a lot of effort making sure you wear the right clothes and listen to the right—

SKAGGS

I don't. I swear to god I don't. Don't tell me I do when I don't.

GARY

Well you just told me.

SKAGGS

Because you told me first.
  (*after a short pause*)
Because clearly you're projecting!

GARY

This is getting out of hand.

SKAGGS

Fuck that, man. Don't tell me it's getting out of hand after you like point your finger at me and accuse me of some vague thing that you're unwilling to admit to yourself!

GARY

  (*holding up his hands*)
Whoawhoawhoa.

SKAGGS

Don't fucking whoawhoawhoa me, man! I hate that shit! Then it seems like I'm attacking you!

GARY

You are attacking me.

SKAGGS

No I'm not!

GARY

I'm gonna go to bed.

SKAGGS

No. No. You stay up and look at whatever sex shit you're looking at on the web, and I'll—

GARY

I was playing a *game*—

SKAGGS

—I'll just go to bed and read or something. I don't want to have this discussion either, man.

GARY

(*after a pause*)
I'm sorry that this happened.

SKAGGS

That what happened.

GARY

This . . . tension.

Skaggs laughs a horrible, forced laugh. Then he puts a CD in the CD player. Elliott Smith's "Roman Candle" plays. He stares at Gary.

SKAGGS

Did it ever occur to you that I might be *effortlessly* Cool?

Gary shakes his head no. Skaggs turns up the music and walks back through the hallway to his bedroom. Blackout. Spotlight on Amanda on the study.

AMANDA

Who *was* Winnie Rosebath? She's gone down in Vermont history as the woman who, um, enchanted Alfred Collins with her
incredible beauty and, ah, mysterious charm . . . but strangely,
there are no existing photographs or paintings of her. We *do* know
that Winnie was married to Gilbert Rosebath, a local architect—
he actually designed the present-day Shirley Inn—and when the
Rosebaths relocated to Shirley from Washington in 1859 there
was a great deal of excitement over Winnie's alleged beauty,
sophisticated clothing, and her love of "amateur theatricals."

(*pause*)

Historians have found several daguerreotypes that were, for brief
periods of time, um, believed to be photographs of Winnie Rosebath.
But all of them have turned out to be fakes, or just pictures of *other*
Winnies in the southern Vermont area . . . . and so it seems like we
just have to imagine for ourselves what she looked like, and the
kind of impression she made on Alfred Collins.

I just . . . I guess I just imagine her to be kind of . . . impossibly
beautiful. But we don't know. The truth is, she could have pretty
much just been—

*The front door clicks open. Amanda sticks her head out of the study.
Skaggs is standing in the doorway.*

AMANDA

Hi.

SKAGGS

I'm not here to ask you out.

AMANDA

Okay.

She steps out into the hallway.

SKAGGS

What were you just doing?

AMANDA

What?

SKAGGS

I looked through the window and you were / like—

AMANDA

I . . . I was practicing. Things have been pretty slow, so I just . . . sometimes I go over the tour by myself / and—

SKAGGS

I, ah, I wanted to ask you if, ah . . . my mom's boyfriend . . . actually, I think he's her fiancé now? They have these like mysterious Irish commitment rings? Anyway, uh . . . every Thursday night he makes this incredibly strange lasagna for my mother and it's like this dinner ritual they have and I sat through it last Thursday and I think if I go through it again alone I'm gonna have a, uh, heart attack or a hernia or something.

AMANDA

What's so strange about the lasagna?

SKAGGS

It's um . . . they use this weird . . . the noodles are like made out of this wheat shit, and he puts, like, squash in it or something?

AMANDA

Is it vegetarian?

SKAGGS

Yeah. Are you a vegetarian?

AMANDA

Mm-hm.

SKAGGS

Huh. Yeah. I guess that's cool.
  (*an awkward pause*)

Oh. Yeah. Do you wanna come over for dinner tomorrow night? I swear to god I'm not hitting on you.

> AMANDA

Why do you keep saying that?

> SKAGGS

Uh . . . I don't know. I guess Meghan would . . . my ex-girlfriend worked at the box office for this dance company? And these creepy guys would come back like the day after the performance and pressure her to go out with them. It always really disgusted me. Because she was stuck in this little glass . . . she was like behind this little glass window and she couldn't go anywhere and they'd be like yelling at her through the little microphone thingie.

Amanda is unimpressed.

> SKAGGS

So. Uh . . . do you wanna come over?

> AMANDA

. . . Yeah.

> SKAGGS

Yeah?

> AMANDA

Yes. Thank you. For the invitation.

> SKAGGS

I can come pick you up in my / mom's—

> AMANDA

No. Um. I have a car. Where do you . . .

Amanda searches her pockets for a pen. She finds one. She looks around for paper.

AMANDA

Um . . .

Amanda picks up Harry Potter and the Order of the Phoenix *and opens to the front.*

SKAGGS

No! Don't write in Harry Potter.
  (*he searches through his pockets*)
I'll find a receipt or something . . .

AMANDA

There are all these blank pages in the front.

SKAGGS

That's where you autograph it if you're J. K. Rowling.

AMANDA

It's okay. Just, uh . . . just tell me.

SKAGGS

Okay. Um . . . you know Pleasant Street?

AMANDA

Yeah.

SKAGGS

Just drive . . . like drive up, up . . .

AMANDA

North?

SKAGGS

Like Burger King is on your . . . right.

AMANDA

  (*writing*)
Okay.

SKAGGS

You drive up, past um, past the bank, past Calvin, past Shay, then
you'll . . . actually, past Northbrook too, and then you'll, the road
will kind of bear right, follow it . . .

AMANDA

I'm still on Pleasant?

SKAGGS

Yes.
   (*pausing as she writes*)
. . . Follow it, over the train tracks, it gets kind of woodsy, there'll
be . . . there's like this little grocery gas station thing on your left,
then you wind a bit, and then Kingman'll be on your right. Take
a right on Kingman. 26 Kingman. We're blue with black shutters.
And there's this, there's this little construction sign in the front
yard. My mom keeps forgetting to take it down.

Amanda writes this all down. Then she looks up.

AMANDA

26?

SKAGGS

26 Kingman. I guess you can always Mapquest it. But I think
those are pretty / accurate—

AMANDA

26 Kingman is Winnie Rosebath's house.

SKAGGS

Uh . . . who?

AMANDA

Winnie Rosebath. Winnie *Rosebath*. Were you *listening* on the tour?

SKAGGS

. . . Yes.

AMANDA

26 Kingman is . . . it's the Rosebath house. I . . . I remember
I found it when I first moved here. I drove past like five times. Oh
my god. Are you kidding me? You live there?

SKAGGS

Uh . . . if it's the same—

AMANDA

It's the same one. It's the same one! They redid it in the 1920s,
but it's basically—I get to go *inside*? Your mother *lives* there?

SKAGGS

It's actually Gary's house. My mom moved in like six months—

AMANDA

That place is like the source of . . . oh my *god*!

Skaggs looks vaguely unhappy.

SKAGGS

Uh . . . I should go.

AMANDA

What time should I be there?

SKAGGS

Uh . . . seven-ish?

AMANDA

Yes!

She beams at him.

SKAGGS

You seem very excited.

AMANDA

I am! This is . . . this place is amazing.

Skaggs nods, starts to exit, then pauses.

                    SKAGGS
What place?

                    AMANDA
This *town.*

Skaggs nods miserably and leaves. Blackout.

Scene Eight

Lights up on Gary putting pillows down on the living room floor.
Skaggs is sitting on the rug looking through his book of CDs. Judy
is in the kitchen, getting out plates and silverware and lecturing
Amanda. Amanda is leaning on the kitchen counter.

                    JUDY
You have to become receptive. You have to be willing to accept
the possibility that you are actually Divine. That you're a Divine
Being.

                    AMANDA
Huh.

                    JUDY
It's . . . we're all so scared of seeming ego . . . egomaniacal or self-
centered, but accepting the fact that you have divinity inside of
you actually allows you to see it in other people. I mean . . . it's
not until . . . *that's* how you begin to practice kindness.
    (after a short pause)
I think you would really like this woman.

Amanda nods. Judy smiles at her.

                    JUDY
You're so pretty.

                              AMANDA
Oh. Well. I don't, um . . . thank you.

Skaggs enters the kitchen, suspicious.

                              SKAGGS
   (to Amanda)
Did she just say something weird to you?

                              JUDY
I said that she was pretty.

                              SKAGGS
Please don't act totally insane.

Skaggs walks back into the living room.

                              SKAGGS
   (to Gary)
What are you doing with those pillows?

                              GARY
Your mother wants to eat on the floor.

Skaggs storms into the kitchen.

                              SKAGGS
Why are we eating on the floor?

                              JUDY
Because . . . okay, you're already mad at me.
   (after a pause)
The radiator is under the kitchen table. And my skin . . . my legs
get incredibly dry and itchy and if you didn't insist on cranking
the heat up all the / time—

                              SKAGGS
I don't think seventy degrees is an unreasonable—

JUDY

And if we're gonna keep it cranked up I just . . .
(*to Amanda*)
He'll walk around in his boxer shorts and then complain about how cold it is.

SKAGGS

She's going through menopause.

JUDY

Wrong. I already have gone through menopause.
(*to Amanda*)
You probably do this when you visit your mother.

AMANDA

My mother is dead.

JUDY

I'm so sorry.

AMANDA

Yeah. It's okay.

JUDY

It's not okay.

SKAGGS

Jesus.

Skaggs walks back into the living room and starts looking through his CD book again.

AMANDA

(*to Judy*)
Do you mind if I . . . is it okay if I look around?

JUDY

Of course. Skaggs should . . .
(*calling out*)
You should give her a tour!

Skaggs ignores them. Amanda begins wandering through the house. She wanders into Skaggs's room. She furtively opens a drawer in his nightstand, peeks inside, and then quickly shuts it. She wanders into the hallway. She peers out the bay window. She fingers the potted flowers.

AMANDA

I love your plants!

No one hears her. Amanda steps into the study and sees the tiny marble bust of a woman sitting on a shelf. Quickly, she slips it into her purse. In the kitchen the stove dings. Gary opens the oven door.

JUDY

Use a potholder.

She hands him one. Gary takes it and takes the lasagna tray out of the stove.

GARY

OUCH.

He slams the tray down on the counter, then takes off the potholder and inspects it.

GARY

This doesn't work.

Gary starts slicing into the lasagna. Judy watches him.

JUDY

(quietly)
Those are very big pieces.

GARY

Okay, you do it.

JUDY

I wasn't saying that.

GARY

No. It's. I *want* you to do it.

He hands her the spatula. She takes it and starts cutting.

JUDY

I'm just gonna split them / in—

GARY

(*inspecting the sweat stains under his arms*)
I have to change my shirt again. This is unbelievable.

JUDY

Skaggs turned up the heat.

SKAGGS

(*from the living room*)
You're both crazy!

Gary walks toward the bedroom, past Skaggs.

SKAGGS

It's like a fucking freezer in here.

GARY

Are you putting on music?

SKAGGS

Yeah.

GARY

Try not to make it too depressing.

SKAGGS

Okay. That's . . . I don't understand what you're talking about.

Gary is already in the master bedroom, unbuttoning his shirt.

SKAGGS

I DON'T UNDERSTAND WHAT YOU MEAN BY THAT!

Amanda wanders into the master bedroom and encounters Gary without his shirt.

AMANDA

Oh my god.

GARY

Uh.

AMANDA

I'm so sorry.

Amanda flees back into the hallway and stands there, traumatized.

JUDY

IT'S READY!

Judy walks into the living room.

JUDY

Where's your little friend?

SKAGGS

Wow. That's like a particularly degrading—

Gary enters.

GARY

Is the salad done?

JUDY

Oh my god. I completely . . . I forgot.

A horrible pause.

GARY

Yeah. It's fine. Wow. Great. Let's just start.
    (*after a pause*)
Fuck it! You forgot to make the salad. It's fine. We'll just eat tiny pieces of lasagna.

SKAGGS

Whoa. Gary. You just casually swore.

Amanda enters the living room. Judy smiles tearfully at her.

JUDY

I forgot to make the salad!

Gary lets out a huge sigh.

JUDY

. . . So we're just having lasagna.

AMANDA

No, no. That's great! I love lasagna. I'm just happy it's vegetarian.

GARY

. . . It's not vegetarian.

AMANDA

Oh. / I—

JUDY

(to Skaggs)
You didn't tell me she was a vegetarian.

GARY

It has ground turkey in it.

SKAGGS

I thought that was like vegetable protein.

GARY

It's turkey.

AMANDA

That's fine. I can eat around it.

GARY

It's pretty . . . it's pretty mixed in.

AMANDA

I feel terrible.

SKAGGS

Why would anyone put ground turkey in lasagna?

JUDY

It's a low-fat alternative to beef. Gary's trying to watch his—

GARY

Okay. Enough.
(*he starts heading toward the kitchen*)
I'll just . . . I'll just throw the salad together as / quickly as—

JUDY

No. You . . . I forgot to buy the . . . we don't have lettuce.
(*after a pause*)
I'm sorry. I've had an incredibly stressful day.
(*after another awful pause*)
I wrote it down but then . . .

GARY

It's actually fascinating. It really is. Because even though you work part-time you're still . . . you're miraculously unable to complete tasks that a full-time-person would be . . . would have no trouble.

SKAGGS

That sentence didn't make any sense.

JUDY

Why are you being so mean?

GARY

I'm not being mean.

JUDY

I had no idea that having someone over would make you this tense.

A pause. Amanda stares at the floor.

GARY

I'm not tense.

Gary plops down—with some difficulty—on a pillow and buries his face in his hands. Judy kneels down beside him and strokes his hair.

AMANDA

I'm sorry . . . should I go?

Skaggs forcefully shakes his head no.

JUDY

   (to Gary, touching his face)
What's going on?

GARY

   (after a long pause)
. . . I think I'm just really, really hungry.

JUDY

What else.

GARY

I don't want to do this right now.

JUDY

Okay.
   (to Amanda)
Please have a seat. Skaggs?

Amanda and Skaggs sit down on their pillows.

JUDY

I'm gonna bring everyone their food.

Gary starts to get up.

JUDY

Sit. Sweetheart. Sit.

Judy exits into the kitchen and starts spooning the lasagna out onto dishes. Skaggs and Gary and Amanda are left sitting on their pillows. Skaggs glances out the window.

SKAGGS

Whoa. It's like a storm out there.

AMANDA

How long have you lived in this house, Mr. Bernstein?

GARY

My last name is Miller.

AMANDA

I'm sorry. Mr. Miller.

GARY

You can call me Gary. Fifteen years.

AMANDA

Oh. Wow.

GARY

I raised my son here.

Amanda nods enthusiastically.

SKAGGS

This house belonged to this nineteenth-century lady she's obsessed with.

GARY

I'm sorry . . . excuse me. I have to go to the bathroom.

Gary exits. Judy enters with two plates.

JUDY

Amanda . . . I, um, this is what I could find in the refrigerator. This is Indian food from the other night. Two nights ago. It's still good. Totally vegetarian. Saag Paneer? Do you know what that is?

AMANDA

Yeah, yeah.

JUDY

It's spinach with the little cheese cubes?

AMANDA

That's great. Thank you.

JUDY

I just microwaved it. It's hot. Be careful.

Judy stops for a second.

JUDY

Do you hear that?

AMANDA

Uh-huh.

JUDY

The website said there were going to be these high-speed winds?
Like a hundred miles an hour?

SKAGGS

Uh . . . that's impossible.

Judy puts the plates in front of them, then exits back into the kitchen.

SKAGGS

They are deeply screwed-up people.

AMANDA

They're nice.

SKAGGS

I think he might be cheating on my mother.

The sound of the toilet flushing from offstage.

AMANDA

Why?

SKAGGS

I'll tell you later.

Gary reenters and settles himself awkwardly back down on the pillows.

GARY

(*pointing to Amanda's sweatshirt*)
I like that.

AMANDA

Oh . . . I came straight from work. It's my, um . . . it's kind of my
uniform.

GARY

"The Pines."

The sound of the wind again.

AMANDA

It's the name of . . . it's what they called it. The Collins house.
Most of the big estates in Shirley had names back then.

GARY

Huh.

AMANDA

This house was actually called "White Flower Farm." Winnie
Rosebath—the woman who lived here? She had this amazing
greenhouse and she . . . she grew this rare white flower called the
Double Narcissus. People used to come from all over to see it.
    (*after a pause*)
Just an interesting, um, tidbit.

*Judy enters with plates for herself and Gary. She settles down on the
pillows. Then Judy jumps up again.*

JUDY

I'm gonna plug in the humidifier. It's so *dry* in here.

She plugs in the humidifier.

GARY

(*to Amanda*)
Where are you from? Originally?

AMANDA

Cincinnati.

GARY

Okay. Great.

Judy settles back down on the pillows.

JUDY

Finally.

They begin to eat. A long, awkward silence while everyone chews.

AMANDA

What do you do for work, Mrs. Bernstein?

JUDY

Miz Bernstein. Judy. Sorry. Call me Judy.
I'm a college and career counselor. At Shirley High. But I'm
getting . . . I'm studying part-time for a certificate in EMDR.

AMANDA

Cool.

They go back to eating. A pause.

AMANDA

I'm sorry—I—what's EMDR?

*All the lights go out. Besides the tiny green glow of the nightlight
next to the couch, it's pitch black.*

JUDY

Oh my god.

All the lights go on again, for a second, then flicker and go out again.

GARY

Jesus.
   (*after a pause*)
They'll go on again in a second.

JUDY

Skaggs?

SKAGGS

Yeah?

JUDY

Are you still there?

SKAGGS

Why wouldn't I be here?

JUDY

You're not saying anything.

SKAGGS

What am I supposed to say?

JUDY

Amanda?

AMANDA

Yeah?

JUDY

   (*after a pause*)
This is *terrible*.

The sound of rummaging. Skaggs takes a lighter out of his pocket and flicks it on. He holds it up in front of their faces, half illuminating everyone.

SKAGGS

Here.

The lighter goes out. Skaggs flicks it on again. Judy takes it.

JUDY

I'm gonna go find candles.

Judy stands up, holding the lighter, and walks into the kitchen. She begins rummaging through the cabinets.

SKAGGS

Hey. You guys. Look at the nightlight.

GARY

It must be battery powered.

AMANDA

It's plugged into the wall.

SKAGGS

MOM!

JUDY

What?

SKAGGS

THE FUCKING NIGHTLIGHT IS STILL ON!

JUDY

Aha.

Judy finds two candlesticks. She lights them and carries them back into the living room, and settles back down on the pillows. Everyone huddles around the candles. A silence.

JUDY

It stands for Eye Movement Desensitization and Reprocessing.

SKAGGS

What the hell are you talking about?

JUDY

Amanda asked about EMDR.

AMANDA

Oh. Right. Okay.

JUDY

It's like . . . people confuse it with it hypnosis but they shouldn't. It's a kind of stress-reduction therapy.

SKAGGS

You realize you sound like a crazy person.

JUDY

Skaggs doesn't like to hear about it. But it . . . it's actually really helped me. I've always had this tendency towards obsessive thinking and now—

AMANDA

Oh my god, me too!

JUDY

—you would love this, then. You would love it. You basically . . .

Judy lifts the candle.

JUDY

You have this little light . . . the technician holds up this little light and you just . . .

Judy moves the light back and forth.

JUDY

. . . you just follow the light back and forth with your eyes. Back and forth. Little movements.
  (*Judy follows the candle with her eyes*)
Little movements. Back and forth.

Do you go into a trance?

JUDY

No. No, not really. You just actively relive certain memories, and it allows you to begin processing the information in a new way. The external stimulus, um . . .

SKAGGS

That makes no sense.

JUDY

It does, though. It's been proven.

SKAGGS

What's the science?

JUDY

The science is that . . . at the beginning you state a positive belief. And then you process the memory using this calming, this alternating process, and even just after a month of treatment there's this like renewed energy in the positive belief.

SKAGGS

I asked what the *science* is.

JUDY

That is the science.

Skaggs buries his head in his hands.

AMANDA

I do this thing when I'm upset where I write these really angry letters? I'll write a whole long horrible thing about someone. But then I never send it to them. It just sort of gets the aggression out.

JUDY

See, that's . . . that's not bad . . . but it actually doesn't get at the root of the problem. Because the cultural—there's this concept that you can get aggression out? But actually . . . it's been proven that acts of aggression only breed more acts of aggression. So it's more of a neurological thing.

SKAGGS

Please . . . Mom?

JUDY

We can talk and talk, or write angry letters, but our brains are still worked up in this frenzy, this like very tightly wound . . .

Judy gestures with her hands around her head.

SKAGGS

Mom.

JUDY

What.

SKAGGS

You're making me want to kill myself.

Judy falls silent. They are all quiet for a while. Amanda reaches out and runs her finger back and forth inside the flame.

JUDY

Ooh. Be careful.

Amanda stops.

AMANDA

So Mr. Miller. Gary. You have a son?

Gary nods.

AMANDA

What's his name?

GARY

Uh . . . Nick.

AMANDA

How old is he?

GARY

Twenty.

AMANDA

Oh great. Where does he go to school?

GARY

He's in the army.

AMANDA

Oh. Okay.

GARY

He's very, uh . . . independent.
   (*after a confused pause*)
I wanted him to go to school but he was very determined to . . .
he really wanted to enlist.

AMANDA

Is he . . . where is he at this—

GARY

He's in Georgia. He uh . . . he's a Ranger? So when they go to, when
they go over they . . . he's never there for more than four or five
months.

AMANDA

I'm . . . that must be hard for you.

GARY

Well.

JUDY

Gary wishes he called home a little more.

GARY

Okay, if I . . . if I wanted to say that . . . if I wanted to share that, I would have said it.

JUDY

Sorry.

GARY

I don't, um . . . I'm trying to be supportive of him. But I don't—

JUDY

Gary was a Conscientious Objector during Vietnam.

Gary exhales in frustration.

JUDY

Sorry.

AMANDA

He must be very brave.

GARY

Yeah. Well. He's a good kid.
    (*pause*)
He's a little closer with his mother . . . they spent more . . . I saw him every other weekend, but my ex-wife's father, his grand—

Skaggs abruptly stands up. They all look at him.

SKAGGS

Sorry. My leg fell asleep.

AMANDA

    (*to Judy and Gary*)
Thanks for dinner.

GARY

(to Judy)
Do you wanna go to bed?

SKAGGS

It's like 8:30.

JUDY

That's funny.
You never come to bed with me this early.

GARY

So?

JUDY

It's because there's no electricity.
    (pause)
You can't get on the computer.

Angry, Gary tries to stand up, but he slips on a pillow and comes crashing back down on the ground.

JUDY

Oh my god!

AMANDA

Are you okay?

GARY

I'm fine.

Gary gets up slowly.

JUDY

Gary!

GARY

It's not a big deal.
    (to Judy)
My laptop has a battery, by the way.

Gary takes the second candle, limps into the bedroom and shuts the door. Inside the bedroom he begins to remove his clothes.

JUDY

Is your father still in Cincinnati?

AMANDA

He lives in L.A.

SKAGGS

Oh, man. L.A is the best.

AMANDA

I don't like it.
　(to Judy)
He's remarried.

JUDY

Uh-huh.
　(whispering)
I should probably go to bed. I think Gary's mad at me.
　(to Amanda)
Are you spending the night?

Inside the bedroom, Gary blows out his candle.

SKAGGS

What are you talking about?

AMANDA

Um . . . no. I'm not spending the night.

JUDY

Well, it was wonderful meeting you. You're very vibrant.

Judy kisses Amanda on the top of the head, then Skaggs, then gropes her way off into the darkness. A long silence.

SKAGGS

Sorry. I'm not normally that . . . I don't know. I'm like a monster version of myself or something.

AMANDA

Don't be sorry.

After a pause.

SKAGGS

Are you depressed?

AMANDA

Um . . .

SKAGGS

Like in general.

AMANDA

Wait. I have a . . . do you *always* talk about how you feel?

SKAGGS

Wait, what?

AMANDA

Is that like the only thing you talk about? Actually . . . sorry. That sounded really judgmental. Never / mind.

SKAGGS

Whatever, man.

He scratches his head self-consciously. A horrible pause.

AMANDA

Um. Depressed. Um . . . well . . . I think I'm sort of sad. Yeah. I think I'm sad. But I don't know if I'm depressed.

SKAGGS

Huh.

AMANDA

There was this one time a couple years ago . . . I don't know.
I graduated from college and my father . . .

(pause)

. . . I was also a teaching fellow at this horrible school . . . anyway.
I don't know. This job kind of saved my life. I guess I have like . . .
I guess I'm somewhat optimistic? But it's an interesting question.
I mean, I might be. Depressed.

SKAGGS

Sorry . . . do you mind if I check email really quickly?

AMANDA

Uh. Sure.

*Skaggs dashes out of the room, holding the candle, leaving her in
the darkness. He goes to his room, picks up his laptop off the floor,
and then comes back into the living room with it tucked under his
arm. He sits back down next to Amanda on the pillows.*

SKAGGS

Fuck. The wireless here is totally unreliable. Come *on*.

AMANDA

Are you expecting something?

SKAGGS

I emailed my ex-girlfriend like three hours ago. I totally shouldn't
have. Okay. Here we go.

He types. She peeks over his shoulder.

AMANDA

One new!

Skaggs clicks. Then waits.

SKAGGS

Okay. Do not poop out on me.
(he clicks on something again. Pause.)
Fuck.

AMANDA

Who's Jill Buxbaum?

SKAGGS

It's just . . . it's a mass email. I always get her fucking show invites.
Wow.
(he pushes the computer off his lap)
I'm an idiot.

AMANDA

What'd you write?

SKAGGS

Uh . . . "I miss you."

AMANDA

Well, give it a day or two. Can I check?

SKAGGS

Sure. Whatever.

Amanda takes the computer onto her lap and starts typing.

AMANDA

So why'd you guys break up?

SKAGGS

Yeah. Well. She, uh . . .
(pause)
We'd been dating almost three years. Things were getting kind of
hard . . . but they're like inevitably hard, right? At the three-year
point? That's like classic, right?

Amanda nods vaguely, still looking at the computer.

SKAGGS

But then she . . . she made out with this guy at a party. And she called me the next day and told me, but I was like . . . I mean, she was basically shitting all over the relationship. Because if . . . if you're in a rough spot, and if you go like drunkenly whatever . . . then in effect you're trying to end it, right?

AMANDA

So you broke up with her?

SKAGGS

Yeah. I was like: You Have In Effect Shat All Over This Relationship. So there's no point.

AMANDA

Wow.

SKAGGS

Then two weeks later I freaked out and called her and I was like maybe we can work through this but she was like no I've had some time to think about it and like the fact that I did that and the fact that you like broke up with me immediately afterwards made me realize that this relationship has a very weak pedestal, base, whatever . . . and . . . yeah. She was like . . . this was in an email she wrote? She said: "You not trusting me made me not trust myself." And then she listed all these ways that I, like . . .
     (pause)
I mean, I clearly did something wrong. I'm still not sure *what* exactly? But the knowledge of that fact just . . . I don't know. It like makes me want to kill myself.
     (after a pause, peering over at the computer)
Anything new?

AMANDA

Nope.

SKAGGS

Who's Kenny Gordon?

AMANDA

My dad.

SKAGGS

He writes you a lot of emails.

AMANDA

He's crazy.

Amanda moves the laptop off her lap and onto the floor. The blue light—along with the candles—shines up at them from below. Skaggs lies down on his back.

SKAGGS

Read one to me.

AMANDA

You want me to read you one of my emails?

SKAGGS

Just read me *something*. I feel like I'm gonna puke.

AMANDA

"Dear Sweetheart. Sorry for writing again. I'm so lonely, Amanda. Can you maybe acknowledge that? I realize everything is my fault but just give me a little love, okay? After all, we both miss and care for each other. Karen reads my hotmail account so write me back at this one. Hugs and kisses, Dad."

SKAGGS

(after a long silence)
Whoa.
(Skaggs picks the laptop back up and starts doing something)
Hey. Is it really sick and twisted that I keep all these old emails and like IM sessions from Meghan in a file on my desktop?

AMANDA

You guys IM'd each other?

SKAGGS

Yeah. She'd be at work all day and I'd be home so we'd just like . . .
(after a pause)
We even had, like, IM sex. Or whatever you call it.

AMANDA

Are you kidding me?

He shakes his head.

AMANDA

How do / you—

SKAGGS

It's like phone sex. But actually easier. Weirdly.

AMANDA

I guess the whole thing is just . . . it's not that appealing to me.

SKAGGS

Well, yeah, in theory it's kind of disgusting, but then you're talking
and you kind of miss the person and picture having sex with them
and then it just like . . . happens.

AMANDA

I just have no idea what I would *say*.

SKAGGS

Wanna read them?

She looks at him.

SKAGGS

I kept everything. You could read the sex ones.

AMANDA

You would show them to me?

SKAGGS

Yeah. Whatever.

She bursts out giggling and covers her face with her hands. He watches her.

SKAGGS

I'm serious.

AMANDA

That just seems incredibly . . . *wrong.*
  (*after a long pause*)
Okay. Yeah. Show me.

Skaggs looks through the computer.

SKAGGS

Uh . . . okay. Here.

Amanda scoots over next to him and he puts the computer between them and props it up on both of their knees.

SKAGGS

Wait. The first part is boring. Like . . . start here.

Amanda reads in silence for a while. Then she starts giggling.

SKAGGS

What? What?

AMANDA

Oh my god. This is just . . . this is so wrong.

SKAGGS

Which part?

AMANDA

Um . . . "I can see your" . . . actually no. I can't say that out loud.

SKAGGS

Say it.

AMANDA

Um . . . oh my god.

SKAGGS

Say it!

AMANDA

Um. Aggh. Okay. Girlfight67: "I can see your cock bulging through your pants."

SKAGGS

(*reading the response*)
MrSkaggs: "I want to suck on your little pink nipples."

AMANDA

Oh my god. We have to stop.

SKAGGS

Read more.

AMANDA

You want to read this out loud?

SKAGGS

Yeah.

AMANDA

Why?

SKAGGS

. . . It's funny.

AMANDA

Um . . . oh my god. I can't believe we're doing this. Okay. Um: "I want you to . . ."

SKAGGS

"Uh-huh"

AMANDA

"unbutton my shirt"

SKAGGS

"okay, I'm unbuddoning it." Ha ha. I spelled that wrong.

AMANDA

"and I want you to bit my nipples."

SKAGGS

"I'm thinking about your sweet breasts. Oh Meg I'm so hard."

AMANDA

(after a pause)
This is really weird.

SKAGGS

Keep going.

AMANDA

"I'm running my hand up and down your leg and I can feel your cock through your pants and it makes me so wet. I'm so wet I'm"

SKAGGS

"I want to shove my hand inside your panties those lacy black ones"

AMANDA

"I'm burning up"

SKAGGS

"I'm taking my cock out of my pants and I'm showing to you."

AMANDA

"I have to put it my mouth. Pleasepleaseplease let me put it in my mouth."

SKAGGS

"I'm jerking off while I look at you—"

AMANDA

Wait! Okay. Stop.

Amanda folds the top of the computer down and puts it on the ground. They're only lit by the candle now.

SKAGGS

What?

AMANDA

It's just . . . it's not actually that funny.

A long pause. Skaggs looks at Amanda. Amanda looks away.

SKAGGS

Hey. When was the last time you were, like, with someone?

AMANDA

Um.
  (*a long pause*)
I guess it's been a year and a half?

Another excruciating pause. Skaggs reaches out and slowly touches her collarbone. She looks at him. He looks at her. She does not move. He launches himself to his knees, then leans down and kisses her. They begin kissing in a desperate, panicked fashion. Amanda falls backward onto the floor. Skaggs falls on top of her. They start feverishly dry humping, their clothes still on.

AMANDA

(sitting up)
Wait. Just. One.

She sits up and blows out the candle. In total darkness:

AMANDA

Okay.

The sounds of dry humping. Amanda begins to moan.

AMANDA

Oh god . . . oh my god.

All the lights in the house suddenly start flickering back on again. Gary is revealed, standing in the doorway to the living room, watching them. Amanda and Skaggs don't appear to notice him. He darts back inside the bedroom. Amanda and Skaggs stop kissing for a second and squint up at the light.

SKAGGS

. . . Weird.

AMANDA

It feels really bright.

SKAGGS

Yeah. But it's just like . . . it's actually not.
   (after a pause)
Can we keep doing this?

AMANDA

Yeah.

They begin kissing again. Blackout.
End of Act One.

Act Two

———

Scene One

The kitchen. Morning. Judy is doing Salutes to the Sun in the middle of the kitchen on her purple yoga mat. After a minute Skaggs walks out of his bedroom in his boxer shorts, holding his bong. He puts it on the kitchen table and starts packing it.

JUDY

This early?

SKAGGS

Trust me.

Skaggs sits down at the table.

SKAGGS

I emailed Meghan.

Judy keeps doing her Salutes. Skaggs takes a hit.

SKAGGS

She hasn't written back.

Amanda walks out of the bedroom, still wearing her clothes from the night before. Skaggs continues cradling his bong, staring off into the distance.

                                    JUDY

   (*shocked*)
Amanda.

                                   AMANDA

Hi.

                                    JUDY

Um . . . would you like some breakfast? Tea or coffee or something?

                                   AMANDA

Oh no . . . I'm . . . I'm actually late for work. I have to go. But uh . . .

                                    JUDY

Maybe like a glass of orange juice?

                                   AMANDA

Um. Okay.

Judy rushes over to the refrigerator and starts getting out the orange juice. Amanda eyes Skaggs. He continues to ignore her. Judy brings her a glass of orange juice.

                                   AMANDA

Thank you so much.

She drinks. Skaggs takes another hit from the bong. Amanda looks at it.

                                   AMANDA

That's pretty big.

                                   SKAGGS

   (*releasing a cloud of smoke, coldly*)
Yes indeed.

Amanda keeps looking at Skaggs. Skaggs keeps staring off into the distance.

JUDY

The power came back on!

AMANDA

Yeah.

JUDY

I thought all the vegetables were gonna go bad. In the fridge. But.

Amanda tries to nod. Her hands begin to shake. She places the glass down on the kitchen table.

AMANDA

I should take off.

Skaggs finally turns and looks at her.

SKAGGS

Yo. Gordon.

AMANDA

Sorry?

SKAGGS

Gordon. That's your last name, right?

AMANDA

Oh. Yeah. That's just . . . they just always call my dad Gordon.

SKAGGS

See you round.

AMANDA

. . . Yes.

Amanda walks toward the door and puts on her coat. She starts to leave, then steps back into the room.

AMANDA

I'm sorry. I keep meaning to . . . is Skaggs your real name?

Skaggs looks at Judy. Judy looks back at Skaggs.

JUDY

He changed it when he was fifteen.
   (pause)
Tell her the story. Come on.

SKAGGS

Ah . . . I had this huge crush on a girl at overnight camp and the whole month we were there she called me Skaggs. Because Boz Scaggs was like her favorite musician? Which now in retrospect is extremely disturbing. Anyway, when I came back I wanted everyone to call me Skaggs. She said that it fit me.

JUDY

It kind of does.

SKAGGS

It's definitely less nerdy.

AMANDA

Than what?

JUDY

   (to Skaggs)
But you *were* nerdy.
   (to Amanda)
He was adorable. He had these big glasses and he had to wear / a—

SKAGGS

Okay, okay.

AMANDA

But what was your original . . .

Skaggs ignores her and takes another enormous hit.

JUDY

Brian.
  (to Skaggs)
Is that okay? That I just told her?
  (to Amanda)
Brian Bernstein.

AMANDA

  (nodding, in some kind of pain)
Huh.

Amanda leaves. Judy looks at Skaggs. Skaggs looks at Judy.

SKAGGS

What?

JUDY

I like her.

Skaggs collapses onto the table, and cradles his head in his arms.

JUDY

And she's just *so* beautiful. I could look at her . . . I mean, she's really gorgeous. In this very interesting way.

SKAGGS

You're just saying that because she's black.

JUDY

I am not.

SKAGGS

Yes you are. You always say black people are beautiful.

JUDY

That is . . . that is not true. How could you . . .

SKAGGS

You do.

JUDY

You're wrong. You're wrong.
She was also extremely sweet. And smart.

SKAGGS

Great. You and Gary should feel free to fuck her. Have a three-some. Whatever.

Judy covers her mouth with her hand. It seems like she might start crying. Instead Judy walks away and rolls up her yoga mat. She puts it in the bedroom. She returns.

JUDY

When are you going to start looking for a job?

SKAGGS

Here? Or in New York?

JUDY

Either.

SKAGGS

I'm not getting some crap job in Shirley.

JUDY

Then . . . .you should at least be playing drums.

SKAGGS

I lost my set, Mom. How many times do I have to say that? I lost my set. I lost my set.

JUDY

But I can lend / you—

SKAGGS

And it's not like . . . this is not like a fucking quest, okay?

JUDY

What are you talking about?

SKAGGS

There's no like *endpoint*! I'm not gonna like suddenly figure shit out / and—

JUDY

How do you know?

SKAGGS

Because I'm not gonna buy into some . . . I am like Fundamentally Against Dogma. I'm not gonna miraculously start believing that everything—

JUDY

You're being kind of dogmatic right now, though.

SKAGGS

I'm depressed.

JUDY

Are you?

SKAGGS

Um . . . yes?

JUDY

You're not so depressed that you can't sleep with someone. And then not be . . . not be a little nice to them the next morning.

SKAGGS

We didn't sleep together. We messed around. I gave her oral sex.

JUDY

Okay. Fine.

SKAGGS

. . . and she didn't reciprocate. Which I found to be extremely weird.

JUDY

She didn't reciprocate?
(*Skaggs shakes his head*)
Maybe she was nervous.

SKAGGS

Whatever.

JUDY

Huh.
(*a pause*)
What were we just talking about?

SKAGGS

I was trying to communicate to you the inherent paralyzing quality
of this thing I'm suffering through and the impossibility / of—

JUDY

Sumi's coming into town next week. On Wednesday.

SKAGGS

Oh my god.

JUDY

I want you to see her. Just one . . . just one of the afternoon
seminars. I'll pay for it.

SKAGGS

Jesus.

JUDY

Just . . . you've got to at least *try* to feel better, Skaggs. Otherwise
I can't keep supporting you living here and—

SKAGGS

Fine. Fine.

JUDY

You'll go?

SKAGGS

. . . Yes.

JUDY

Also let me do some EMDR on you.

SKAGGS

. . . Maybe.

JUDY

I'm gonna go take a shower.

Judy starts walking toward the master bedroom.

SKAGGS

You do believe me, right?

JUDY

Believe you what?

SKAGGS

Everything I say. When I tell you how bad I feel.

Judy nods, then exits. He watches her. Blackout. Lights up on Amanda in the center of the kitchen. She takes her cell phone out of her pocket and dials. After a while:

AMANDA

Hi. Skaggs. It's Amanda. Um . . . I'm calling on the off chance you didn't get my first message . . . there was like this weird beep while I was leaving it and I wasn't sure if your machine cut me off? So just ignore this if you already . . . *(she trails off)*
Um . . . I finished *Order of the Phoenix.*
    (pause)
Anyway. I felt like we left on a weird note this morning so I wanted to check in and . . . I don't know. Maybe I'm being paranoid. Okay.

I just ate a peanut butter sandwich. I don't know why I'm telling you that. Um. Okay. Bye.

She hangs up and cringes. Blackout.

Scene Two

Lights up on Skaggs rummaging through Judy and Gary's room. He is lifting up blankets, opening drawers. Gary walks in.

GARY

Hi.

SKAGGS

Oh. Hey.

GARY

Do you want to explain to me what you're doing in here?

Skaggs shakes his head.

GARY

Okay, well, would you?

SKAGGS

Yeah. No. Sorry. I'll leave.

Skaggs starts to walk out.

GARY

Tell me what you were just doing.

SKAGGS

. . . I was looking for a CD.

GARY

Why would . . . that doesn't make any sense.

Skaggs shrugs.

GARY

Okay. You know what? I have something to say.

SKAGGS

Shoot.

GARY

You have to be nicer to us. If you're going to live here, you have to . . . you have to have a better attitude.

SKAGGS

. . . The *point* is that I have a bad attitude. That's exactly why I . . . I will be the first to admit that I'm a fucking asshole, Gary.

GARY

Well, you need to treat people you love with respect. Even if you're depressed. Even if you hate yourself.

SKAGGS

Okay . . . um . . . I actually do think I treat Mom with respect. I spend like two hours a day listening to her spiritual hypnosis crap.

GARY

Well, what about me?

SKAGGS

What about you?

GARY

Come on, Skaggs. I hate it when you play dumb.

SKAGGS

I don't love you. Is that what you're asking?
    (*after a pause*)
Because I totally believe in the love respect dichotomy thing or whatever. I just don't love you.
    (*pause*)
You are like a strange man who is living with my mother.

Annie Baker

GARY

I'm her partner.

SKAGGS

Okay. Then why do you . . . you avoid her like the plague, man.
You're always sitting at your computer at like four in the morning.
I mean, do you guys even have sex? Never mind. I don't want to
know the answer to that question.
   (*a short pause*)
And "partner" makes you sound like a gay couple, by the way.

GARY

I want you to start being nicer to me.

SKAGGS

Define "nice."

GARY

You acknowledge me when I walk in the room. You say hello. You
ask me questions about my day. About my life. You—

SKAGGS

Okay. You want me to ask you a question about your life? How
many, like, Iraqi children has your son blown up in the past year?

A terrible pause.

GARY

I don't think he's blown up anyone, actually.

SKAGGS

How many has he shot in the head? Or like tortured?

GARY

I don't think he's—

SKAGGS

Or, okay, how many times has he stood by and watched some
incredibly fucked up shit happen? Without like saying anything?
Just like participating in like the total devastation of—

324

GARY

That's not . . . that's not what he's doing. He's putting his life at risk. Do you know what that's like when . . .

(he takes a deep breath)

I'm proud of him. And he's—

SKAGGS

No you're not. You're ashamed, man. I can tell. You're ashamed you have like this weird fascist soldier kid. It's like, what did you do wrong?

Gary just stares at him.

SKAGGS

He's part of an atrocity, man! And I'm sorry I'm like bringing it up right now, but I actually think it's been pretty respectful of me to refrain from commenting on it every time we speak to each other!

GARY

(after a very long pause, quietly)

Nick is . . . he's twice the person you are.

SKAGGS

Whoa. Okay. Uh . . . that doesn't make any sense. But okay.

GARY

You're a parasite.

SKAGGS

. . . I'm sorry. What the fuck is that supposed to mean?

GARY

You know what exactly what it means. You use up resources and you don't contribute in any way to . . . anything.

SKAGGS

I make music, Gary. I make art.

GARY

No you don't. It's . . . it's so obvious, Skaggs, that you're not an artist. Do you know that?

SKAGGS

(*genuinely thrown*)
That's, uh . . . that's pretty bold, Gary. Because what the fuck do you know / about—

GARY

You don't practice. A real artist would find a way to . . . there are drumming pads. I know about those. How much do they cost? Next to nothing. Your mom is even willing to help you buy a new *set*. But you don't want to. Something inside you. You just don't want it.

A long pause. Skaggs sits down on the bed.

SKAGGS

(*holding back tears*)
I'm really fucked up about Meghan, man. I wrote her an email on Thursday . . . it's been two days. I'm . . . I'm falling apart and I—

GARY

I don't think this is about Meghan.

SKAGGS

. . . Fuck you.

GARY

I think this is you realizing that your life has no meaning. That you don't know how to work hard. And it scares the shit out of you. Because you have no idea how to change.

A pause while Skaggs starts to cry. Then, through his sobs:

SKAGGS

Well, you're a pervert.

GARY

Okay. We should stop.

SKAGGS

You . . . you're a fucking sex addict.

GARY

No, I'm not, actually.

SKAGGS

You're cheating on Mom.

GARY

I'm not. Why do you think I'm—

SKAGGS

You leave in the middle of the night, I hear you like fucking leaving in the middle of the night and you're always supposedly playing *video* games somewhere but I checked on your laptop and you look at like disgusting *porn*, man—

GARY

Okay, most people look at porn. You never look at porn?

A pause. Skaggs clears his throat and wipes away his tears.

SKAGGS

I know you were there. Watching us. Listening to us.

GARY

What are you talking about?

SKAGGS

Me and Amanda. Did it turn you on?

GARY

I stepped out of the room to . . . it was not intentional.

SKAGGS

Did it turn you on?

GARY

I was there for literally less than a minute.
  (*a pause*)
I'm sorry. Okay? I'm being honest here. I'm sorry.
  (*a longer pause*)
Listen. I. I love you, Skaggs.

SKAGGS

Are you kidding me? You're telling me you love me after like *lambasting* me and—

GARY

I love you. I truly do.

SKAGGS

I'm flabbergasted, man.

GARY

And . . . .listen. I'm a different person than I was five years ago. I'm grappling with stuff, but . . .
  (*pause*)
People can change. I . . . that's what I think I'm trying to communicate to you. I really . . . I believe you can change. I have faith in you.

Skaggs walks out of the room. After a second, he walks back in.

SKAGGS

Sock drawer.

GARY

I don't know what you're talking about.

SKAGGS

She keeps chocolate in her sock drawer.

Skaggs walks out of the bedroom and slams the door. Gary sits down on the bed. After a second, he walks over and pulls open the sock drawer. He paws through its contents, takes out the bar of chocolate and looks at it. Outside the bedroom, Skaggs walks over to the couch, unplugs the nightlight, and throws it at the bedroom door. It makes a horrible sound. Gary jumps.

SKAGGS

(screaming)
ABANDON HOPE, DICKWAD!

Gary sits back down on the bed. After a second, he starts eating the chocolate and crying a little. Blackout.

Scene Three

Amanda is sitting on her bench, staring into space. After a minute, the front door opens. It's Skaggs.

SKAGGS

Hey.

Amanda turns around and stares at him.

SKAGGS

So-o . . . I did like a little reconnaissance mission on his computer and found some very weird stuff. You can imagine. There was like a *particularly* disturbing Google history. But, ah . . .
(pause)
I think I was actually wrong about . . . yesterday he said he was going to his office? So I took my bike out of the garage and I followed him? And, uh . . . he just like went to his office for eight hours. So I don't think he's having an affair or anything. I think it's just . . . I think he just spends like all his time playing video games. Which is . . . I mean, it's really scary, man. Because when I look at this guy I can like see all the like pathetic directions my life could go in by the time I turn sixty.
(pause)

Also Meghan hasn't emailed me back. Which . . . I mean, I'm trying to be stoic about it. But I have this like nauseous stomachache and it's like . . . it's pretty persistent.

AMANDA

I thought you've had a nauseous stomachache for weeks.

SKAGGS

Yeah. I mean. Yeah. How are you?

She shrugs.

SKAGGS

How's life post–Harry Potter?

AMANDA

You didn't call me back.

SKAGGS

Yeah. I just . . . I've been like a real mess.

AMANDA

Um . . . I actually don't understand.

SKAGGS

Wait, what?

AMANDA

I called you and I asked you to call me back.

SKAGGS

Yes.

AMANDA

So I don't . . . I don't know why someone wouldn't . . . I don't understand how you could get a message from someone asking you to call them back and then not call them back.

SKAGGS

Huh. Um . . . I guess I didn't know I was, like, *obligated* to?

AMANDA

That's not what I'm saying.

SKAGGS

I mean, I'm here now. I like stopped in to say hello.

AMANDA

Two days later.

SKAGGS

Whoa. You're like *pissed* at me?

AMANDA

I just . . . I don't get it.

SKAGGS

Why is it such a big deal?

AMANDA

It's not a big deal.
   (she stares down at her lap)
I guess I've just been like . . . waiting. And it sucks when you're like sitting around waiting for someone to call. I mean, you should know. You're like . . . I mean, you're sitting around freaking out about Meghan.

SKAGGS

Yeah, but she's my girlfriend. Ex-girlfriend.

AMANDA

I'm sorry. We just . . .

SKAGGS

What?

AMANDA

We were like . . . naked together?

SKAGGS

Yeah?

AMANDA

Oh my god. This is. This is really humiliating.

SKAGGS

I'm sorry. I don't get / what's—

AMANDA

You're like . . . you invite me over for dinner with your family?
And then we—

SKAGGS

Dude, I said it wasn't a date!

AMANDA

(burying her face in her hands)
Wow. This is like . . . this is exactly what I . . . this is my worst
nightmare.

SKAGGS

Whoa. *Whoa.*

AMANDA

It's just like . . . I don't even . . . I don't even like you that much!
I just . . . I just wanted to get to know you better and I wasn't
even . . . I wasn't even that *interested* in you but then that thing
happened and then I told myself, okay, cool, maybe we'll get to know
each other and spend time together and figure out if maybe it's
something that could work or whatever but you didn't even . . . I
mean, now I just feel like an idiot because I called you just to say
hello and you didn't even call me back!

SKAGGS

Uh . . .

AMANDA

I guess I just didn't expect that you would be this *rude*.

SKAGGS

I'm not *rude*! Why is . . . why is everybody like *attacking* me all of a sudden?

AMANDA

You're . . . you're really rude. You're really rude and you're just . . . you're totally self-involved. I can't . . . I can't believe I'm being this person. I don't even *like* you that much.

SKAGGS

Okay. Thank you. You don't have to keep saying that.

AMANDA

But now I'm . . . this is . . . now I feel like I do with my dad where he'll email me ten times in a row and tell me he misses me and then I write back being like okay, sure, I guess let's give it a try, and then I don't hear from him for two years!

SKAGGS

Um . . . this is not like that at *all*, man.

AMANDA

You just . . . and now I'm this person! And you're just . . . you're just some immature asshole!

A very long pause.

SKAGGS

Wow. Wow.
I mean . . . who do you think you are? I'm not even like . . .
    (*a long pause*)
I was doing you a *favor*, man.

AMANDA

Excuse me?

SKAGGS

I mean, come on, man. You're like this weird little Vermont hobbit who's obsessed with dead white women . . . you clearly have no friends . . . you haven't been laid in like a million years . . . so I thought to myself, wow, this chick really needs some guy to go down on her, and, you know, why not, Skaggs, maybe you need to become a better person and start acting altruistically for once in—

AMANDA

(screaming)
STOP IT!

They both stand there. Skaggs's cell phone rings. He takes it out and looks at it. Then he shuts the phone and puts it back his pocket.

AMANDA

You should go.

SKAGGS

Listen. Amanda. You're not . . .
   (a pause)
. . . You're not a hobbit, man.

AMANDA

Oh my god. Just stop. Please.

SKAGGS

I, uh . . . I'd like to be friends with you.

AMANDA

Okay. Thanks. No.

SKAGGS

I . . .
   (he scratches his head)
My mom is making me go to this like spirituality talk on Wednesday? The crazy hugging woman? Did she tell you about her?

Amanda shrugs.

SKAGGS

We could like go together and make fun of it.

AMANDA

I don't really want to see you anymore.

SKAGGS

. . . Okay.

Skaggs starts to walk out the door, then stops and clasps his stomach.

SKAGGS

Jesus. I, uh . . . I feel like I'm gonna throw up.

AMANDA

Granted.

SKAGGS

No. Um. I think I might throw up.
  (*after a pause*)
Do you have . . . do you have some sort of like baggie?

Amanda doesn't respond.

SKAGGS

Amanda. I'm . . . uh . . . I'm serious.

AMANDA

Um . . .

SKAGGS

I don't think you want me to puke on the one-hundred-twenty-five-year-old wallpaper.

Amanda starts rummaging through her book bag.

SKAGGS

Oh Jesus.

Amanda pulls out a brown paper lunch bag, takes a sandwich out of it, throws the sandwich on the ground, and hands Skaggs the bag. He crouches down on the ground, his back to her, and bends over it.

SKAGGS

Oh my god.

AMANDA

You're not actually gonna throw up.

Skaggs begins to throw up inside the bag. His back convulses. Amanda turns away, repelled. He throws up for a while. There is a long pause after he finishes. Amanda picks up Harry Potter and the Order of the Phoenix *and opens it to the first page. Slowly, Skaggs stands up and twists the top of the bag shut. He looks at Amanda. Her eyes still on the book:*

AMANDA

Do you feel better?

Skaggs takes a deep breath and looks around at the house.

SKAGGS

. . . Um. Yes. I do.

Amanda nods, still staring at the book.

AMANDA

Good.

Skaggs takes a deep breath, then turns and walks out of the house. Blackout.

Scene Four

Lights up on Skaggs sitting on the couch in the living room, eating saltines and drinking directly from a huge bottle of ginger ale. Judy is sitting next to him with a cup of tea.

SKAGGS

Do you ever think about what people will say about you at your funeral?

Judy nods.

SKAGGS

You like fantasize about it?

JUDY

Sure.

SKAGGS

Good. That makes me feel like less of an asshole.

Gary enters the room, sits down in an armchair, and turns on his laptop.

SKAGGS

Do you want to be cremated or buried?

JUDY

Um . . . cremated.

SKAGGS

Okay. See, I'm glad I asked. Cause if you like got run over by a car today Gary and I would have had no idea like . . . what your wishes are.
    (*calling out*)
Cremated, Gary!

Gary nods, not taking his eyes off the computer.

SKAGGS

Buried for me.

JUDY

Okay . . . I don't want to think about that.

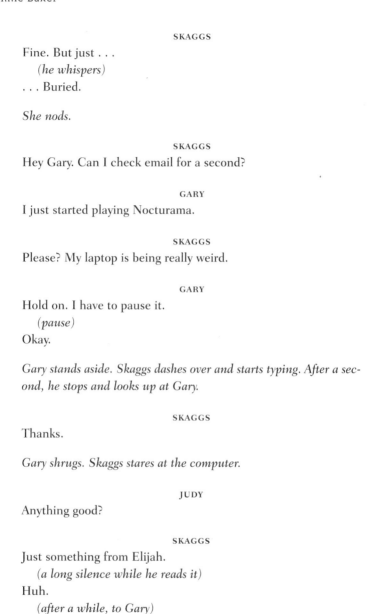

SKAGGS

Fine. But just . . .
(he whispers)
. . . Buried.

She nods.

SKAGGS

Hey Gary. Can I check email for a second?

GARY

I just started playing Nocturama.

SKAGGS

Please? My laptop is being really weird.

GARY

Hold on. I have to pause it.
(pause)
Okay.

Gary stands aside. Skaggs dashes over and starts typing. After a second, he stops and looks up at Gary.

SKAGGS

Thanks.

Gary shrugs. Skaggs stares at the computer.

JUDY

Anything good?

SKAGGS

Just something from Elijah.
(a long silence while he reads it)
Huh.
(after a while, to Gary)
Okay. Thanks.

Skaggs stands there, thinking. Gary goes back to playing his game.

JUDY

What did he say?

SKAGGS

Weird.

JUDY

What?

SKAGGS

He's moving to L.A.

JUDY

I thought he was working for that photographer downtown.

SKAGGS

Yeah. No. I mean, he was. But he, uh . . . his older brother is like a reality TV producer? Apparently he's gonna move there and be a PA for this new show. He's like driving there in his car next week.

JUDY

Ech. Reality TV.

SKAGGS

Some of it isn't that bad, Mom.

JUDY

It's awful.

SKAGGS

You don't even watch it. You just think it's bad cause you read articles about it.
    (after a pause)
Anyway. He said he could get me a PA gig if I want it.

Gary and Judy both look up.

JUDY

You're not gonna say yes, are you?

SKAGGS

No. I'm not . . . I can't have a job right now. I mean, I'm totally dysfunctional.

    (*pause*)

That would be insane, right?

They don't respond. Skaggs scratches his head.

SKAGGS

That's great that he's going, though. L.A is cool.

JUDY

I don't know. It's not so cool if the job is meaningless and you're not helping anyone or creating anything worthwhile.

SKAGGS

. . . Yeah.

A pause. Skaggs peers over Gary's shoulder.

SKAGGS

So that's Nocturama?

GARY

Uh-huh.

SKAGGS

What . . . like . . . what is it?

GARY

What do you mean?

SKAGGS

Like what . . . what's the game?

GARY

It's uh . . . well, you're kind of in this underground world.

Gary is still focused on the game. He doesn't take his eyes off the screen.

SKAGGS

Okay.

GARY

And, uh . . . you can't really see much, because you're moving through these caves?

SKAGGS

(peering over Gary's shoulder)
Are you in a cave now?

GARY

Yeah. And, uh . . . you can . . . I mean, it's complicated. You . . . you can buy different sources of light from the priestesses, and, well, there's this underground sort of church? It's hard to explain. But, uh . . . that red thing I'm holding . . .

SKAGGS

You're the muscle-y guy?

GARY

Yeah. That's a divinity ball. I earned that on the first level. You're basically . . . Hold on.

A fit of tapping on the keyboard.

GARY

I had to kill that shaman.

JUDY

(from the couch)
You killed a *shaman*?

GARY

He was evil.

Judy sighs and shakes her head.

GARY

Anyway, you're descending, you're descending into the, uh, heart of this underground world, and the lower you go the darker it gets, so the more protection and, uh, light you need? And there are these . . . there are these killer rats, and, uh, cave beasts? But if I'm . . . I'm pretty well-stocked so I can just . . .

SKAGGS

Whoa. You just killed that rat.

GARY

Well, I eliminated him.

SKAGGS

What's the difference?

GARY

He might come back later.

Gary keeps playing the game while Skaggs watches, rapt.

SKAGGS

Those graphics are insane, man.

GARY

Yeah. It's pretty good.

A long silence while Judy watches Skaggs watch Gary play.

SKAGGS

What's, like, the goal?

GARY

Oh. Well. You don't really know until you get to the . . . but I've played it before, so I know. You . . . you enter the core, you go in—

SKAGGS

The core of what?

JUDY

Core of the world?

GARY

Well. Kind of. You go in, and there's this, uh, sorceress, she's the
one who removed all the light . . . that's why you've had to buy it
on the black market the whole time . . .

SKAGGS

Okay . . .

GARY

. . . and, anyway, you, you go against her, you have this big fight,
and then if you kill her—

SKAGGS

Wait. You've actually killed her?

Gary nods, still playing.

GARY

Yeah. If you kill her . . . she sort of melts away and she turns into
this little boy. Lying on the ground. And you—

JUDY

You kill a little boy?

GARY

Well, you don't know you've killed a little boy until after you've
killed him. But then . . . you pick up his dead body—

SKAGGS

How do you know to do that?

GARY

The game just does it for you. It's a graphic. You take him in your
arms, and you absorb his curse so he can live again.

SKAGGS

That's the end of the game?

GARY

Uh-huh.

SKAGGS

Whoa.

Judy gets up and goes into her bedroom. She opens the sock drawer and starts looking through it.

SKAGGS

What are you doing now?

GARY

I'm negotiating with a spearwoman.
    (after a pause, quietly)
You should take that job.

SKAGGS

What?

GARY

Don't tell your mom I said that.

Judy reenters.

JUDY

Where's my chocolate?

Skaggs and Gary both look up.

JUDY

My chocolate is gone.
    (to Gary)
Did you find it?

Gary doesn't say anything.

JUDY

GARY.

Gary doesn't respond. He keeps staring at the computer.

JUDY

Oh my god. That is . . . I've . . . you can't . . . I can't believe this!
You've never . . . I *hid* that so you wouldn't be tempted to—

SKAGGS

Chill out, man. I ate it.

JUDY

No you didn't.

SKAGGS

I did. Yesterday. I ate the whole thing. I needed like a sugar high
or whatever.

JUDY
   (after a pause)
It's really expensive chocolate, Skaggs.

SKAGGS

I'll buy you a new one.

JUDY

It's six dollars a bar.

SKAGGS

Whatever. You said I could have some.

JUDY

I didn't mean the whole thing.
   (after a pause, to Gary)
Sorry.

GARY

It's okay.

Judy walks back over to the couch and sits back down, dejected. Skaggs's cell phone, which has been sitting on the ground, emits a small beep.

JUDY

Your phone just beeped.

SKAGGS

Yeah.

JUDY

Does that mean you have a message?

SKAGGS

Yeah. Meghan called.

JUDY

Are you gonna listen to it?

SKAGGS

Eventually.

JUDY

You're kidding me. You've been pining away for a month and you don't want to—

SKAGGS

It's . . . the prospect of actually like hearing her voice in my ear after all this time is like . . . and she has this condescending thing she does? When she like knows she's fucked up or in power or something? She sounds all kind of drippy and apologetic and like . . . I don't know if I want to listen to her be like *Heey, I got your email* or whatever.

JUDY

I thought you missed her.

SKAGGS

I do. I do. But I miss . . . I like miss the time we went to visit her dad in Point Reyes. I mean, that was like two years ago. But I keep thinking about it. We were just really happy and relaxed and . . . I don't know. I mean, it kills me, cause like that version of us is like totally dead.

GARY

(*not looking up from the computer*)
So you miss yourself.

SKAGGS

Yeah.
I mean, her, too.

JUDY

This is . . . this is perfect for EMDR. I'm telling you.

SKAGGS

Aggh.

JUDY

Because . . . it's . . . you keep focusing on this memory. It's obsessive thinking. What you need to do is find a way to process the memory and acknowledge it without causing yourself pain.

Skaggs shakes his head.

JUDY

I'm gonna do it.

Judy gets up and runs out of the room. Gary keeps playing Nocturama.

SKAGGS

Hey Gary.

GARY

Uh-huh.

SKAGGS

I wanted to, uh . . .

Judy comes back in with her little EMDR contraption.

JUDY

Okay. We're gonna do it.

She dims the lights.

JUDY

Do you want to . . . hm. You need to be relaxed. Why don't we . . .
  (*she throws a bunch of pillows onto the floor*)
You can just kind of prop yourself up on these.

SKAGGS

Jesus. You're really excited about this.

*Skaggs sits on the ground in front of the couch. Judy puts a pillow
beneath his head and surrounds him with other pillows.*

JUDY

Are you comfortable?

SKAGGS

I don't know. Yeah.

*Judy turns on the little green light. Gary pauses Nocturama and
watches.*

JUDY

Okay. I'm gonna . . . just follow this with your eyes. Back and forth.
  (*Skaggs follows it with his eyes*)
Yup. Now. Before we . . . before we go into the memory, I want
you to ask yourself a question. Ask yourself: "What is the best way
I could feel, to be at my best in this situation?"

SKAGGS

Wait, what?

JUDY

When you're . . . the next time you experience this memory, how would you like to react? Don't stop following the light.

SKAGGS

Uh . . . I guess I'd like to not feel depressed?

JUDY

Can you state that positively?

SKAGGS

Uh . . . I guess I'd like to feel not . . . sorry. Um. I'd like to feel calm?

JUDY

Good.

SKAGGS

And . . . uh . . . hopeful?

JUDY

Good.

SKAGGS

I thought I wasn't supposed to feel hopeful.

Judy stops moving the light.

JUDY

Why?

SKAGGS

You said to Abandon Hope.

JUDY

That's . . . that's about living in the present. It's okay to feel hopeful, um, in a memory.

Gary shakes his head. Skaggs sees him and grins. Judy starts moving the light again.

JUDY

Okay. Now . . . take your time . . . but just . . . just start going through the memory. Start narrating it.

SKAGGS

The whole thing?

JUDY

Just . . . live it again. But don't close your eyes.

SKAGGS

Okay. Um . . . we'd been dating for like ten months. We were staying in L.A. . . . and, uh, we decided to drive all the way up Highway 1 to her father's house in Point Reyes.

JUDY

Just be back in it. Try to be back in it.

SKAGGS

Okay. Uh. We're driving. We're in her aunt's Jetta. We leave L.A. We take 10 West to Santa Monica and then we put on, okay so as we're turning onto 1 we put on Joni Mitchell and we play "California" like right as the ocean comes into view and we start laughing at ourselves at like how cheesy we're being but it's actually, like I actually feel kind of incredible and like the ocean is on my left and Meghan is driving and her window won't roll up so her hair is like in her mouth and I keep putting my hand on her leg.

JUDY

You're doing really good.

SKAGGS

Okay . . . so we drive up up up and like through Malibu and the hills are all brown and we almost turn off in Topanga Canyon but, uh, then we don't . . . and there are all these little people down by the ocean and she keeps being like should we stop here? and I'm like we're gonna be driving past beach for the next nine hours, wait until we get to Big Sur.

A pause.

JUDY

Keep going.

SKAGGS

I'm just remembering how fucking bossy I was.

JUDY

Stay in it.

SKAGGS

. . . So we drive and we drive and, uh, we stop in Santa Barbara cause her cousin is a bellhop at the Four Seasons and he . . . he was actually a pretty cool guy, and he like worked all these extra hours to get us a free room, which is crazy, cause the Four Seasons is like two thousand dollars a night . . . so we drive into the parking lot and this like guy in a suit takes our car and Meghan's cousin leads us to this villa building or something covered in red flowers and we have this huge room and we just go fucking nuts and run around in little circles on the carpet. We've like never been anywhere this nice in our lives. We both came from these like weird single mothers who live in cold places in New England and never take vacations.
No offense.

JUDY

I'm not here.

SKAGGS

So we're in this gigantic like amazing hotel room and there are all these little shampoo bottles in the bathroom and we jump up and down on the bed and then we have sex and she starts like crying during it but in this really nice way and I remember she—

JUDY

No "I remember." Stay in the present.

SKAGGS

. . . She like bites my shoulder while we're having sex and it leaves this little mark and I look in the mirror afterwards in the bathroom and see this like pink circle on my shoulder and I smiled, sorry, I smile, and I look at my reflection smiling, I'm smiling like a dumb shit, so happy, and I'm like: who is this guy? Like I don't even recognize myself. And for a second this fear goes through my body. This weird icicle of fear. I'm like: why am I here. What am I doing. I should be back in Brooklyn practicing and like maybe having a beer with Elijah but instead I'm at the Four Seasons with this person who like, I look into her eyes, Jesus Christ, it's so cheesy—

JUDY

It's not cheesy.

SKAGGS

—and it's like all the moments in my life have led up to this one. Blah blah blah.

(pause)

Anyway. We're like these happy assholes and the next day we keep driving, we drive up to Big Sur, we stop and look at these fucking seals, or sea lions or something, I forget, and at some point we stop in, uh, San Luis Obispo and after that Meghan starts calling me Obispo . . . which now that I think about it is such an infantile stupid thing to call someone but at the time I thought it was incredibly charming or something and then we switch places and uh . . .

He pauses.

JUDY

What?

SKAGGS

I'm censoring a certain part of the story.

JUDY

Don't.

SKAGGS

Yeah. I actually should.

JUDY

I'm not judging you.

SKAGGS

Okay . . . uh . . .
I start driving and then like somewhere just before we're coming into San Francisco she gives me a blow job and it like feels so fucking good and I keep saying: the top of my head is coming off. I can't stop saying that: the top of my head is coming off and I'm driving / into—

JUDY

This happened while you were driving?

SKAGGS

Yeah. See. That's / why—

JUDY

She gave you oral sex while you were driving?

SKAGGS

Yes.

JUDY

(*quietly*)
You're lucky you didn't get into an accident and her head didn't go flying through the windshield.

SKAGGS

Great.

JUDY

Sorry.

SKAGGS

Jesus, Mom.

JUDY

Please keep going.

SKAGGS

This is exactly why I didn't—

JUDY

Just . . . when you're done? I have a story about something like that . . . sex in the car? And um . . . one of the people actually died.

Skaggs stands up, throwing the pillows aside.

SKAGGS

I'm done.

JUDY

Skaggs.

SKAGGS

I'm done. It's over.

JUDY

I want to hear about Point Reyes!

SKAGGS

No way. No way. And you know what? I don't give actually give a fuck anymore. About any of it. So good job.

Skaggs gets up and walks to his bedroom. Judy and Gary look at each other.

JUDY

Have you ever done that?

GARY

What?

JUDY

Sex in the car.

Gary nods. Judy sighs and shakes her head. Skaggs storms back in and snatches his cell phone off the floor.

> JUDY

Are you gonna listen to Meghan's message?

> SKAGGS

I'm calling Elijah.

He storms back into his bedroom and shuts the door. Judy shrugs.

> JUDY

. . . I don't know. I think maybe it helped.

Blackout. Lights up on Amanda, standing in the center of the living room.

> AMANDA

Okay. Well. I hope this was enjoyable, and I hope some of the myths surrounding Elizabeth Collins and her, um, reclusive life-style have been, um, dispelled today. I mean, we'll never exactly know why she refused to show anyone her poems . . . or why she chose to end her life when she did. But it does seem like from a very early age Elizabeth Collins simply felt like she didn't *belong*. In Shirley, or, really, anywhere. I mean, a lot of people go through periods of *feeling* like they don't belong, but then after a while they feel like they do again. With Elizabeth . . . she just . . . it seems like she spent her whole life watching everything without participating . . . seeing everything with this painful, um, clearness . . . and knowing that no one was really seeing *her* at all.

(*a pause*)

Um. There's this letter she wrote to her older sister Athel . . . in 1863 . . . right before Alfred headed out west with Winnie Rosebath . . . I'm just gonna . . .

(*Amanda takes a piece of paper out of her pocket and reads it out loud*)

"I am exhausted tonight, Athel, and weak of heart . . . Alfred took me to a dinner at White Flower Farm, and afterwards there was a small theatrical and some dancing. Lucy Boltwood played the piano. I stood next to the bay window and watched the party as if from a great distance—the dancing—the laughter—Alfred waltzing with the Rosebath girl—and then—Athel—I don't know what came over me—something terrifying—a kind of beast in my heart—and I took up one of the jasmine flowerpots and smashed it to the ground. I suppose I wanted someone to look at me. But then the worst happened—*no one took notice at all*—the dancing continued—the music—and Athel—there has never been a darker pall across my mind."

(*she clears her throat and puts the piece of paper back in her pocket*) Okay. Well. I don't want to leave on a really heavy note or anything, but . . . I think that's about it. Make sure you look at the painting on your left as you go out the door . . . it's an example of the Hudson River School of Luminism Elizabeth loved so much. A lot of landscapes, with dappled light, and, uh . . . just take a look. It's pretty cool. Okay. Thank you for coming to The Pines. You've all been great. Don't forget to collect your free tote bag on the way out.

Amanda steps out of the living room, into the hallway, and opens the front door. Blackout.

Scene Five

Lights up on Skaggs hauling his duffel bags out into the hallway one by one and piling them next to the door. Judy and Gary are standing and watching him. Skaggs drops the last duffel bag on the floor.

SKAGGS

What time is it.

JUDY

4:30.

SKAGGS

Aw man. This is totally a mistake.

GARY

Why?

SKAGGS

I dunno. I guess I don't feel like I'm gonna puke my brains out anymore. But I still feel dead. Is it really bad to like rejoin society if you feel like a dead person?

GARY

No.

SKAGGS

What if I start feeling suicidal?

GARY

You won't.

SKAGGS

What if I lose my mind and turn into some like crazy dude with a beard wandering up and down Sunset Boulevard?

JUDY

I just wish you were working for a more . . . for something more inspiring.

SKAGGS

Yeah. I don't know. It's money, man.

JUDY

Are you even gonna have time to drum?

SKAGGS

I guess. At night or whatever.
And like . . . I don't know. My name will be in like little white letters on the TV screen. At the end of the show. Which is like . . . I don't know. You guys can watch it. That's kind of cool, right?

They don't respond.

SKAGGS

Uh. Well. Thanks for having me?

JUDY

Did you tell Meghan?

SKAGGS

Nah. I just . . . Her message was all . . . she was like . . . "I miss you too but I'm so confused" and I was like: I don't know. Fuck that. Her tone or whatever. She's so manipulative.

His cell phone rings. He looks at it.

SKAGGS

Shit. It's Elijah.

He peeks out the window.

SKAGGS

He's here.

Judy starts to cry.

SKAGGS

Aw, Mom.

GARY

Jude.

JUDY

(*sobbing*)
Don't commit suicide.

SKAGGS

Jesus. I probably won't commit suicide, okay?

She starts crying harder. Gary glares pointedly at Skaggs. Skaggs sighs.

SKAGGS

Mom.

JUDY

(still sobbing)
What?

SKAGGS

I promise I won't commit suicide.

JUDY

What if you start feeling—

SKAGGS

I'll call you and you can coach me out of it. You'll stay, like, fully informed. If I decide to do it I'll tell you in advance and you and Gary can like fly out there and we'll all have a bonfire on the beach beforehand.

Judy nods shakily and holds her arms out. Judy and Skaggs hug.

SKAGGS

Uh. Bye, Gary.

GARY

I'm proud of you.

SKAGGS

Uh . . . you shouldn't be.
(after a pause)
Say hi to Nick.

Skaggs shoulders his duffel bags and is gone. The door slams behind him. A long silence. Judy slowly walks into the living room and sits down on the couch. Gary walks over and sits next to her. He puts his arm around her. After another long silence:

GARY

I miss dancing with you.

Judy begins to cry again. She crawls into Gary's lap and sobs into his shoulder.

GARY

Hey. You did a good job.
  (pause)
You did a good job.

Judy gasps for breath.

GARY

Good.

Judy sits up and wipes her face. They look at each other.

JUDY

I miss it too. He just . . . I didn't want him to make fun of us.

Gary nods. Then he gets up, takes a CD off the shelf, and puts it in the CD player. Judy stares out the bay window.

JUDY

Ooh. Look at the sunset.

Gary presses play. "Djembe Ni Bara" from the world music CD Spirit of South Africa *begins to play. He walks over to Judy and stands in front of her.*

GARY

Come on.

Gary starts dancing. He has a very particular way of dancing. He takes small steps and waves his hands above his head in slow, beatific movements. Eventually Judy gets up and joins him. She jumps up

*and down and snaps her fingers. She uses Gary's negative space,
darting in and out of his armpits and weaving her hands around
his waist. After a minute, there is a knock on the door. They stop
dancing. Gary presses stop on the CD player.*

JUDY

Oh my god. It's him.

She runs to the door and opens it. Amanda is standing there.

AMANDA

Hi.

JUDY

. . . Hello! I . . . Come in!

AMANDA

Um. I can only stay a minute.

JUDY

Skaggs is . . . have you talked to Skaggs?

AMANDA

I . . . he's at the spirituality seminar, right? That's why / I—

JUDY

He left. For Los Angeles. He didn't tell you?

AMANDA

No.

JUDY

Oh dear.

AMANDA

No. It's okay. I actually . . . I don't care. Not to sound callous or
anything. But it's . . .

Gary waves at her.

GARY

Hi!

AMANDA

Hi.
(*after a pause*)
I just . . . I wanted to return something. This is really embarrassing.
I can't believe I . . . I have no idea how it happened. But I . . .

She takes the small marble bust out of her bag.

AMANDA

I took this the night I came over for—

JUDY

It's Sumi!

AMANDA

Who?

JUDY

It's Sumi. My spiritual teacher. The one who's speaking at the
college. I didn't even realize this was missing!

AMANDA

Oh. Yeah. I, uh . . . I saw it, and I thought . . . I don't know. It's . . .
it's your spiritual teacher?

JUDY

She's . . . you would love her. She actually . . . this sounds crazy,
but she actually *materialized* this for me at her conference last
summer.

AMANDA

(*after a confused pause*)
Ah. Okay. I just . . . for some reason I thought it was an antique
and I thought it was this, um . . . I thought it was an old . . . I can't

believe I took it. I'm so sorry. It's the worst thing I've ever done.
I've been a mess. About it. And I wanted to—

GARY

That's the worst thing you've ever done?

AMANDA

. . . Yes.

*Gary chuckles and walks over to the CD player. He crouches down
and paws through the CDs.*

AMANDA

Um. Okay. I should get back to work.

GARY

Stay and dance with us!

JUDY

Gary.

GARY

What? *She* wouldn't make fun of it.

JUDY

We . . . it's sort of our thing. We use it as a way to exercise together.
I do yoga, too.

GARY

Hold on. You said you're interested in antiques?

AMANDA

Well, I . . . I'm actually just interested in Shirley history and—

GARY

I might have something for you. One minute.

Gary dashes off. Judy smiles awkwardly at Amanda.

JUDY

I have no idea what he's talking about.
  (*a pause*)
Why don't I take down your email address so Skaggs / can—

AMANDA

No, no. Please.

Gary comes back holding a tiny gold-framed picture in his hands.

GARY

This is . . . Nick found this in the basement about ten years ago.
We were cleaning it out after the divorce. And he found . . . I have
no idea who this is.

JUDY

Ooh, it's tiny!

Gary hands it to Amanda. She stares at it.

JUDY

What is it, Gare?

GARY

It's just . . . it's a little photograph. Of this very beautiful woman.
It looks like it's from—

AMANDA

  (*her hands trembling*)
It's a daguerreotype.

GARY

Daguerreotype. Huh. Anyway. I don't know if it interests you.

AMANDA

I . . . yes.
  (*she takes a deep breath*)
I'm sorry. This is . . .

GARY

Have it! If you like. It's just been sitting in the basement.

AMANDA

I do. I. I will. Thank you.

Amanda keeps staring at the picture, bereft. A pause.

GARY

Have you ever heard of "Djembe"?

AMANDA

I'm sorry. What?

GARY

They're this amazing music collective from South Africa?

JUDY

No, wait! Play her "Welcome Children"!

GARY

Okay . . . one minute.

Gary puts a new CD in. "Welcome Children" by African Vibes begins playing. Judy cheers. She and Gary start dancing.

JUDY

Isn't it great?

Amanda stands there, still clutching the daguerreotype and staring at it.

GARY

Wanna join in?

AMANDA

Uh . . . no . . . I don't—

JUDY

(*breathless*)
We were always too embarrassed to do this in front of Skaggs!

Amanda looks up.

AMANDA

I see.

Amanda stands in front of the bay window, watching them. They keep dancing while the sun sets and the room gets darker and darker. Amanda glances over at the jasmine flowerpots sitting on the windowsill. She reaches out and touches one of the blossoms. Then she quickly takes her hand away.

JUDY

(*panting*)
Should we turn on a light?

GARY

I don't know. This is kinda nice.

JUDY

Come on, Amanda! Don't be shy! We won't judge you!

Amanda shakes her head and tries to smile. Judy and Gary's dance becomes more and more uninhibited and joyful. Amanda keeps watching. They keep dancing.
A few seconds later, the room goes black.

END OF PLAY

Body Awareness

———

Production History

Body Awareness received its world premiere at the Atlantic Theater Company (Neil Pepe, Artistic Director; Andrew D. Hamingson, Managing Director) on June 4, 2008. The production was directed by Karen Kohlhaas; the set design was by Walt Spangler, the costume design was by Bobby Frederick Tilley II, the lighting design was by Jason Lyons, the sound design was by Anthony Gabriele and the production stage manager was Jillian M. Oliver. It was performed by:

JOYCE	JoBeth Williams
JARED	Jonathan Clem
PHYLLIS	Mary McCann
FRANK BONITATIBUS	Peter Friedman

Characters

JOYCE, fifty-five
JARED, her son, twenty-one
PHYLLIS, Joyce's girlfriend, forty-six
FRANK BONITATIBUS, fifty-nine

Setting

Stage left is Joyce and Phyllis's kitchen. There's a sink and a stove, a table with chairs, and a bookshelf with a multi-volume set of the OED.
Center stage is a queen-sized bed. This is Joyce and Phyllis's bedroom.
Stage right is a blackboard.
The characters should wander freely in and out of the sets during the scene transitions, turning on lights, removing props, etc.

Time

2005

Note

A slash (/) indicates where the next speech begins.

Lights up on Phyllis standing in front of the blackboard, clutching a microphone and a few index cards. She is nervous. Written across the blackboard is the word "MONDAY." Phyllis takes a deep breath.

PHYLLIS

The goal for Body Awareness Week is threefold.

(*pause*)

One: it's a catalyst for discussion.

Two: it's a chance for everyone here at Shirley State to just kind of *check in*: first with ourselves, and our own bodies, and then with our thoughts and judgments about other people's bodies. We live in a very harsh culture, a culture that encourages a real obsession with appearance, and, um, healing from this culture, healing ourselves, can only really take place once we're able to step back and examine the culture itself from a critical viewpoint. Deepak Chopra uses a, what I think is a really great example of flies stuck in a jar: if you keep the lid on for long enough, when you finally take it off, only a few flies are actually brave enough to leave the, ah, *confines* of the jar. The rest just keep flying around inside.

(*she takes a deep breath*)

Three: we've invited some really fabulous guest artists to campus this week, so it's a great opportunity for all of us to really look at art in a new way. I mean, if you think about it, so *much* of art is about body awareness, or at least gaze awareness . . . so faculty members, if any of this is applicable to your class work . . . don't make it a source of stress or anything, but there is just *so much* potential discussion surrounding these issues.

(*after a pause, peering out*)

Wow. It's really snowing out there.

(*she smiles nervously*)

I guess that's it. It's Monday! We've got five very eventful days ahead of us. I'm, ah . . . I'm really excited about this.

Blackout on Phyllis.

Joyce and Phyllis's kitchen. Joyce and Jared sit at the table. Jared wears his McDonald's uniform. After a long silence:

JOYCE

We're fine with you masturbating, Jared.

Jared does not respond.

JOYCE

This is not about the fact that you masturbate.

Another silence.

JOYCE

The thing is . . . you can't rack up those charges. We see them on the bill.

JARED

Okay.

JOYCE

You're free to use the internet, or purchase whatever yourself . . .

(*another awkward pause*)

. . . We just can't afford the Pay Per View.

JARED

This is really gross.

JOYCE

What's gross?

JARED

Talking about this.

JOYCE

Yeah, well, I think women with no body hair? I think that's gross.

Jared is silent.

JOYCE

You know people don't really look like that, right? It will be extremely hard for you to find a real person who looks like that.

Jared refuses to look at her.

JOYCE

Those women have had extensive plastic surgery and really painful hair waxing procedures. I assume you know that we all have pubic hair for a reason.

A long pause.

JOYCE

What are you thinking about?

JARED

Why do you care?

JOYCE

I love you . . . ? I think you're fabulous . . . ?

JARED

OED stuff.

JOYCE

Any specific word?

JARED

I was thinking about the definition for "imbecile."

JOYCE

That sounds like a fun one.

Jared gazes at her suspiciously, then continues.

JARED

Nowadays "imbecile" just means someone stupid. But it used to mean "physically weak." It originally comes from the Latin for "without a supporting staff."

JOYCE

Huh.

JARED

What's weird is that this implies there was a time when "physically weak" and "stupid" were synonymous.

JOYCE

Yeah. I avoid using the word "stupid" whenever possible. It's kind of judgmental, don't you think?

Jared abruptly stands up, takes a book out of his backpack, and puts it down on the table.

JOYCE

Wow. You read the whole thing?

JARED

Yes. Well. I perused it.

JOYCE

And?

JARED

It was extremely well written.

JOYCE

It's a fast read, right?

JARED

I don't really care about whether something is a "fast read."

JOYCE

No, I just meant . . . Phyllis says he's an incredible psychologist. Like, renowned.

A *pause.*

JOYCE   JARED
    Do you think—   I don't have it.

JOYCE

. . . Okay. We don't need to jump to any conclusions right now. I . . . Phyllis and I just wanted you to think about it, and then—

JARED

I can tell you with one hundred percent certainty that I don't have it.

JOYCE

That's great. That's great.
    (*after a pause*)
I just think that if we all went and met with a psychologist he or she could give us a more definite—

JARED

I AM NOT FUCKING RETARDED.

JOYCE

Tone Of Voice.

JARED

I am not fucking retarded.

JOYCE	JARED
It doesn't mean you're retarded. It's a social—	I don't have it.

JARED

They give that example. If an Asperger's person walks in the front door and sees a loved one crying they don't stop and ask, What's Wrong?

JOYCE

Uh-huh.

JARED

I can say with one hundred percent certainty that I would stop and ask, What's Wrong?

JOYCE

Really? The last time you saw me crying you told me to stop and make you a snack.

JARED

You were crying for a stupid reason.

JOYCE

I was crying because you threatened to stab me in the eye.

JARED

I just . . . I'm obviously a really smart person.

JOYCE

It doesn't mean you're not smart. It just means you have trouble relating to people.

Jared picks up his backpack.

JARED

I have to go to work.

JOYCE

I love you. Hey. Don't forget. Our guest artist is coming tomorrow. So keep things neat.

JARED

Is it a man?

JOYCE

I don't know.

JARED

I would prefer that it not be a man.

JOYCE

I really don't have any control over that, sweetheart.

Jared walks out of the room. After a few seconds, he walks back in.

JARED

Maybe you have Asperger's.

JOYCE

Jared.

JARED

Because you're kind of an idiot.

JOYCE

I'm not an idiot, honey.

JARED

You've never read *Crime and Punishment*. You're fifty-five and you've never read *Crime and Punishment*.

JOYCE

Have *you* ever read *Crime and Punishment*?

Jared roars in frustration, then takes an electric toothbrush out of his pocket. He turns it on and starts passing the toothbrush back and forth between his hands. Joyce watches him.

JOYCE

If you're angry at me just say it. You don't have to insult me. You can say: I'm feeling really angry right now, Mom.

JARED

I'm not angry. I'm surrounded by imbeciles. You don't even . . . you don't even read the dictionary!

JOYCE

You're going to be late.

Jared stops and stares at her, seething with rage.

JARED

I could kill you.

JOYCE

Warning One.

JARED

I could kill Phyllis.

JOYCE

Warning Two.

JARED

I could garrote both of you in your sleep.

JOYCE

Warning Three. If you make one more physical threat I will call the police.

JARED

I have First Amendment Rights.

JOYCE

You are not allowed to physically threaten people and you know that.

JARED

First Amendment says I can physically threaten people.

JOYCE

No it doesn't.

JARED

Yes it does.

JOYCE

No. It doesn't.

JARED

BABBLING CRETIN!

Joyce collapses onto the table and buries her face in her arms. It's unclear whether or not she's crying. Jared stands there and watches her for a while. He turns off the toothbrush.

JARED

I won't kill you.

Silence.

JARED

I was joking.

Silence.

JARED

What's wrong?

Joyce does not respond.

JARED

See? I asked.

Blackout.
Joyce and Phyllis's bedroom. Joyce and Phyllis sit up in bed together, lit by the bedside lamp. Phyllis is reading the Asperger's book. Joyce is clipping her toenails and depositing them on the nightstand.

JOYCE

There's this weird *crud* all over my toenails.

PHYLLIS

(*not looking up from her book*)
What color is it?

JOYCE

Gray-ish?

PHYLLIS

Ew.

After a pause, Phyllis puts down the book.

PHYLLIS

If he doesn't think he has it how does he explain the fact that he still lives with his mother?

JOYCE

There are lots of cultures where children live with their parents through adulthood.

PHYLLIS

And rack up porn bills?

JOYCE

America is very strange. We're so focused on independence. It's like, you can't need anybody. You have to be this totally autonomous . . . *person*.

PHYLLIS

Hey. Speaking of other cultures. I finally met the Palestinian dance troupe kids.

JOYCE

Oh! Cute!

PHYLLIS

They were amazing. They've been living in these refugee camps since they were babies? And they were / all—

JOYCE

Wait. I don't get it. How do they relate to Body Awareness?

PHYLLIS

Well. They're a dance troupe. For one thing.

JOYCE

Huh.

PHYLLIS

And they're very political.

JOYCE

Right.

Joyce goes back to clipping her toenails.

PHYLLIS

Hey. My eye is twitching. Can you tell?

Joyce looks at her.

JOYCE

Where?

PHYLLIS

Left one.

JOYCE

Nope.

PHYLLIS

I can feel it, um . . . it's sort of pulsing? Just like this little pulsing—

JOYCE

I don't see anything.

Jared yells from offstage:

JARED
(offstage)
I CAN HEAR YOU GUYS TALKING AND I'M ATTEMPTING
TO FALL ASLEEP!

Phyllis and Joyce look at each other, amused.

JARED
(offstage)
I HAVE TO GET UP AT SIX IN THE MORNING!

JOYCE
(calling out)
Okay, okay, we hear you!

JARED
(offstage)
I ACTUALLY HAVE A JOB!

PHYLLIS
(yelling back good-naturedly)
We have jobs too!

JARED
(offstage)
IN ACADEMIA!

PHYLLIS
(laughing)
YOUR MOTHER'S JOB DOES NOT COUNT AS ACADEMIA!

Phyllis grins at Joyce. Joyce stares at her for a few seconds, then:

JOYCE
What do you mean, it doesn't count as academia?

PHYLLIS
A high school teacher is not an academic.

JOYCE

Why not?

PHYLLIS

An academic has a PhD.

JOYCE

Who says?

PHYLLIS

Um. It's common knowledge?

JOYCE

I've never heard that before.

PHYLLIS

Joyce. A public school teacher is not an academic. An academic publishes articles. An academic—

JOYCE

You are such a snob.

PHYLLIS

What? No. I'm the *opposite* of a snob. How am I a snob?

JARED

(*offstage*)

WILL BOTH OF YOU KINDLY CEASE SPEAKING!

Phyllis and Joyce fall silent. After a short pause, the buzzing sound of the electric toothbrush is heard from offstage.

PHYLLIS

(*softly*)

Oh please. He's not sleeping. He's sticking his toothbrush up his ass.

JOYCE

Phil.

PHYLLIS

What?

JOYCE

He likes rubbing it against his gums. He finds it soothing.

Phyllis holds up the Asperger's book.

PHYLLIS

Did you read the part where it says that they get really dependant on certain objects and rituals?

JOYCE

Yeah.

PHYLLIS

Also they have an unbelievably sensitive sense of smell. *Totally* Jared.
  (*after a pause*)
I can't get over the fact that you never made him see a therapist.

JOYCE

He refuses to go.

PHYLLIS

Yeah, but with certain kids you just have to insist / on—

JOYCE

(*defensively*)
For a while it seemed like he was gonna be fine.

Phyllis sighs.

JOYCE

For a while it seemed that way!

PHYLLIS

I'm gonna turn off the light.

JOYCE

He had friends in elementary school. This little clique of boys?

Phyllis reaches over and turns off the lamp. They're barely visible in the moonlight. After a pause, quietly, out of the darkness:

JOYCE

He was a *very* cuddly baby.

PHYLLIS

Okay, okay.

A pause.

JOYCE

Will you spoon me?

PHYLLIS

Mmm.

*The sound of sheets rustling. They settle into a comfortable position.
After a few seconds:*

JOYCE

God. I can't stop thinking about this girl in my B period class.
Loreen? I told you about her.

PHYLLIS

I'm really tired, sweetheart.

JOYCE

She's so *makeup-y*. I don't know. It's weird. There's something
really nervous and sexualized about her.

PHYLLIS

Mm-hm.

JOYCE

I think maybe she was molested.

PHYLLIS

You think everyone was molested.

JOYCE

Well, one out of four / women—

PHYLLIS

Yeah, but you think EVERYONE was molested.

JOYCE

That's not true.

PHYLLIS

You thought I was molested. When you met me.

JOYCE

Well, you seemed kind of . . . molested.
  (*after a long pause*)
Will you do it again?

PHYLLIS

Oh my god. I'm so tired.

There is a rustling underneath the covers.

JOYCE

Higher.

After a pause:

JOYCE

Yeah. There.

PHYLLIS

Okay.

JOYCE

Is that weird?

PHYLLIS

Yeah, Joyce.

JOYCE

Is that thigh? Or is it crotch?
  (*after a long silence*)
Is it weird for someone to put their—

PHYLLIS

It's weird.

JOYCE

It could have been nothing.

PHYLLIS

It's weird, honey.

JOYCE

He could have just . . .

PHYLLIS

Your father was *definitely* a bastard. Can we go to sleep?

JOYCE

Yeah. Yeah. Sorry.

The two women shift around in bed and embrace each other. Slowly, morning light comes through the window.
Phyllis gets up out of bed and walks over to the blackboard. She writes "TUESDAY" on the blackboard, then turns to the audience and speaks into a microphone.

PHYLLIS

It's an honor just to stand here and introduce the next performers. They've flown across oceans, and, um, continents to perform for us, and they're an unbelievably strong, brave group of children. People. They came together in a refugee camp in Palestine, where, well . . . the word that comes to my mind is "hopelessness." In a place of hopelessness they formed a community, and they created this work of dance . . . it's pretty mind-blowing. So without further ado—
  (*she hesitates*)
Oh. Sorry. One more thing. Just a nomenclature issue. This week, um, February 20th to the 27th, is, officially, National Eating Disorder Awareness Week. But I wanted to reiterate that here at Shirley State College we've chosen to call it Body Awareness

Week. There's still gonna be the roundtable discussion on eating disorders, but we feel it's important to take a more positive tack and make the whole thing about the larger issue of Self Image in general. And this way we get to see incredible groups like Idbaal perform! So just a reminder, it's not Eating Disorder Awareness Week at Shirley State, it's *Body Awareness* Week. If we could correct the mistake on any posters or publicity materials, that would be great. Okay. Prepare to be . . . very moved. I'd like to welcome Idbaal!

She steps aside. Pounding Palestinian music starts playing.
Blackout.
Joyce and Phyllis's kitchen. Frank Bonitatibus stands in the middle of the kitchen, playing the recorder. Joyce is sitting at the table and watching him, utterly enchanted. He finishes, lowers the recorder and smiles at her. After a pause:

JOYCE

Oh. My. God.

FRANK

You enjoyed it?

JOYCE

That was *otherworldly.*

FRANK

Mmm.

They grin at each other for a while. Finally Joyce shakes her head, as if to clear her thoughts.

JOYCE

I should start making dinner.

Joyce gets up from the table and starts getting vegetables out of the fridge. Frank trails her around the kitchen while she prepares the meal. He continually munches from a bowl of baby carrots on the kitchen table.

FRANK

So you teach high school?

JOYCE

Yup.

FRANK

What do you teach?

JOYCE

Cultural Studies.

FRANK

Is that like Social Studies?

JOYCE

It's a little different.

FRANK

How?

JOYCE

Um, well, we sort of take more of an anthropological perspective?

She starts cutting up the vegetables. Frank peers at some of the pictures on the refrigerator.

FRANK

How long have you and your girlfriend been together?

JOYCE

Three years.

FRANK

Wow. Great.

JOYCE

It is great.

FRANK

Do you call her that? Your "girlfriend"? Is it okay? To call her that?

JOYCE

Um, well, some people—

FRANK

Do you prefer "partner" or something?

JOYCE

Oh. I don't know. Well, actually, / yes. I—

FRANK

"Partner" sounds so *dippy*, though. You know what I mean?

JOYCE

Um—

FRANK

Have you always been . . . ?

Frank makes a vague gesture.

JOYCE

Uh. No. I have a son. You'll meet him. Yeah. I was married. To a man. Years ago. Phyllis was actually my first, um, female partner.

FRANK

What about her?

JOYCE

Oh, Phyllis. Yeah. Phyllis knew she was gay when she was in kindergarten.

FRANK

Three years together. Huh.
    (*after a pause*)
You really feel like you know each other after three years.
    (*Joyce nods*)

But then one day the person says something really weird and you're like: DO I actually know you? Or are you this total stranger?

Joyce doesn't respond. She finishes chopping vegetables and starts putting them into a pot on the stove.

FRANK

Anyway.

JOYCE

Are you in a relationship?

FRANK

No. I'm actually incredibly happy to be single. Just taking stock of things.

Joyce nods.

FRANK

You live here. That's so strange.

Joyce nods again.

FRANK

"Shirley, Vermont." This is a weird town.

JOYCE

It's small.

FRANK

Yeah. Small and weird.

Joyce starts stirring and seasoning.

FRANK

Is everyone really PC? Are people like, don't say "black person," say "person of color"?

JOYCE

Oh. Well. I don't know. I / think—

Annie Baker

FRANK

Don't say "retarded," say "mentally disabled"?

JOYCE

Actually—

FRANK

People in towns like this always seem to find my work threatening.

JOYCE

But your pictures are so moving!

FRANK

It's like you're not allowed to do anything involving naked women anymore. If a woman is naked, you're a misogynist.

JOYCE

But you have so many *types* of women—

FRANK

I know—

JOYCE

—that one photo of the old lady? With the mastectomy?

FRANK

Yeah.

JOYCE

It was gorgeous. The way she was smiling?

The buzzing sound of Jared's toothbrush is heard from offstage.

FRANK

Do you hear that?

JOYCE

My son must be home.

FRANK

Yeah, but what's that sound?

Joyce hesitates.

JOYCE

Um. You should probably know. Jared is kind of . . . special.

Frank looks at her.

FRANK

Special meaning what?

JOYCE

Um. I think he has something called Asperger's? I'd like him to
see a therapist about it. He refuses to, / but—

FRANK

I've heard of that. It's like lack of empathy, right?

JOYCE

There are less negative ways to put it.

FRANK

No, I just—

JOYCE

There's this thing called Theory of Mind? It's our ability to know
that other people don't know what we're thinking . . . that we each
have these independent mental states? People with Asperger's
have a hard time—

Jared enters the kitchen, sucking on his toothbrush.

JARED

The whole house smells like meatloaf.

JOYCE

No one's making meatloaf.

JARED

It smells like meatloaf.

Annie Baker

                        JOYCE
Jared. This is Frank Bonitatibus.

*Frank extends his hand. Jared lifts his hand up in a limp salute, but
doesn't touch Frank. After a second, he turns off the toothbrush.*

                        JARED
I don't have Asperger's.

                        JOYCE
You were eavesdropping.

                        JARED
Stop telling everyone I'm retarded.

                        JOYCE
I never said you were retarded.

                        JARED
   (to Frank)
She made me take classes with the retarded kids in high school.

                        JOYCE
I made you take one Organizational Skills class.

                        JARED
   (to Frank)
I'm incredibly smart—

                        FRANK
   (nervously)
Of course—

                        JARED
—and she made me take this class with the Special Ed kids. This
one guy kept going like this:
   (he bobbles his head back and forth)
"You owe me three dollah. You owe me three dollah."

Jared starts laughing.

394

JOYCE

Okay. Enough.

FRANK

Are you a student at Shirley State?

JARED

College is stupid. Buncha frat girls and guys having sex with each other.

FRANK

That's not what my college experience was like.

JARED

People do drugs and go to parties.

FRANK

Where is he getting this stuff?

JOYCE

I don't know. I told him how much I loved Brandeis.

JARED

It doesn't really matter anyway. I'm an autodidact.

FRANK

Oh yeah?

JARED

Do you know what that means?

FRANK

I think so.

JARED

It comes from the Greek.

FRANK

You know Greek?

JARED

I know etymology.

FRANK

What's that?

JARED

Ha.
(to Joyce)
He doesn't know what etymology means.

JOYCE

It's a big word, Jared.

FRANK

Wait. I think I know what it means. The beginning of things? / The—

JARED

WRONG.

JOYCE

Why don't you tell him?

FRANK

I don't need him to tell me.

JARED

The origins and histories of words.

FRANK

Sure. Of course.

JARED

It's my strength. It's proof that I'm not a retard.

JOYCE

Please stop saying retard.

FRANK

(to Jared)
You ever seen *Rain Man*?

JARED

No.

FRANK

Dustin Hoffman is this retarded guy, but he's like a genius in certain subjects. He's always freaking out and doing these little flappy—

JOYCE

(getting upset)
That's autism. I think you're talking about autism. Jared has Asperger's. It's on the autism spectrum, but it's actually a much milder—

JARED

I DON'T HAVE IT. FUCKING SHIT!

Frank looks at Joyce, expecting her to say something. Joyce goes back to stirring the soup.

FRANK

(to Jared)
Uh . . . if you don't go to college what do you do?

JARED

Lots of things. I'm an autodidact.

JOYCE

I think he means where do you work.

JARED

I work at McDonald's.

FRANK

Oh, hey, good, great. Hard-workin' man!

JARED

Everyone there is an idiot.

FRANK

I'm sure that's not true.

JARED

It smells like meatloaf in here. Also like glitter. That glue and glitter smell?

Joyce ignores him. Jared takes a volume of the OED off of the bookshelf, sits down at the kitchen table, and starts reading it.

FRANK

This is an interesting family.

JOYCE

Mmm. We're very open.

Phyllis enters through the backdoor.

JOYCE

Phil! This is our guest artist!

PHYLLIS

Hey! Oh great! I'm Phyllis. I'm one of the, ah, many organizers.

They shake hands.

FRANK

Frank Bonitatibus. It's incredibly generous of you to let me—

PHYLLIS

Oh, no! Please. Thank *you.*

Phyllis beams happily at him, then walks over to Joyce and kisses her.

PHYLLIS

Hey, ladybug.

FRANK
(inserting himself back into the conversation)
. . . It's just so nice to stay in an actual *house*. Usually I just end
up sitting alone in a hotel room and drinking beer.

PHYLLIS
We don't drink in this house.

FRANK
No, that's fine, that's not / what—

JARED
(looking up from his book)
Yes we do. We drink milk. We drink water.

PHYLLIS
I mean alcohol, Jared.

JARED
We drink Cranberry Raspberry Cocktail.

FRANK
(nervously)
Sounds fine, sounds fine.

JARED
We drink our own urine.

A *horrible pause.*

JARED
Just kidding.

FRANK
Great.

JARED
I was being ironic.
(to Frank)
The book said people with Asperger's don't know how to be ironic.

PHYLLIS

What's your medium, Frank?

FRANK

I'm a photographer.

PHYLLIS

Oh! Wonderful! I've just been working with the performance artists, / so—

JARED

Do you make daguerreotypes?

FRANK

Ah. No.

JARED

Do you know what a daguerreotype is?

FRANK

Yes.

JARED

Do you know the etymology of daguerreotype?

FRANK

No. I—

JOYCE

(pointedly, ignoring Jared)
Tell Phyllis about your photographs.
(to Phyllis)
I saw them this afternoon. They're amazing.

FRANK

Uh. Well. I take pictures of women.

JOYCE

(giggling)
Naked women.

Phyllis looks at Joyce, confused.

> PHYLLIS

I'm sorry—?

> JOYCE

They're actually incredibly moving. You have to see it. Everyone was / just—

> PHYLLIS

(ignoring Joyce; to Frank)
Wait, why? Why do you take pictures of naked women?

> FRANK

Why does anyone take pictures of anything?

> JOYCE

Explain it to her. It's actually wonderful.
(to Phyllis)
He goes around—

> FRANK

I go around the country. I don't pay anyone. Women volunteer to pose for me. It's a way for them to, uh, reclaim their own body image.

> PHYLLIS

Why don't men pose for you?

> JOYCE

It's not just, like, model types. He takes pictures of old women, little girls—

> PHYLLIS

Excuse me?

> FRANK

With parental permission.

A pause.

JARED

The word "daguerreotype" actually comes from the French inventor of the daguerreotype himself. Louis Daguerre.

PHYLLIS

Sorry. I just—

JOYCE

Phyllis is very sensitive.

PHYLLIS

Um, I don't think I'm that sensitive, Joyce. You're the one who's, like, the language police.

An awkward pause.

JOYCE

You know, Sally Humphries loves his stuff. She's really crazy about it.

PHYLLIS

Uh-huh.

JOYCE

(to Frank)
Phyllis was on the search committee that brought Sally Humphries into the psychology department. It was such a white-male-dominated little boy's club, and Sally is this like fabulous *fiery* African-American woman. She's actually part Native American, too, I think . . .

FRANK

Oh yeah?

JOYCE

. . . and she's just fabulous.

A defeated pause.

PHYLLIS

(to Frank)

How do you know it isn't just exhibitionist? Or exploitative?

FRANK

It's neither.

PHYLLIS

How do you know?

FRANK

Because I'm not exploiting them, and they don't do it for exhibitionist reasons.

PHYLLIS

(trying to sound light-hearted)

Well, I'm not posing for you.

FRANK

Don't worry, honey. I'm not asking.

PHYLLIS

Did you just call me "honey"?

JARED

(looking up from the OED)

I refuse to get naked in front of anyone.

PHYLLIS

Frank wouldn't be interested anyway, Jared, because you're a man.

JARED

I don't want anyone to see me naked. Even if I get a girlfriend. I don't want her to look at me.

Jared goes back to reading.

JOYCE

(after an awkward pause)

Okay! Let's eat! I made this great winter soup.

> JARED

It smells like meatloaf.

> JOYCE

Please try to be polite. We have a guest.

Everyone sits down at the table.

> JOYCE

(*to Jared*)
Can you put that away?

Jared puts the OED volume on his chair and sits on it. He's perched about five inches higher than everyone else. Joyce ladles out soup.

> FRANK

Sorry. Do you all say grace?

> PHYLLIS

We're not religious.

> JOYCE

I'm actually Jewish. Well. I'm half Jewish. Phyllis / is—

> FRANK

Fantastic. That's so great.

> JOYCE

But I'm not observant.

> FRANK

No, that's wonderful! Jews are wonderful. My parents are Greek.

> JOYCE

Very nice!

> FRANK

. . . But I personally take a sort of nonreligious Buddhist view of things. Still. Judaism is so beautiful. It's such a dialectical religion, you know?

JARED

I never got a bar mitzvah.

JOYCE

He just wanted one so people would give him money. I thought
that probably wasn't the right reason to go through with it.

FRANK

Hey. You know what? We should do a Shabbas.

JOYCE

Oh. Um. We don't really do that kind of thing.

PHYLLIS

Also it's not Friday.

FRANK

It would be such a treat for me.

JARED

Religion is stupid.

JOYCE

Jared! That's a close-minded thing to say.

FRANK

Come on.

JOYCE

It's a little embarrassing. I just . . . I don't think I even know how
to do Shabbas.

PHYLLIS

Why is that embarrassing?

FRANK

Ah-ha. See, I do. You got any red wine?

PHYLLIS

We don't drink.

JOYCE

We have grape juice . . .

FRANK

Perfect.

PHYLLIS

Sorry. I . . . um . . . no one else thinks that doing Shabbas on a Tuesday is a little disrespectful? Possibly sacrilegious?

Joyce gets some grape juice out of the cupboard and puts it on the table. She gets out four wine glasses.

JARED

Booze. Goody.

He laughs.

PHYLLIS

I don't want any.

JOYCE

Oh, come on.

She grins happily at Phyllis. Phyllis shakes her head. Joyce pours her a glass of grape juice.

FRANK

Okay. Now sit. Please.

Joyce sits. Frank takes his recorder out of his pocket and plays an "A." Phyllis looks on in disbelief. Frank puts his recorder back in his pocket, takes a deep breath, and closes his eyes.

FRANK

(*singing*)
Baruch atah adonai
Elohaynu melekh ha-olam
Borey pree hagofen.

Frank opens his eyes and smiles serenely.

> FRANK

That was the prayer for wine.

> PHYLLIS

How do you know the prayer for wine?

> FRANK

I was married to a Jew for ten years.

> JOYCE

Me too!

He and Joyce burst into giggles. Phyllis and Jared are unamused.

> PHYLLIS

Why is that funny?

> JOYCE
> *(ignoring her; to Frank)*

That was gorgeous. Thank you.

> FRANK

It's not over. Do you have any candles?

> JOYCE

I actually do!

Joyce gets up and gets out two candles and two candlesticks. She puts them on the table.

> PHYLLIS

This is great. A goy teaching a Jew how to do Shabbas. On a Tuesday.

> FRANK

I hope I'm not being presumptuous.

> JOYCE

No, no. Not at all.

> FRANK

Okay. Light the candles.

Joyce lights the candles.

> FRANK

Wave your hands around.

Joyce jiggles her hands.

> FRANK

No, like you're bringing the heat towards you.

He mimes. She obeys.

> FRANK

Good.

> JOYCE

Oh yeah! It's like that scene from *Fiddler on the Roof*!

> JARED

I hate musicals.

> FRANK

Now put your hands over your eyes.

Joyce puts her hands over her eyes. Frank takes out his recorder, gives himself another "A," and then sings the following in a pleasant monotone:

> FRANK

Baruch atah adonai
Elohaynu melekh ha-olam . . .

> JARED

You said that before.

> FRANK

. . . this one is different . . .

Asher kid-shanu
B'mitzvotav v'tzivanu
L'had'like neir shel Shabbat. Amein.

A pause.

                         FRANK
   (softly)
Can we all sing that last word together?

            PHYLLIS *(reluctantly)*, JOYCE AND FRANK
A-*a-a-a-mein.*

                         FRANK
Now take your hands away.

Joyce takes her hands away. They all look at her.

                         PHYLLIS
You're crying. Jesus Christ.

                         JOYCE
It's just . . .
   (to Frank)
Thank you.
   (she sits down, shakily)
My Bubbie used to sing like that.

                         PHYLLIS
You were raised by atheists.

                         JOYCE
Not my parents. My Bubbie.

                         FRANK
It's nice, right? Connecting with your roots.

                         JARED
This soup is not as gross as I thought it would be.

JOYCE

I really love listening to people sing. Phyllis never sings. She's too self-conscious.

Phyllis stares at Joyce, hurt.

JOYCE

What? It's true.

FRANK

Singing is very meditative.

JOYCE

(*nodding*)
I wish I meditated more.

FRANK

We're all so *wound-up* all the time.

JOYCE

Exactly.

FRANK

We, uh . . . we walk around in these little circles, and we forget to pay attention to what we could see if we just stopped using our brains so much.

PHYLLIS

Sorry . . . I'm a little confused. What do you mean / by—

FRANK

There's a lot of stuff happening around us. Stuff we're not aware of most of the time. You know what I mean. We don't live in this perfectly linear universe.

PHYLLIS

I actually have no idea what you're talking about.

JOYCE

Do you mean thoughts and dreams? Or . . .

                    FRANK

Sure. Both. Also visions. Visitations.
   (*after a pause*)
If you make yourself open.

                    JARED

You sound dumb.

                    JOYCE

Jared.

                    FRANK

I don't think I sound dumb.

                    PHYLLIS

   (*to Joyce*)
The soup is great.

                    JOYCE

Thanks.

                    PHYLLIS

The squash is so, um—

                    FRANK

When I was eight I was hit by a car. I had to wear a body cast for
ten months.

                    JOYCE

Oh my god.

                    FRANK

Funny things happen when you're stuck in bed for that long. I'd
wake up after a nap and there would be a dozen people standing
around my bed. Old-fashioned people. With the big hats? Men in
suits. Women with those little frilly umbrellas. They'd be talking
to each other like they were at a cocktail party or something. They
didn't even pay attention to me. I'd sit up in bed and scream GO
AWAY. They'd turn to look at me, with these disappointed faces,
and then they'd disappear.

PHYLLIS

Cool dream.

FRANK

Oh come on. It wasn't—please. Don't condescend to me.

PHYLLIS

Excuse me?

JOYCE

Phyllis has a PhD in psychology. She teaches "Brain and Behavior."

FRANK

I don't see how that's relevant.

PHYLLIS

It sounds like a great dream. What's wrong with me saying that?

FRANK

Ah . . . I just find it frustrating when people who refuse to acknowledge certain ambiguities in the universe look down on those of us / who—

JOYCE

How many times did you see the, um, the people?

FRANK

They came back every few months. Eventually I realized they weren't going to hurt me.

PHYLLIS

So what are you trying to say? They were ghosts?

FRANK

I'm not trying to say anything.

A pause.

PHYLLIS

What's the difference between a ghost and an incredibly realistic hallucination?

Frank taps his stomach.

PHYLLIS

What's that supposed to mean?

FRANK

Your gut. You feel it in your gut.

JARED

(*to Frank*)
You're not being very logical.

FRANK

I don't care for logic.
(*after a pause, to Joyce*)
Thank you for dinner. I feel very comfortable here.

JARED

Logic comes from the Greek for the "the art of reason."

FRANK

You're a smart kid, Jared.

JARED

Actually, I'm not a kid. I'm twenty-one. I could have sex with an adult woman.

JOYCE

Jared.

JARED

I could.

A pause. They all go back to eating. Blackout.
Joyce and Phyllis's bedroom. Nighttime. Joyce is in bed. Phyllis is pacing up and down the floor, infuriated.

PHYLLIS

Okay, so what, some prepubescent girl comes into his studio and takes off her clothes and he's like: I'm going to help you reclaim your body image?

413

JOYCE

Could you please lower your voice? He's right down the hall.

PHYLLIS

It's totally, it's disgusting, I mean, there are gonna be male college students walking around the Student Union looking at photos of naked prepubescent girls. Oh my god! I'm gonna lose my shit!

JOYCE

It's very very hard for me to have sympathy for you when you haven't even taken the time to look at the photographs.

PHYLLIS

He goes around the country doing this? What a scam. What a pervert! Someone needs to, like, eliminate him from the face of the planet.

JOYCE

Okay. You know I find that kind of talk upsetting.

PHYLLIS

Using art to . . . oh my god. It's so manipulative. It's so obviously manipulative and *evil*. This guy is like . . . evil manifest!

JOYCE

What about it is so threatening for you?

PHYLLIS

Threatening? Nothing. I find nothing threatening about it. I find it repulsive and disgusting and exploitative and crazy. I think this guy is like a psycho killer. I think he chops women up and buries them in his backyard!

Jared appears in the doorway, holding the Asperger's book.

JARED

I have something to say.

PHYLLIS

Jared, how do you feel about a middle-aged man traveling around the country and asking women to take their clothes off?

JOYCE

(ignoring her)
What do you have to say, sweetheart?

JARED

I know why you guys think I have Asperger's.

They look at him.

JARED

I've never had sex and you think that's weird.

JOYCE

. . . I don't think it's weird at *all* that you haven't had sex.

PHYLLIS

I didn't have sex until I was in college.

JARED

You're a lesbian.

PHYLLIS

How does / that—

JOYCE

Listen. It's good to wait. It's good to wait until you're ready, and you've met somebody you really like, / and—

JARED

The book says people with Asperger's have a hard time forging physical and romantic relationships because of their lack of empathy and social prowess and I know that's why you think I have it but you're wrong. I'm just shy, and introverted, and I have better things to do than go to a frat party and get drunk and make out with some stupid girl.

JOYCE

. . . And I'm proud of you for that, sweetheart.

PHYLLIS

Hold on. Why does the idea of having it upset you so much?

JARED

It upsets me because I don't have it.

PHYLLIS

What makes you so sure?

JARED

I've read most of the book and I've thought about it and I don't have it. And they say there's not a foolproof test you can do anyway.

PHYLLIS

(*sighing*)
Okay. That's true. But Jared? You line up with pretty much every single one of the symptoms. You have this formal way of talking, you freak out if there's any change in your daily routine, you haven't had a friend in more than—

Jared throws the Asperger's book at Phyllis's head. She screams and dodges.

PHYLLIS

WHAT THE HELL!

Joyce leaps up and grabs Jared's arms.

JOYCE

No. No. You cannot do that.

JARED

(*shouting at Phyllis*)
Okay, well, you have Down syndrome! I read a book on Down syndrome and I decided that you have it!

PHYLLIS

You can test for Down syndrome, you little jerk!

JOYCE

Phyllis.

JARED

You're stupid and you have no idea how stupid you are and you're like totally oblivious and ugly so I think you have Down syndrome!

JOYCE

Both of you stop it!

Joyce slides to the floor and sits there, crying.

PHYLLIS

(to Jared)

Listen. I'm . . . a psychology professor is telling you that you most likely have this thing and that maybe you can get help for it. Someone could help you work on your social skills and then maybe you'd actually get a girlfriend and have sex and it could be pretty great, but no, you refuse to go to therapy and you won't admit that maybe, just maybe, you have it! Why are you holding yourself back?

JARED

Because I know. Like that guy Frank was saying. I know it in my gut.

PHYLLIS

I give up.

JARED

I'm going to have sex. Without anyone's help. Just wait and see.

JOYCE

Oh my god. Jared? Do not go out and have sex to prove something to Phyllis.

JARED

You think I have it, too.

JOYCE

. . . I'm not sure. Okay?

PHYLLIS

Oh, come on, Joyce.

Joyce shoots her a look.

JARED

I'm going to get a girlfriend and I'm going to have doggy-style sex with her.

JOYCE

Please. Please don't talk that way. That's not going to make you happy, honey.

Jared walks out of the room, then immediately turns around and walks back in.

JARED

She's going to be impressed by how much etymology I know.

He walks out. Phyllis and Joyce look at each other.

JOYCE

I am feeling very very angry at you right now.

PHYLLIS

That's fine. Because I am feeling very angry at you right now.

JOYCE

No you're not. You're feeling angry at Frank Bonitatibus. And you took it out on Jared.

PHYLLIS

(*after a pause*)
Were you flirting with him?

JOYCE

Who?

PHYLLIS

Frank Bonifuckhead.

JOYCE

No. Jesus, Phyllis. You have totally lost it.

PHYLLIS

I feel like you were kind of flirting with him. Do you miss male attention or something?

JOYCE

I said no. You're allowed to ask, but then you have to believe me when I say no.

PHYLLIS

Sometimes you can flirt without realizing it.

JOYCE

If I was flirting without realizing it then you have no reason to be mad at me.

PHYLLIS

I beg to differ.

Joyce stands up.

JOYCE

I'm turning off the light.

PHYLLIS

I want to read more.

JOYCE

I don't give a shit.

Joyce turns off the light. There's a knock on the door. After a second, the door creaks open. Frank is standing in the doorway in a bathrobe.

Annie Baker

FRANK

Is everything okay?

PHYLLIS

Hunky-dory, Frank.

FRANK

I heard Jared yelling.

PHYLLIS

Thanks so much for checking.

Frank nods and walks away. Joyce and Phyllis lie in the darkness.
After a while, daylight comes in through the window.
Phyllis gets out of bed, walks over to the blackboard, and writes
"WEDNESDAY." She faces the audience and reads the following
from an index card:

PHYLLIS

Patricia Feinstein began her career as a psychiatrist, but a sab-
batical at UC Berkeley in 1975 inspired her to move towards a
focus in sexology and sex therapy. Since then, she has worked as
a psychologist at Beth Israel Hospital in Boston, a co-director at
the Fort Collins Sex and Gender Clinic, and now she's Assistant
Professor of Psychiatry at the Cornell School of Medicine.
    (Phyllis looks up at the audience)
One thing I really like about Doctor Feinstein is the way she criti-
cally examines the modern feminist movement, and the different
ways women today are trying to, um, reassert, or, um, reclaim
their self-image and sexual identity. Are all of these efforts con-
structive? Or do some of them just continue our legacy of self-
objectification? Take the, um, the new, allegedly "feminist" trend
of burlesque dancing. The woman's sexuality is still determined
by her onlooker, and to make the, um, common excuse that the
dancer *enjoys* exposing and depersonalizing herself is to remain
willfully ignorant of the fact that—
    (she suddenly stops and looks into the wings, confused)

What? Oh. Okay.
We're running out of time.
Sorry about that. Patty Feinstein, everyone. Please give her a warm
welcome.

She steps out of the light. Blackout.
Joyce and Phyllis's kitchen. Jared is alone, reading the OED at the
table. Phyllis enters with a book. After a pause:

PHYLLIS

Are you mad at me?

JARED

No.

PHYLLIS

Because of last night?

JARED

It's not worth my time to be mad. I've got better things to do.

PHYLLIS

I want to apologize for being / so—

JARED

Whatever. I don't care.

Phyllis sits down at the kitchen table with her book. She glances
over at Jared.

PHYLLIS

What word are you looking at?

JARED

I'm reading one of the brief introductory essays.

PHYLLIS

Oh yeah? What's it about?

JARED

Prescriptivism versus descriptivism.

Phyllis gives him a blank look.

JARED

It's like a really really big deal in the dictionary world.

PHYLLIS

Well, I've never heard of it.

Jared sighs disgustedly.

PHYLLIS

Just tell me, Jared.

JARED

Prescriptivism is the dictionary telling you what the correct definition is. Even if people in the outside world use the word differently.

PHYLLIS

That's what dictionaries are supposed to do, right?

JARED

Well, descriptivism says there shouldn't be any editorial judgment. It says a dictionary should just record what people are saying and writing in the real world, no matter how weird it is. A descriptivist strives to be a Totally Neutral Observer.

PHYLLIS

What are you?

JARED

What?

PHYLLIS

Are you a descriptivist or a prescrip—

> JARED

I don't know. The descriptivists have a good point about being anti-ideology, but prescriptivists say that that's not actually possible.

> PHYLLIS

I'm anti-ideology.

Jared shrugs.

> PHYLLIS

. . . So you're a prescriptivist?

> JARED

I guess. I also just hate people who misuse words.

Phyllis laughs. Jared continues reading.

> PHYLLIS

That was funny.

> JARED

I was being somewhat ironic.

> PHYLLIS

I know.

Jared puts down the OED.

> JARED

I have the ability to empathize.

> PHYLLIS

Uh-huh.

> JARED

I'm very good at empathizing.

> PHYLLIS

Well.

JARED

It must be hard to be a lesbian. Right? People make fun of you?

PHYLLIS

Uh. Not that much anymore. Not to my face, at least.

JARED

It must be hard to not be that pretty anymore. To get old.

PHYLLIS

Are you trying to be mean?

JARED

No! I'm telling you that I see how your life is hard.

PHYLLIS

Okay, that's . . . that's not how you empathize with people. You don't sit there and speculate about random things that might be hard for them.

JARED

What do you do?

PHYLLIS

You listen and you try to see things from their perspective.

JARED

So if you empathized with me maybe you wouldn't think I have Asperger's?

Phyllis sighs and flips through her book.

JARED

What're you reading?

PHYLLIS

Women's Bodies, Women's Wisdom.

> JARED

Why are you reading it?
> *(after a short pause)*

I'm listening and asking questions.

> PHYLLIS

Great.
> *(after a pause)*

I have to make the closing speech on Friday. So I'm trying to compile a list of quotes I can use.

> JARED

Do you want to use anything from the OED?

> PHYLLIS

No. Thanks.

> JARED

I hope you're going to provide the audience with concrete information.

> PHYLLIS

Definitely. This book has some incredible stories. Like this one woman? She was in her fifties, she'd already gone through menopause, and her daughter was leaving for college. So she started having all these weird empty-nest dreams, like dreams about her daughter being a baby again and nursing, and then she went to the doctor and there were, like, these *cysts* in her breasts.

> JARED

Disgusting.

> PHYLLIS

Hold on. When the doctor removed the cysts . . . she found that they were filled with milk!

Jared stares at her.

                              PHYLLIS

Milk cysts!

                              JARED

That sounds imaginary.

                              PHYLLIS

Isn't that amazing?

                              JARED

It's like a story Frank would tell.

                              PHYLLIS

   (stiffening)
No it's not.

                              JARED

Yeah. Like, oh there was a ghost, or like this woman gave birth to
a flower or something.

                              PHYLLIS

It's actually not the same at all.
   (after a pause, touching her eye)
Shoot. Jared. Look at me.

He looks at her.

                              PHYLLIS

Can you see my eye twitching?

                              JARED

No.

                              PHYLLIS

The bottom lid? It's sort of jumping around?

                              JARED

No.

PHYLLIS

Weird.
(after a pause)
Where *is* Frank?

JARED

The Visual Artists' Tea and Reception.

PHYLLIS

Oh god. Just the thought of it makes me sick.
(after a pause)
By the way, I went to see his photographs this morning.

Jared goes back to reading the OED.

PHYLLIS

They were totally offensive and horrible. No surprise.

No response.

PHYLLIS

And aesthetically? Not that good. I mean, as aesthetic statements
they were just . . .

She trails off. A pause.

PHYLLIS

I mean, even if they were of men and women both, I still wouldn't
like them.

JARED

It's good they're not of men.

PHYLLIS

No. Why do you say that?

JARED

Men are ugly.

PHYLLIS

That's crazy. What are you talking about?

JARED

Penises are ugly.

PHYLLIS

No, no. That's a common misconception. Penises are beautiful.

JARED

You don't really think that.

PHYLLIS

Yes I do.

JARED

But you don't want to have sex with a penis.

PHYLLIS

I can still think they're beautiful.
   (*after a pause*)
Vaginas are kind of weird-looking, too, you know.

JARED

Ew. Gross.

PHYLLIS

What?

Jared goes back to reading the OED.

PHYLLIS

Hey. Don't you ever want to read other stuff? Like a novel or something?

JARED

I need to prepare.

PHYLLIS

For what?

JARED

I told Frank that I wanted to write for the dictionary and he said: "What are you waiting for?" So now I'm preparing to be a lexicographer.

PHYLLIS

How do you prepare to be a lexicographer?

JARED

You read the dictionary.

PHYLLIS

Don't you need a degree?

Jared looks at her.

JARED

I'm an autodidact.

Phyllis looks at her watch.

PHYLLIS

It's three. Don't you have a shift this afternoon?

He doesn't respond.

PHYLLIS

Jared?

JARED

I quit.

PHYLLIS

You're kidding me.

JARED

I want to devote all my time to the OED. McDonald's was a distraction. I don't want to be a dilettante.

PHYLLIS

Oh my god.

JARED

Sorry if that pisses you off.

PHYLLIS

Your mom is . . . are you just expecting that your mom is going to support you for the rest of your life?

JARED

Just until I become a lexicographer.

PHYLLIS

You need to go back there and tell them you want your job back.

JARED

Too late.

PHYLLIS

I'll go with you. Do you want me to go with you?

JARED

I was also fired.

PHYLLIS

Did you quit or were you fired?

JARED

I knew I wanted to quit but I didn't want you guys to make me go back so I arranged it so they'd fire me.

PHYLLIS

What did you do?

JARED

It's not a big deal.

PHYLLIS

Oh my god.

Jared goes back to reading the dictionary.

PHYLLIS

Your mother is going to freak out, Jared. She is going to *freak out.*

JARED

Yeah, well. I'm hoping she'll empathize.

Blackout.
In front of the blackboard: Frank is sitting on a table, eating leftover
cheese cubes and drinking from a plastic cup of wine. Joyce walks
in. He looks up and smiles affably.

FRANK

You missed the reception.

JOYCE

Yeah.

FRANK

Want a cheese cube?

JOYCE

I'm lactose intolerant.

FRANK

Okay.

He continues munching away. After a pause:

FRANK

Why are you here?

JOYCE

Oh. I. Sorry. I—

FRANK

No. I'm glad you're here. I'm just wondering *why* you're here.

JOYCE

Um. I guess I wanted to see the photographs again.

FRANK

(gazing at her)
Uh-huh.

JOYCE

(looking around the room)
Phyllis thinks your work is pretty offensive.

FRANK

I got that feeling.

JOYCE

It's funny. The two of us are usually so . . . on the same page, you know? I mean, we've always prided ourselves on being, I don't know, politically sensitive without being overly PC? I don't really like to use the phrase PC, though, right?

FRANK

I don't mind.

JOYCE

It's just . . . I think your pictures are really beautiful. And I feel the women come across as very *strong*.

FRANK

So do I.

JOYCE

It's weird to be told you're wrong, you know? That something you think is beautiful is actually—

FRANK

It's okay for the two of you to disagree.

JOYCE

I know.
(after a pause)
Hey. Do you ever . . . would you ever take a picture of *us*?

FRANK

Who's "us"?

JOYCE

Me and Phyllis and Jared. We don't really have any good pictures
of the three of . . . of, um, our family. A family portrait. We'd pay
you, of course, / and—

FRANK

I don't let people pay me.

JOYCE

Oh. Then . . . would you be willing to—

FRANK

That's not really the kind of work I do, Joyce.

JOYCE

Oh.

FRANK

Sorry.

JOYCE

No. No. I was . . . I was just wondering.
    (after a long pause, trying to sound jokey)
So you swear you're not a sleazeball?

FRANK

That's a completely crazy question.

JOYCE

Well—

FRANK

What does "sleazeball" even mean?

JOYCE

. . . Um. I don't know.

She giggles and covers her face with her hands. Through her fingers, muffled:

JOYCE

Iguesslikeifyoujerkedofftothem?

FRANK

What did you say?

She uncovers her face.

JOYCE

Like if you jerked off. If you jerked off to your own photographs.

FRANK

What if I did?

JOYCE

That would be creepy.

FRANK

That would make me a sleazeball?

JOYCE

. . . Yeah.

FRANK

That's a very dangerous thing to say, Joyce.

JOYCE

Why?

FRANK

Because then art is all about the intentions of the artist and not the effect that the art has on the audience. Which I think is the more important part.

JOYCE

Oh.

FRANK

I mean, what if Michelangelo masturbated to the statue of David? Does that make him a bad sculptor?

JOYCE

Oh. Sorry. Yeah. I guess I don't know very much about art.

FRANK

I mean at that point you're getting into mind control.

JOYCE

Oh, no, no, I didn't mean—

FRANK

It's just a very dangerous arena.

JOYCE

I'm sorry.

FRANK

Don't be sorry. It's just: do you like the photographs. Do you think they're beautiful.

JOYCE

Definitely. Definitely. But. I mean. Okay. Hypothetically. What if you were like this psycho rapist murderer and you took the pictures right before you raped and killed all these women?

FRANK

You're asking important questions.

JOYCE

But what's the right answer?

FRANK

Do you want to pose for me, Joyce? Alone?

A silence.

FRANK

I've just been getting that vibe from you.

JOYCE

Um.
　(after a long pause)
I guess I'm curious about what it would be like.

FRANK

Well, I'm here for the next two days. I have my equipment.

JOYCE

I don't really know *why* I'm curious.

FRANK

It's a tremendous opportunity.

JOYCE

Yeah.

FRANK

It's both a very individual personal thing and an opportunity to become part of something really large and important.

JOYCE

Would you even *want* me to pose for you?

FRANK

What does that mean?

JOYCE

I don't know.

FRANK

I think you're beautiful.

JOYCE

Yeahyeahyeah.

FRANK

I do.

JOYCE

Phyllis would kill me.

FRANK

Why do you think Phyllis is so defensive?

JOYCE

I don't know. Defensive? I mean, yeah. Also protective, I think. She's really protective of me.

FRANK

Why?

JOYCE

Oh. Well. Stuff. I mean, both Phyllis and I have really long histories. I don't know. Um . . .

FRANK

This is making you uncomfortable.

JOYCE

No. I just think I should . . . I guess I don't really know *why* I want to pose for you. I don't know if it's, um, for the right reason.

FRANK

Is there such thing as a right reason?

JOYCE

Well. Yeah.
  (*after a pause*)
Yeah. I mean, yeah. I think so.

He nods. Blackout.
Joyce and Phyllis's kitchen. Phyllis is sitting at the table reading Women's Bodies, Women's Wisdom. *Her feet are propped up on a chair. She is studiously ignoring Jared and Joyce, who are standing at the stove. Joyce is making dinner while Jared hovers behind her.*

                         JARED

You always said: pursue your dream.

                         JOYCE

You are not allowed to quit your job and lie around the house reading the dictionary unless you agree to go into therapy.

                         JARED

I don't need therapy.

                         JOYCE

Are you happy living like this? Sitting around the house all day? Doing nothing?

                         JARED

Well, I find most people to be insufferable. My co-workers were imbeciles. And I want to be a lexicographer. Also I'm working on finding a girlfriend. So I'm actually being quite productive.

                         JOYCE

How are you working on finding on a girlfriend?

                         JARED

Uh.
    (after a pause)
. . . do you think I could talk to Frank?

                         JOYCE

Why?

                         JARED

Because.

                         JOYCE

Because he's a man?

                         JARED

I guess.

JOYCE

Oh, sweetie. I'm sorry. I'm sorry your dad's not around.

JARED

I wouldn't want to talk to Dad. He's an imbecile.

JOYCE

I don't know about imbecile. I do think he's a sociopath.

PHYLLIS

(looking up)
You're going to let Jared talk to that crazy pervert about sex?

JOYCE

I don't think Frank is a crazy pervert.

PHYLLIS

(to Jared)
I thought you didn't like him. You said he was illogical.

JARED

He is. But he said he's been married twice. So clearly he's had some measure of success with women.

JOYCE

If you want to talk to Frank that's fine. He'll be back later tonight.

PHYLLIS

You're kidding me.

JOYCE

No. I actually think it might be a good idea.

PHYLLIS

Jared, this guy is a real scumbag.

JARED

I just want advice on how to get someone to be my girlfriend.

PHYLLIS

I've had a lot of girlfriends.

JARED

It's different for you.

PHYLLIS

You want some good advice? Ask lots of questions. Pay attention. *Like* yourself. Don't have sex just to have sex. Have sex because there's nothing you'd rather be doing, in that moment.

A pause.

JARED

I want different advice.

PHYLLIS

Frank Bonitatibus is a loser.

JOYCE

I disagree.

PHYLLIS

And he wants to get in your mother's pants.

JOYCE

He does not want to get in my pants.

JARED

Who would want to get in your pants? You're old.

JOYCE

Frank's older than me, Jared.

PHYLLIS

This is great. Jared is going to get love and sex advice from the guy who single-handedly ruined Body Awareness Week.

JOYCE

What are you talking about?

PHYLLIS

The whole thing is like a joke now. I bring in a nutritionist, I bring in a race and gender panel, I bring in a fucking domestic violence quilt, and then we have exploitative nude photographs of little girls hanging in the Student Union. It's perfect. It's just perfect.

JOYCE

(to Jared)
I'll talk to him about it tonight.

PHYLLIS

Have the two of you been hanging out a lot?

JOYCE

Stop interrogating me!

PHYLLIS

I'm not interrogating you!

JOYCE

You always do this. You pretend it's out of some kind of cold intellectual curiosity but actually you're just jealous and tyrannical.

PHYLLIS

I am not tyrannical!

JOYCE

Always pretending you know more than me. Like you know my own *thoughts* better than me.

PHYLLIS

Well, sometimes you're just so transparent, Joyce! Your motivations are so unbelievably—

JOYCE

You think I'm transparent?

PHYLLIS

You're / just—

> JOYCE

Can you guess what I'm doing on Friday?

> PHYLLIS

Um. I don't know. Flirting with straight men? Making organic soup?

Joyce gives her an icy stare.

> JOYCE

I'm posing.

> PHYLLIS

What?

> JOYCE

I'm posing for a photograph.

Phyllis stares at her.

> PHYLLIS

You're not. Don't screw with my head.

> JOYCE

I might change my mind. But I'm pretty sure I want to do it.

> PHYLLIS

Why?

> JOYCE

Because it would be freeing.

> PHYLLIS

From what?

> JOYCE

What?

> PHYLLIS

Freeing from what?

JOYCE

I don't know what / you—

PHYLLIS

WHAT WOULD IT FREE YOU FROM?

JOYCE

. . . Well, my own embarrassment. My own self-consciousness.
All that stuff you always talk about. Like being able to look in the
mirror? And feel proud? I want to—

PHYLLIS

When I talk about looking in the mirror I'm talking about looking
in the mirror *in private*. I'm talking about being able to get away
from the male gaze. Do you get it, Joyce? Are you stupid? THE
POINT IS BEING ABLE TO GET AWAY FROM THE FUCKING
MALE GAZE! AND YOU'RE WALKING RIGHT INTO IT!

JOYCE

Don't call me stupid.

PHYLLIS

If you pose for Frank Bonitatibus you're an idiot!

JOYCE

God. I just . . . why do I surround myself with . . . ? The *two* of
you. Calling me stupid. Telling me I'm an imbecile. Why is my
family . . . aren't we supposed to support each other?

JARED

I don't care if you pose for Frank Bonitatibus.

JOYCE

Gee, thanks, Jared. I'll just wait until tomorrow when you tell me
that I'm stupid for not having read *War and Peace*.

JARED

Crime and Punishment.

443

PHYLLIS

Okay. Listen. If it's that important to you, the two of us should go buy a Polaroid camera. I'll take as many pictures of you as you want. Sexy naked pictures. You can take pictures of me, too. Okay?

JOYCE

It's not the same.

PHYLLIS

So it . . . see? It *is* about objectification! You want some old white guy to take your picture and get a hard-on / from—

JOYCE

The fact that he's white is irrelevant!

PHYLLIS

No. Wrong. It's part of . . . of COURSE he's white. This is about POWER.

JOYCE

You're not making any sense.

PHYLLIS

If you pose for that man I don't think I can continue being in this relationship.

JARED

Oh boy.

JOYCE

You've got to be joking.

PHYLLIS

I just . . . I can't imagine it. It makes me sick to my stomach.

JOYCE

You just . . . are you making an ultimatum, Phil?

PHYLLIS

I'm telling you how it'll make me feel.

JOYCE

And it'll make you feel like you can't be in this anymore?

PHYLLIS

I'm being honest.

JOYCE

Okay . . . you *know* how destructive you're being.

PHYLLIS

No. No. You are *so* in denial, Joyce. You *have* to know this is all about your dad. You can't admit to yourself that he did something really bad, but now you want to strip naked in front of some random sleazy guy and have him take your picture and this just . . . this like you compensating for some very, very weird shit!

After a long, upset silence:

JARED

Are you guys going to break up?

JOYCE

That would . . . that would be the dumbest breakup of all time.

PHYLLIS

It's how I feel.

JOYCE

Great. Thanks.

Phyllis goes back to Women's Bodies, Women's Wisdom.

JARED

(*to Joyce*)
Can I go play video games now?

JOYCE

Wait a second. What did you do to get yourself fired?

JARED

(*after a pause*)
I called someone a retard.

PHYLLIS

That got you fired?

JOYCE

Who did you call a retard?

JARED

The retarded guy who makes the salads.

PHYLLIS

You called the retarded guy a retard?

JARED

Yeah.

Phyllis titters.

JOYCE

It's not funny.

Phyllis puts her head in her hands and shakes with silent laughter. Jared and Joyce look at her.

JARED

If you think about it, I was just telling the truth.

Blackout. Then moonlight. Then daylight. Phyllis walks over to the blackboard. She writes "THURSDAY." She takes out her microphone. She is tired.

PHYLLIS

Well, that was incredible. I just . . . god. I love puppet theater. Those big masks? Um . . . the whole performance was just addressing so many things, and doing it in such an accessible manner. Thanks to Gary for arranging it.

(*a pause, reluctantly*)

Oh. Before you all leave, I'm also supposed to remind everyone to head over to the Student Union and take a look at some of the, um, visual art we have on display this week.

But, ah . . . well, don't forget, as a sort of interesting exercise, to think about who made each, um, piece of art. It doesn't . . . it doesn't *invalidate* it, of course, if—for instance—using a hypothetical situation—a white man went to Africa and painted pictures of all the, ah, Bushmen he met there. Not at all. But as a, um, as the viewer, don't forget to think about that. Did a Bushman paint the Bushmen?

Or did a white man?

Okay. Hopefully I'll see you all tomorrow at three for the closing ceremony.

Thanks.

Blackout.

Joyce and Phyllis's kitchen. Frank and Jared sit at the kitchen table with mugs of hot chocolate.

FRANK

Your mother tells me you threaten to kill her.

JARED

That's an exaggeration.

FRANK

Well, it's unacceptable.

JARED

Why?

FRANK

You know who threatens to kill their mothers?

JARED

Who?

FRANK

Retards.

JARED

I'm not a retard.

FRANK

I know you're not. That thing your mother says you have?

JARED

Asperger's.

FRANK

I don't think you have it.

JARED

I don't.

FRANK

I do think you've been spoiled. I think you've been weakened. No one has ever told you: If You Do That One More Time, Kiddo, I Will Fucking Kill You.

JARED

My mom threatens to take away my video game allowance.

FRANK

That's not enough. But I understand. It must be hard, not having a father.

JARED

It's okay. Will you tell me how to get a girlfriend?

FRANK

You've never had a girlfriend?

JARED

No.

FRANK

You ever ask anyone out?

JARED

No.

FRANK

You ever have sex?

JARED

No.

FRANK

You ever think you're gay?

JARED

No way.

Joyce peeps her head in through the door.

JOYCE

How's it going in here?

FRANK

Great.

JOYCE

Can I make you guys more hot chocolate?

FRANK

I think we're good.

JOYCE

Okay . . .

She gazes worriedly at Jared.

JARED

No listening in.

JOYCE

Okay, okay.

Joyce darts out.

FRANK

So what's stopping you?

JARED

From . . . ?

FRANK

From asking some girl out on a date.

JARED

I find myself repulsive.

Joyce peeks her head in again.

JOYCE

Sorry to interrupt again. Um, Jared? I'm going to Stop & Shop. Do you want me to buy some more of those microwaveable burritos you like?

JARED

Nah. I'm sick of those.

JOYCE

How about the frozen blintzes?

JARED

Those are okay.

JOYCE

All right. How do you feel about spinach / lasa—

Frank clears his throat impatiently.

JOYCE

I'm gone, I'm gone.

Joyce leaves.

FRANK

You ever help your mother out around the house? With cooking? Cleaning?

JARED

No.

FRANK

You should.

JARED

Sometimes she makes me do the dishes.

FRANK

You should help her with shopping.

JARED

I hate supermarkets.

FRANK

You should go anyway. Ah. Okay! Here's a good starting-off point. Life is sometimes about doing things you don't feel like doing.

JARED

Okay.

FRANK

It's also about being confident. You're not repulsive. You're smart. You're self-educated. You've got a lot to share.

JARED

I guess I mean, like . . .
    (*quietly*)
. . . do you ever look at yourself naked?

FRANK

Sure, sure.

JARED

Is that a weird thing to do?

FRANK

No, no. I mean when you get out of the shower? You kind of . . .
why not, right?

JARED

I just think I look gross.

FRANK

Well. All men look sort of gross.

JARED

Phyllis said men are beautiful.

Frank buries his head in his hands.

FRANK

Oh Jesus. Listen. You're a straight guy. You're attracted to women.
You don't have to find yourself attractive.

JARED

Phyllis said it's important to find yourself attractive.

FRANK

Why is Phyllis giving you love advice? She's a lesbian.

JARED

That's what I said.

FRANK

Lesbians are like . . . I don't mean this in a bad way. But they're like a different species.

Jared nods.

FRANK

Listen. When it comes to dating, don't be afraid to be aggressive. I mean, don't be a creep. But you can say stuff like: "Hey, I like you." "Hey, I think you're beautiful. Can I buy you dinner?" You can tell women you like them. That's okay.

JARED

How do you know when you can have sex?

FRANK

Well, first try kissing them. If they kiss you back, you can touch their breasts. I mean, this is obvious stuff. If they like that, you can touch their stomach. If they like that, if they squirm around or moan or whatever, then you can start touching their, uh, crotch.

Jared starts scratching his hair.

FRANK

Are you okay?

Jared nods.

FRANK

Do you know about eating women out? Do you know what that is?

JARED

Yeah.

FRANK

I would recommend it. Seriously.

JARED

Okay.

FRANK

If you don't, she'll tell her girlfriends and they'll say: "He didn't eat you OUT?"

JARED

Does it taste weird?

FRANK

Depends.

JARED

What if I get grossed-out?

FRANK

Don't be a baby.
(*after a pause*)
I recommend eating the woman out before you actually try intercourse for the first time.
(*after a pause*)
Also try to focus on acting like a grown-up.
(*after a pause*)
Also don't forget to tell her she looks beautiful.

Jared nods.

FRANK

Hey. You look freaked-out. Listen. Don't be scared of eating some girl out. That's the easy part. If I were you, I would worry about getting too excited / and—

JARED

Do you think I'm retarded?

FRANK

No. I already said no. Jesus.

JARED

I guess, um . . .
(*quietly*)
I guess sometimes I think they're right.

> FRANK

You're not retarded. You're living with two women.

> JARED

No, but . . . I mean, it's not . . . it's not like having Down syndrome or something. It just means you have a hard time picking up on social cues.

> FRANK

So what are you saying? You think you have this thing?

> JARED

No. I just . . .

> FRANK

Saying you have it would be taking the easy way out, Jared.

> JARED

Yeah?

> FRANK

Don't take the easy way out.

Jared nods.

> FRANK

Now give me your toothbrush.

Jared freezes.

> JARED

What. Why.

> FRANK

The only thing about you that seems retarded is the fact that you walk around sucking on an electric toothbrush. It's really weird, man.

> JARED

I'd rather not.

> FRANK

It'll be a symbolic gesture.

Jared shakes his head no.

> FRANK

Okay. Fine. Not a symbolic gesture. A, ah . . . a *necessary action*. If I'm some chick there is no way I'm having sex with some guy who walks around sucking an electric toothbrush.

Frank holds out his hand. Jared looks at him. After a few seconds, Jared reaches into his pocket and takes out the toothbrush. He puts the toothbrush in Frank's hand.

> FRANK

My man.

> JARED

I find it soothing. I don't see what's wrong with that.

> FRANK

It's not sexy.

> JARED

I thought men didn't have to be sexy.

> FRANK

No, no. We have to be sexy. You misunderstood me.
We don't have to be beautiful.

> JARED

Oh.

> FRANK

You're a good man, Jared.

Jared nods. After a pause:

> JARED

You really can see ghosts?

FRANK

Yep. I see my dead mother everywhere.

Blackout.
Joyce and Phyllis's bedroom. Joyce is lying in bed reading. There is a
small white line across Joyce's upper lip. Phyllis enters the bedroom.

PHYLLIS

You missed the puppet theater.

Joyce doesn't respond.

PHYLLIS

Are you giving me the silent treatment or something?

No response.

PHYLLIS

What's on your lip?
   (*another long pause*)
Is that bleach? Oh my god. Are / you—

JOYCE

   (*not looking up*)
Please get off my case.

PHYLLIS

Why are you *doing* that?

JOYCE

I've bleached my mustache many times before. This is not a new
development.

PHYLLIS

But you don't even *have* a mustache.

JOYCE

It just looks like that because I bleach it. I do it when you're not
around.

Annie Baker

PHYLLIS

You're kidding.

JOYCE

Nope. I knew you'd give me shit.

PHYLLIS

So why are you—

JOYCE

I'm in trouble anyway. You're threatening to break up with me anyway. So why shouldn't I bleach my mustache in front of you while I still have time?

PHYLLIS

You're still doing it?

JOYCE

Doing what?

PHYLLIS

You're still going to strip completely naked for our houseguest?

JOYCE

Yes.

PHYLLIS

Jesus Christ.

JOYCE

And you're not allowed to threaten me anymore.

PHYLLIS

You're killing my soul!

JOYCE

Oh my god.

PHYLLIS

You're like the one person! The one person I always felt was on my side!

458

JOYCE

I am on your side.

PHYLLIS

No. You've joined the enemy.

JOYCE

There is no enemy.

PHYLLIS

THERE IS NO ENEMY?

JOYCE

Shhh. Think about it. Who's the enemy?

PHYLLIS

Um, prejudice? Misogyny? Exploitative . . . exploitativeness?

JOYCE

Those are concepts. Not people. You think I've joined those concepts?

Phyllis stares at her.

JOYCE

Come on, Phil.
   (*a pause*)
You just don't want Frank to take a picture of something that's *yours*.

Phyllis sits down on the bed, dejected. A pause.

PHYLLIS

Are you attracted to him?

Another pause.

PHYLLIS

Be honest with me.

Another pause.

JOYCE

. . . I don't know. Okay?
And that's . . . that's actually beside the point.

A silence. Phyllis lets out a long, shaky sigh.

PHYLLIS

My eye is twitching again.

Joyce cups Phyllis's face in her hands and stares at her.

JOYCE

I can't see it.

PHYLLIS

   (starting to weep)
It's there! I swear to god!

JOYCE

Okay, okay.

PHYLLIS

I just feel so . . .

She starts to cry harder.

JOYCE

What?

PHYLLIS

Abandoned. Or something. The past four days. I don't know.

JOYCE

Oh Phil.

PHYLLIS

I don't want to give the stupid closing speech tomorrow.

JOYCE

I'll sit in the front row. You can look at me the whole time.

Joyce opens her arms. Phyllis collapses into them and weeps.

PHYLLIS

Body Awareness Week has not gone the way I planned.

JOYCE

I know, sweetheart. I know.

Joyce reaches over to the lamp and turns it off. Moonlight comes through the window, then daylight.
Phyllis gets out of bed and walks over to the blackboard. She writes "FRIDAY." She faces the audience, holding her microphone. She clears her throat, then closes her eyes.

PHYLLIS

"If we ever are to create safety in the outside world, we must first create safety for ourselves right in our own brains."
 (*she opens her eyes and smiles*)
I really like that quote.
Safety in our own brains.
First of all. Everyone. Thank you. Thank you for coming, and thank you for participating in, um, whatever fashion you've participated in this week's activities.
I hope that Body Awareness Week has helped to . . . raise consciousness in some way. In each of us. By consciousness I don't mean self-consciousness, of course. What I mean is, ah . . .
 (*after a pause*)
. . . Because we want to see ourselves without feeling *seen*. Or, um, I guess, to put it, ah, differently, we want to feel *seen* without feeling *judged*. If that's possible. I'd like to think it is, right?

Phyllis stops and smiles to the front row. She is looking for Joyce. She does not see her. She frowns.

PHYLLIS

Sorry. Um . . .

(She looks out into the audience for a while, then:)
Joyce?

She waits. No response.

PHYLLIS

Oh god. Um.
Sorry. I was just . . . sorry.
Okay.
Ah . . .
Well. Maybe it isn't possible. Because there's the male gaze, right, and then there's the *white* gaze, and then there's the *white male* gaze . . . and all of these relate back to the idea of image-ownership, right? Of actually, by looking at something, by observing something, *possessing* it in some way. So if you're like a nineteenth-century-painter guy and you've painted this female nude . . . or if you're a rich guy in the nineteenth century and you've COMMIS-SIONED a painter to paint a female nude, and it's like hanging in your, ah, VERANDAH . . .
   (she pauses)
That's not the right word. Um . . .
   (she reaches up and briefly touches her left eyelid)
I guess the question is . . . how do we remain neutral?
How do we observe ourselves, and other people, without partici-pating in the legacy of image-ownership?
I mean, maybe the male gaze is . . . um . . . maybe it's not like a spotlight. I've always thought of it as this, ah, evil, moving spot-light . . . but maybe it's more like, ah . . . the *sun.* Like it's our solar system and we're revolving around inside of it.
   (pause)
But I don't know. I want . . . I want so badly for there to be a right answer. Because it's just, ah . . . I mean, I was thinking: if there's no right answer . . .
Why does the dictionary even exist?

She is overwhelmed. She reaches up and touches her left eyelid. She stays that way for a while. Eventually she removes her hand and smiles bravely out at the audience.

PHYLLIS

For our final, closing performance, I'm thrilled to introduce to you Moonlight and Morning Bird, Vermont's favorite multiracial husband-wife singing duo. They cover everything from klezmer to gospel, and . . . they're fabulous. They're just really fabulous. Please give them a warm Shirley State welcome.

Blackout.
Joyce is in front of the blackboard, sitting on a stool. She is self-conscious. Frank is setting up his equipment.

JOYCE

When do I take off my clothes?

FRANK

Whenever you want.

A pause.

JOYCE

I have a confession.

FRANK

Yeah?

JOYCE

I, uh, I shaved my legs this morning.

FRANK

What's wrong with that?

JOYCE

I shaved my legs because I knew I'd be doing this.

FRANK

I don't understand.

JOYCE

The point of it is, like, this is what real women look like, and I'm gussying myself up? It kind of defeats the point.

FRANK

I really wouldn't worry about it.

JOYCE

I also plucked these little bellybutton hairs I have.

FRANK

Joyce. It's okay.

JOYCE

And I . . . I trimmed my pubic hair.

FRANK

I think most women probably do that before they pose for me.

JOYCE

But that's BAD, right?

FRANK

Whatever you need to do to make yourself feel beautiful.

JOYCE

But the point is . . .

Frank looks at her, bemused.

JOYCE

Never mind.

FRANK

Don't beat yourself up about it.

JOYCE

So I get a free print?

FRANK

Yup. I'll send it to you in the mail.

She giggles.

JOYCE

Am I supposed to hang it up in the living room or something?

FRANK

Some women do.

JOYCE

Oh my god. That's insane.
  (after a pause)
Sorry. That sounded judgmental.

Frank is concentrating on setting up the tripod.

FRANK

I'm almost ready.

A pause.

JOYCE

My heart is beating really fast. I guess I'm nervous.

FRANK

That's pretty typical.

JOYCE

Most women get nervous?

FRANK

Before they take their clothes off. Once they're naked it's pretty exhilarating.

JOYCE

Ah.

Frank finishes setting up the tripod.

FRANK

I think we're ready.

JOYCE

O-*kay*.

Joyce bends down and unlaces her shoe. She takes it off and throws it dramatically onto the ground.

JOYCE

Ta-da!

Frank nods, unimpressed, his arms folded. Joyce bends down to untie the other shoe. Frank watches. Joyce drops the other shoe to the ground. She looks up at him.

JOYCE

Should I take off my socks?

FRANK

It's up to you.

JOYCE

Huh. Okay. Um . . . I'm gonna leave the socks on.

Frank nods impatiently.

JOYCE

No! Wait! I'm gonna take them off.

Joyce takes her socks off. She begins to unbutton her cardigan.

FRANK

You're gonna do great.

A pause. Joyce toys nervously with the buttons on her cardigan.

JOYCE

I have this um . . . I have this little paunch? I just wanted to prepare you. No matter how much I exercise, I still have this horrible um . . .

FRANK

Most women your age do.

JOYCE

Yeah. Well.

FRANK

Joyce. I think you're an extremely attractive woman. Please don't get all self-conscious.

JOYCE

Sorry.

FRANK

Don't apologize.

JOYCE

Oh. Yeah. No. I'll just . . . sorry.

She starts unbuttoning her sweater again. She takes a deep breath.

JOYCE

Who gives a shit, right?

She rips off her sweater, and looks down at herself, in her bra.

JOYCE

(*tearfully*)

I mean, what's the big fucking deal?

Jared suddenly walks in. He is soaking wet and shaking.

JARED

Mom.

Joyce almost falls off her stool.

JOYCE

Jared!
   (to Frank)
Do you have a towel?

FRANK

Ah . . . no. / Sorry. I—

JOYCE

Sweetie! What happened? Were you *swimming*?

Jared just clutches his elbows and stares at her, shaking.

JOYCE

Jared?

He doesn't respond.

JOYCE

Oh my god.

Joyce starts drying Jared's body with her sweater. He stands there, passively, letting her touch him. She finally wraps her shirt around his shoulders and embraces him. Frank watches them.

JOYCE

Did someone hurt you?

JARED

I won't threaten to kill you anymore.

Jared buries his face in Joyce's shoulder.

JARED

(muffled)
I did something wrong.

JOYCE

Wait, what?

JARED

I did something wrong.

JOYCE

What did you do?

Jared suddenly turns to Frank.

JARED

Give me back my toothbrush.

FRANK

Sorry?

JARED

GIVE ME BACK MY TOOTHBRUSH IMMEDIATELY.

FRANK

It's . . . I threw it away.

Jared looks at Frank for a long time. Eventually he turns to Joyce.

JARED

If I don't go to jail, can I go to college?

JOYCE

(to Frank)
I'm sorry. I can't do this right now.

FRANK

Don't worry about it.

JARED

(*starting to cry*)
I think I'm retarded.

Joyce takes his face in her hands.

JOYCE

You're not retarded.

Blackout.
Joyce and Phyllis's kitchen. Joyce and Jared sit at the kitchen table.
Jared is wrapped in a towel. Phyllis is standing at the kitchen
counter and microwaving something. A long silence.

JOYCE

How old was she?

JARED

I don't know.

JOYCE

Okay . . . how old did she *look*?

JARED

She looked like a Popular Kid.

JOYCE

I don't understand what you were doing there.

JARED

I wanted to meet someone. I wanted to talk to a girl.

JOYCE

So you went to the *pond*?

JARED

First I went to the mall. To the arcade. But there were only guys
there. And this one really fat girl.

Joyce shakes her head.

JARED

Then I remembered how the cool kids used to hang out at the pond. They would go there in the winter and make bonfires.

JOYCE

So she was a high school student?

JARED

Maybe. I don't know.
  (after a pause)
How bad is it to show someone your penis?

JOYCE

It's bad.

JARED

Is it illegal?

JOYCE

Yes.
  (after a pause)
Did you touch her?

JARED

Uh . . .

PHYLLIS

Oh shit. You *touched* her?

JARED

No. I was . . . she was there all alone. She was standing near the water. She said she lived nearby. She was nice. I told her the root of "pond," that it comes from the archaic Old English "pound," and she laughed and said I was funny, and then I just . . . I showed it to her for like a second. It was literally for like a second.

(*a pause*)
I was trying to be sexy.

The microwave dings. Phyllis opens it and reaches inside.

PHYLLIS

Anyone want a defrosted blintz?

Jared and Joyce both nod, numbly. Phyllis takes out three plates, puts the blintzes on them, and puts the plates on the table. She gets out forks and hands them to Jared and Joyce. She sits down at the table. They all sit, staring at their plates.

JOYCE

Did she say anything?

JARED

She screamed and then I ran into the water. When I came out she was gone.

JOYCE

All right. Well. After dinner we'll put in a phone call and let someone know what happened.

PHYLLIS

You want to *report* this?

JOYCE

This girl could be one of my students!

PHYLLIS

Yeah, but how do we know she's going to tell someone?

JOYCE

Phyllis.

PHYLLIS

She might be kind of grossed-out, but okay, you know? And even if she does tell someone, how're they gonna know it's Jared?

JARED

I have distinctive glasses.

PHYLLIS

I don't know. When I was in grad school this old guy on the subway exposed himself to me and it was disgusting and I was really upset, but I don't know if it would warrant someone like Jared getting in, like, legal trouble.

A pause.

JARED

It's just . . . if I were her? That would kind of be scary.

PHYLLIS

Well, of course it would be *scary*.

JARED

But if someone did that to me . . .

A long pause. Jared is thinking.

JARED

. . . I would want that person to . . .
   (to Joyce)
It's so much better if the person admits to doing it, right? So then you don't have to spend the rest of your life thinking about it.

Joyce nods.

JARED

Also I don't want this to turn into a Raskolnikov-type situation.

JOYCE

What's that?

JARED

Raskolnikov? The main character in Dostoyevsky's *Crime and Punishment?*

Joyce looks at him blankly. Jared shakes his head and sighs in disgust.

PHYLLIS

(quietly)
Do you remember her name?

JARED

L something. Lauren.

JOYCE

Loreen?

JARED

Maybe.

A pause.

JARED

I'm going to jail.

PHYLLIS

You are not going to jail.

JOYCE

I, um . . . I don't think I can handle this.

JARED

(to Joyce)
It's okay. When I get out of jail I'll get a job at the OED and you can come visit me in England.
(to Phyllis)
You were right about needing a degree. I researched it online.

Jared begins to eat his blintz. Joyce and Phyllis watch him in silence for a while.

JOYCE

There's a right thing to do in this situation. I just have no idea what it is.

Jared keeps eating. After a long pause:

PHYLLIS

Hey. It's Friday.

JARED

So?

PHYLLIS

It's Shabbas.
  (after a pause)
Joyce.

Joyce slowly looks up.

PHYLLIS

Why don't you get out the candles and grape juice?

JOYCE

Are you trying to make fun of me?

PHYLLIS

No! I'm serious. I think it would be nice.
  (after a pause)
Please?

After a long pause, Joyce slowly gets up and gets out a candle and a bottle of grape juice. She pours three glasses. Shakily, she lights the candle.

JOYCE

I forget what to do.

JARED

You sing the prayer for wine.

JOYCE

Oh. Um.

(*she starts tentatively whisper-singing and approximating Hebrew*)

Baru ama adenoid, emo hey . . .

Jared starts laughing.

JARED

Adenoid? He did not say adenoid.

JOYCE

Well, I don't remember. Sorry. What am I supposed to say?

PHYLLIS

Um. Here.

Phyllis fishes Women's Bodies, Women's Wisdom *out of her bag.*

JOYCE

What is that?

PHYLLIS

Women's Bodies, Women's Wisdom. I wanted to use part of it in my speech today . . . but, I, ah . . . I totally fucked up.

JOYCE

Oh my god.

PHYLLIS

Yeah.

JOYCE

Your speech. I . . . I completely forgot.

PHYLLIS

It's okay.

A pause.

JARED

I can have Asperger's and not be retarded, right?

PHYLLIS

Of course.
   (to Joyce)
Read something out loud. Pretend it's a prayer.

She hands Joyce Women's Bodies, Women's Wisdom. *Joyce opens it.*

JOYCE

Um . . .

PHYLLIS

Anything.

Joyce opens the book to a random page and starts reading.

JOYCE

"Some menopausal women complain of vaginal dryness and thin-ning, which cause—"

JARED

SOMETHING ELSE.

JOYCE

Okay, okay.

Joyce opens to a different page and starts reading.

JOYCE

Um . . . *"Understanding the Bodymind.* Our entire concept of 'the mind' needs to be expanded considerably. The mind can no longer be thought of as being confined to the brain or to the intellect; it exists in every cell of our bodies."

While Joyce is reading, Jared takes something out of his pocket. It's Frank's recorder. Jared starts tentatively blowing into it. Joyce stops and looks at him.

JOYCE

Where did you get that?

Jared continues to try out notes.

JOYCE

Is that Frank's?

Jared nods, still playing.

JOYCE

Did you steal it?

Jared briefly lifts his mouth off the recorder to speak.

JARED

He took my toothbrush.

Jared goes back to playing. He messily begins to pick out the notes to "Jingle Bells."

JOYCE

Oh my god. Jared. What is *wrong* with you?

JARED

I might have Asperger's.

JOYCE

That's not an excuse!

PHYLLIS

It's not a big deal. We'll just give it back to him. He can't be too mad, anyway. I'm about to write him a big check.

JOYCE

Why?

PHYLLIS

I want a copy.

JOYCE

A copy of what?

PHYLLIS

I want a copy of your exploitative nude photograph.

Joyce stares at Phyllis.

PHYLLIS

What?

JOYCE

It's just—

PHYLLIS

I thought me saying that would make you happy.

Joyce looks like she might cry. Phyllis reaches over and strokes her hair.

PHYLLIS

Why don't you keep reading.

Joyce picks up Women's Bodies, Women's Wisdom *and continues reading out loud. During this next passage, Jared puts down the recorder and starts ceremoniously waving his hands over the candle's flame. Frank appears in the doorway with a suitcase. No one notices him.*

JOYCE

"Every thought we think has a biochemical equivalent. Every emotion we feel has a biochemical equivalent. One of my colleagues says, 'The mind is the space between the cells.' So when the part of your mind that is your uterus talks to you, through pain or excessive bleeding, are you prepared to listen to it?"

JARED

(quietly, still waving his hands)

Yes.

Joyce puts down the book and watches her son wave his hands over the candle. She is deeply sad. Still unnoticed, Frank observes the family for a while, then slowly pulls out his camera and takes their picture. There is a blinding flash of white light.

END OF PLAY

The author would like to thank Playwrights Horizons, the Soho Rep Writer/Director Lab, Rattlestick Playwrights Theater, Atlantic Theater Company, The Greens, Mac Wellman, Sam Gold, Linda Baker, and Ben Nugent, who wrote the excerpt from "The Hands Of That Cold Child."

ANNIE BAKER is an Obie Award–winning playwright and teacher. Her full-length plays include *Circle Mirror Transformation* (Playwrights Horizons, Obie Award for Best New American Play, Drama Desk nomination for Best Play), *The Aliens* (Rattlestick Playwrights Theater, Obie Award for Best New American Play), *Body Awareness* (Atlantic Theater Company, Drama Desk and Outer Critics Circle nominations for Best Play/Emerging Playwright), *Nocturama* and *The Flick* (Playwrights Horizons). Her plays have been produced outside of New York City at South Coast Repertory, the Guthrie, Victory Gardens, Artists Repertory, Huntington Theater Company, Seattle Repertory, Studio Theatre in D.C., Hyde Park Theatre, San Francisco Playhouse, and more than one hundred other theaters across the country. They have been produced internationally in England, Australia, Argentina, Bolivia, Chile, Peru, Venezuela, Mexico, Latvia and Russia. Recent honors include a United States Artists Fellowship, a New York Drama Critics Circle Award, a Lilly Award, a Time Warner Storytelling Fellowship, and a Master Artist Residency at the Atlantic Center for the Arts. Baker is a member of New Dramatists and a Residency Five playwright at the Signature Theatre.